BELLE BOYD

IN

CAMP AND PRISON.

BELLE BOYD

IN

CAMP AND PRISON.

WRITTEN BY HERSELF.

WITH AN

INTRODUCTION,

BY GEORGE AUGUSTA SALA.

B

——————

NEW YORK:
BLELOCK & COMPANY,
19 BEEKMAN STREET.
1866.

CONTENTS.

CHAPTER V.

CHAPTER VI.

CHAPTER VII.

CHAPTER VIII.

CHAPTER IX.

CHAPTER XVII.

CHAPTER XVIII.

CHAPTER XIX.

CHAPTER XX.

CHAPTER XXIV.

CHAPTER XXV.

CHAPTER XXVI.

INTRODUCTION.

BY A FRIEND OF THE SOUTH.

———◆———

" WILL you take my life ?"

This was the somewhat startling question put to me by Mrs. Hardinge—better known as *Belle Boyd*—on my recent introduction to her in Jermyn Street.

" Madam," said I, " a sprite like you, who has so often run the gauntlet by sea and land, who has had so many hair-breadth escapes by flood and field, must bear a ' charmed life :' I dare not attempt it." Then, placing in my hands a roll of manuscript, she said, " Take this ; read it, revise it, rewrite it, publish it, or burn it—do what you will. It is the story of my adventures, misfortunes, imprisonments, and persecutions. I have written all from memory since I have been here in London; and, perhaps, by putting me in the third person, you can make a book that will be not only acceptable to the public and profitable to myself, but one that will do some good to the cause of my poor country, a cause which seems to be so little understood in England."

I took the manuscript, promising to look it over, and return it with an estimate of its merits. I have done so; and hence the publication of "*Belle Boyd, in Camp and Prison.*" The work is entirely her own, with the exception of a few suggestions in the shape of footnotes—the simple, unambitious narrative of an enthusiastic and intrepid school-girl, who had not yet seen her seventeenth summer when the cloud of war darkened her land, changing all the music of her young life, her peaceful "home, sweet home," into the bugle blasts of battle, into scenes of death and most tumultuous sorrow.

Believing, with all the people of the South, in the sovereignty of the States, and the absolute political and moral right of secession, our young heroine, like Joan of Arc, inspired and fired by the "tyranny impending," resolved to devote her hands and heart, and life, if need be, to the sacred cause of freedom and independence. How much she has done and suffered in the great struggle which has crimsoned the "Sunny South" with the "blood of the martyrs," we shall leave the reader to gather from the narrative itself.

But, by way of introduction, I have a few incidental facts to relate; and it is proper to add, that I do it entirely on my own responsibility, and without consulting "our heroine" in the matter.

At the time of my presentation to Mrs. Hardinge, above alluded to, I found the lady in very great distress of mind and body. She was sick, without money, and driven almost to distraction by the cruel news that her husband was suffering the "tender mercies" of a Federal prison. Lieutenant Hardinge was in *irons;* and his friends were prohibited from sending him food or clothing! Letters ad-

dressed to his young wife, containing remit-
tances, were intercepted; and thus I found her,
not quite friendless, in this great wilderness
of London, but, what is worse, absolutely desti-
tute of that indispensable and all-prevailing
friend—MONEY.

The sight of a pair of flowing eyes, that
for thirteen long months had refused to weep
in a Northern prison, were enough to call forth
the following communication, addressed to the
Morning Herald, that able and consistent
defender of the Southern cause :—

"A WORD TO CONFEDERATE SYMPATHIZERS.

"SIR:—Your readers cannot have forgotten
the glowing description of the recent romantic
wedding of 'Belle Boyd' (*La Belle Rebelle*),
so pleasantly celebrated a few months since at
'a fashionable hotel in Jermyn Street.'

"Alas, poor Belle! Her bridal bliss was
'like the snow-fall on a river.' Her husband
of a day is now tasting the sweets of a Yankee prison, and she (who 'was made his wed-

ded wife yestreen') all the bitterness of poverty and exile. After enduring for many a long and weary month the insults, sufferings, and persecutions of the 'Old Capitol Prison,' I heard the afflicted lady say yesterday that she 'had rather be there as she was than here as she is.' And why? Cut off from all pecuniary resources at home, she has had to part with her jewellery piece by piece, including her 'wedding presents,' to pay her weekly bills.

"We can well understand how trouble like that would smite the heart of a high-toned woman, the daughter of affluence and luxury, even more cruelly than the tortures of a Federal prison.

"Without further comment, I will only add that Madame Hardinge (Belle Boyd) has prepared for publication a narrative of her adventures, imprisonment, and sufferings, for which there are no lack of publishers ready to advance a handsome sum; but she has recently received threatening intimations that her husband's life depends upon the suppression of her story !

"The father of 'Belle Boyd,' a most respectable Virginian gentleman, has lately died, at the age of forty-six, from a disease induced by his daughter's sufferings. These are the sad, simple facts of the case, and I commend them to the kind consideration of Confederate sympathizers in England. Surely poverty, in a young and accomplished woman, is not only a sacred claim to the protection of society—it is also the very highest credential of honor."

The above was copied by one of the London morning papers, with the following sympathetic comments:—

"We are in a position to verify all that is here stated, and a great deal more. Probably the history of the world does not contain a parallel case to that of this newly married lady, who has just only emerged from her teens. Her adventures in the midst of the American war surpass any thing to be met with in the pages of fiction. Her great beauty, elegant manners, and personal attractions generally, in conjunction with her romantic history before her marriage, which took place

only three months ago at the West End, in the
presence of a fashionable assemblage of affectionate and admiring friends, concur to invest
her with attributes which render her such a
heroine as the world has seldom, if ever, seen
in a lady only now in her twentieth year."

Several of the New York journals also
copied the above, and one of them, *The
World* published the following communication :—

"I would respectfully ask the use of a small
space in the columns of *The World* to say
a word regarding these statements.

"Within the past few months Mrs. Hardinge's agent in the United States has sent
her bills of exchange on London bankers to
the amount of eight hundred pounds sterling,
or nearly ten thousand dollars in greenbacks.
She has never received a sou of this money.
Her letters have been opened here and the
drafts extracted before going on to her, and
this is the reason she is in distress. Too
proud to beg, too honorable to borrow, she

pawned her jewels and wedding presents,
piece by piece, until her situation became
known to her friends. Cut off from pecuniary resources, a stranger in a strange land,
her husband in a Northern prison, what
could she do? 'Surely poverty in a young
and accomplished woman is not only a sacred
claim to the protection of society, but is also
the very highest credential of honor.'

"I received during the week a letter from
this poor lady; and she says, 'I think it is so
cruel in the Yankees to intercept my letters
and stop my money, and I don't know why I
am thus persecuted.' It *is* cruel, and it is
beneath the dignity of any Government to
stoop to such means of revenge. Such things
'n the dark ages would be called unchivalrous.
Good God! can this be the nineteenth cen-
tury?

"Mr. Hardinge came here, as a peaceable
citizen would come, to attend to his private
business and return to England. He had no
Confederate duties. Having nearly completed
his labors, he went to Martinsburg to see his

wife's mother, and while returning thence, with all the necessary papers and passes in his possession, was arrested this side of Harper's Ferry. Confined in nondescript guard-houses, in jails, and dragged about like a convicted felon, he was finally lodged in the Carroll Prison at Washington, and from thence taken to Fort Delaware. After suffering two months' confinement, he was unconditionally released, and sailed for Europe on the 8th February. She will not be in want or distress when he arrives in London. For what he was arrested and confined is to him yet a mystery.

"The intimation to Mrs. Hardinge that the publication of her work would endanger the life of her husband was not without foundation, as there are officials high in power at Washington of whom she knows more than is generally known, and who will be shown up in their true light and colors in her book. They fear the truth."

It is pleasant to add, that the moment Belle Boyd's necessities became known in

London the most generous offers of assistance were literally showered upon her by ladies and gentlemen of the highest and best classes in England. And here I cannot refrain from saying that, after several years of observation and experience, I cannot but regard the real nobility of England as the noblest and most hospitable people in the world. The Southern planters rank—or, alas! did rank—next.

But this is a digression. Let us glance a moment at Belle Boyd in prison, sketched by other hands than her own.

In the month of August, 1862, the editor of the *Iowa Herald*, D. A. Mahony, Esq., a strong Anti-Black Republican, but an able and eloquent supporter of the Constitution and the Union, was taken from his bed, and, without arraignment or trial, and without even being informed of "the things whereof he was accused," hurried away to Washington, and thrust into the "Old Capitol Prison." What he saw and suffered there he has already told the world, in words that ought to burn and brand forever his lawless and infamous persecutors.

The following extracts from Mr. Mahony's journal, published by Carleton, of New York, give us characteristic glimpses of Belle Boyd in prison :—

"Among the prisoners in the Old Capitol when I reached there was the somewhat famous Belle Boyd, to whom has been attributed the defeat of General Banks, in the Shenandoah Valley, by Stonewall Jackson. Belle, as she is familiarly called by all the prisoners, and affectionately so by the Confederates, was arrested and imprisoned as a spy. . . . .

"The first intimation some of us newcomers in the Old Capitol had of the fact of there being a lady in that place was the hearing of 'Maryland, my Maryland,' sung the first night of our incarceration, in what we could not be mistaken was a woman's voice. On inquiry, we were informed that it was Belle Boyd. Some of us had never heard of

the lady before; and we were all inquiring
about her. Who was she? where was she
from? and what did she do? . . . .

"Belle was put in solitary confinement, but
allowed to have her room-door open, and to
sit outside of it in a hall or stair-landing in
the evening. Whenever she availed herself
of this privilege, as she frequently did, the
greatest curiosity was manifested by the victims of despotism to see her. Her room
being on the second story, those who occupied
the third story were civilians from Fredericksburg. . . . .

"But we must not lose sight of Belle
Boyd. I heard her voice, my first night in
prison, singing 'Maryland, my Maryland,' the
first time I had ever heard the Southern song.
The words, stirring enough to Southern hearts,
were enunciated by her with such peculiar
expression as to touch even the sensibilities
which did not sympathize with the cause
which inspired the song. It was difficult to
listen unmoved to this lady, throwing her
whole soul, as it were, into the expression of

the sentiments of devotion to the South, defiance to the North, and affectionately confident appeals to Maryland, which form the burden of that celebrated song. The pathos of her voice, her apparently forlorn condition, and, at those times when her soul seemed absorbed in the thoughts she was uttering in song, her melancholy manner, affected all who heard her, not only with compassion for her, but with an interest in her which came near, on several occasions, bringing about a conflict between the prisoners and the guards.

" Fronting on the same hall or stair-landing on which Belle Boyd's room-door opened, were three other rooms, all filled to their capacity with prisoners, mostly Confederate officers. Several of these were personally acquainted with Belle, as she was most of the time, and by nearly every one, called. In the evenings these prisoners were permitted to crowd inside of their room-doors, whence they could see and sometimes exchange a word with Belle. When this liberty was not allowed, she contrived to procure a large mar-

ble, around which she would tie a note written
on tissue-paper, 'and, when the guard turned
his back to patrol his beat in the hall, she
would roll the marble into one of the open
doors of the Confederate prisoners' rooms.
When the contents were read and noted a
missive would be written in reply, and the
marble, similarly burdened as it came, would
be rolled back to Belle. Thus was a correspondence established and kept up between
Belle and her fellow-prisoners, till a more convenient and effective mode was discovered.
This occurred soon after some of us were
transferred from room No. 13 to No. 10.

One day Mr. Sheward and I were rummag-
ing in an old, dirty, doorless closet in No. 10,
when we discovered an opening in the floor,
and, looking down, perceived the light in the
room below, which happened to be that occupied by Belle Boyd. Here was a discovery!
No sooner was it made, than we set to writing
a note, which was tied to a thread and dropped down through the discovered aperture.
It happened to be seen by Belle, who soon

returned the compliment. Thenceforth a
regular mail passed through the floor in No.
10; and though Lieutenant Miller and Superintendent Wood prided themselves on being
well informed of every occurrence which took
place in prison contrary to the rules, with all
their vigilance, aided by the presence, as they
admitted, of a detective in every room of the
prison, except that of Belle Boyd, they never
discovered this through-the-floor mail. It
would not be the least interesting chapter in
the history of the Old Capitol to give in it
these letters of Belle Boyd. But the time is
not yet."

These last words of Mahony remind me
of the fact that Belle Boyd, the "rebel spy,"
is in possession of a vast amount of information implicating certain high officials at Washington, both in public and private *scandals*,
which she deems it imprudent at present to
publish. "*The time is not yet.*"

"Belle usually commenced her evening
entertainment," writes Mahony, "with 'Mary-

land.'" Up to this time this patriotic and
spirit-stirring song, written by young Randall,
of Baltimore, must be regarded as the "Mar·
seillaise" of the South. And as it is as yet
but little known in England, I will here quote
it entire—

AS SUNG BY BELLE BOYD IN PRISON.

"The despot's heel is on thy shore,
            Maryland!
    His torch is at thy temple door,
            Maryland!
    Avenge the patriotic gore
    That flecked the streets of Baltimore,
    And be the battle queen of yore,
            Maryland! my Maryland!

"Hark to a wandering son's appeal,
            Maryland!
    My Mother State, to thee I kneel,
            Maryland!
    For life and death, for woe and weal,
    Thy peerless chivalry reveal,
    And gird thy beauteous limbs with steel,
            Maryland! my Maryland!

"Thou wilt not cower in the dust,
            Maryland!

Thy beaming sword shall never rust,
                Maryland!
Remember Carroll's sacred trust,
Remember Howard's warlike thrust,
And all thy slumberers with the just,
                Maryland! my Maryland!

"Come! 'tis the red dawn of the day,
                Maryland!
Come with thy panoplied array,
                Maryland!
With Ringgold's spirit for the fray,
With Watson's blood at Monterey,
With fearless Lowe, and dashing May,
                Maryland! my Maryland!

"Dear mother! burst the tyrant's chain,
                Maryland!
Virginia should not call in vain,
                Maryland!
She meets her sisters on the plain:
Sic semper, 'tis her proud refrain,
That baffles minions back amain,
                Maryland! my Maryland!

"Come! for thy shield is bright and strong,
                Maryland!
Come! for thy dalliance does thee wrong,
                Maryland!

Come to thine own heroic throng,
That stalks with Liberty along,
And gives a new *Key* to thy song,
      Maryland! my Maryland!

"I see the blush upon thy cheek,
      Maryland!
And thou wert ever bravely meek,
      Maryland!
But, lo! there surges forth a shriek,
From hill to hill, from creek to creek:
Potomac calls to Chesapeake,
      Maryland! my Maryland!

"Thou wilt not yield the Vandal toll,
      Maryland!
Thou wilt not crook to his control,
      Maryland!
Better the fire upon thee roll,
Better the shot, the blade, the bowl,
Than crucifixion of the soul,
      Maryland! my Maryland!

"I hear the distant thunder hum,
      Maryland!
The Old Line's bugle, fife, and drum,
      Maryland!
She is not dead, nor deaf, nor dumb,
Hurrah! she spurns the Northern scum!
She breathes, she lives; she'll come, she'll come!
      Maryland! my Maryland!"

"The singing of this song," says Mahony, "often brought Belle in collision with the guard who passed to and fro in front of her room-door. It was, of course, provoking; but was such a place a proper one in which to imprison a female, and especially one who, whatever may have been her offence, was, in the estimation of the world, a lady?" . . .

Many a patriotic lady of Baltimore has been arrested by Federal officers for singing the patriotic song of "Maryland." But what will the English reader say when he learns the following fact? At one of the most celebrated eating, drinking, and singing saloons in London, the classical resort of authors, actors, poets, and wits, for these hundred years at least, the famous band of boys, who sing better than any choir outside the Sistine Chapel in Rome, after having got "the words and air of 'Maryland' by heart," are not allowed to sing it, *for fear of giving offence!* OFFENCE TO WHOM? It might possibly "offend" *somebody*, were they to chant the "Marseil-laise."

To return again to our caged bird:—

"Belle was allowed to go in the yard on Sundays, when there was preaching there. On these occasions she wore a small Confederate flag in her bosom. No sooner would her presence be known to the Confederate prison-ers, than they manifested towards her every mark of respect, which persons in their situa-tion could bestow. Most of them doffed their hats as she approached them, and she, with a grace and dignity that might be envied by a queen, extended her hand to them, as she moved along to her designated position in a corner near the preacher. We Northern prisoners of state envied the Confederates who enjoyed the acquaintance of Belle Boyd, and who secured for her such glances of sympathy as can only glow from a woman's eyes.

"Belle's situation was a peculiarly trying one. If she kept her room, a solitary prisoner, her health, and probably her mind, would become affected by the confinement and solitude; if she indulged herself by sitting outside her room-door, she became exposed to the gaze of more than a hundred prisoners, nearly all of them strangers to her, and many of them her enemies by the laws of war. Nor was this all. She could not help hearing the comments made on her, and the opinions expressed of her, by passers-by; some of them complimentary and flattering, it is true, but oftentimes couched in expressions which were not what she should hear. The guards, too, were sometimes rude to her, both by word and action. At one time, especially, one of the guards presented his bayoneted musket at her in a threatening manner. She, brave and unterrified, dared the craven-hearted fellow to put his threat into execution. It was well for him that he did not, for he would have been torn into pieces before it could have been known to the prison authorities what had happened.

"Belle was subjected to another worse annoyance and indignity than even this. Her room fronted on A Street, and, as usual with all the prisoners whose rooms had windows opening towards the street, Belle would sit at her window sometimes, and look abroad upon the houses, streets, and people of the city named after Washington. It happened frequently that troops were moving to and fro, and it was on such occasions especially that Belle, prompted by that curiosity which seems to be a law of nature in mankind, would look through her barred window at the soldiers. No sooner would they perceive her, than they indulged in coarse jests, vulgar expressions, and the vilest slang of the brothel, made still more coarse, vulgar, and indecent by the throwing off of the little restraint which civilized society places upon the most abandoned prostitutes and their companions. . . . .

"Did the officers of the troops passing by permit the soldiers to thus insult a female, and subject themselves to such scornful and contemptuous reproof? the reader will be apt to inquire. Yes; and participated with the soldiers in uttering the most vulgar language and indecent allusions to the imprisoned woman;

and that, too, without having the remotest idea of who she was, or of what she was accused. It was enough for them that she was a defenceless woman, to insult and outrage her by such language as they would not dare to apply in the public streets to an abandoned woman who had her liberty. And these men were going forth to fight the battles of the Union! They had just parted with mothers, wives, and sisters. It would seem that, in doing so, they turned their backs upon the virtues which give beauty to woman and dignity to man. . . . .

"At the general exchange of prisoners, which took place in September, Belle Boyd was sent to Richmond. As soon as it became known in the 'Old Capitol' that she was about to leave, there was not one, Federalist or Confederate, prisoner of state, officer of the 'Old Capitol,' as well as prisoner of war, who did not feel that he was about to part with one for whom he had, at least, a great personal regard. With many it was more than mere regard.

"Every inmate of the 'Old Capitol' tried to procure some token of remembrance from Belle, and there was scarcely one who did not bestow on her some mark of regard, esteem, or affection, as their sentiments and feelings influenced them severally, and as the means at their disposal afforded them an opportunity to manifest their sensibility. While every man who had any delicacy of feeling for the apparently forlorn prisoner rejoiced at her release from such a loathsome place, and from being subjected, as she continually was, to insult and contumely, there was not a gentleman in the 'Old Capitol' whose emotions did not overcome him, as he saw her leave the place for home."

Thus kindly and warmly writes the veteran editor of the *Iowa Herald*, one of the victims of Seward's "little bell," for whose improvement and release the "Powers" at Washington, "clothed with a little brief authority," have given no reason or explanation. But was not Mr. Mahony "guilty" of being the Democratic nominee for Congress?

A somewhat more poetic picture of "*La Belle Rebelle*" is given by the accomplished author of "Guy Livingstone," in his "Border and Bastille," written while tasting the sweets of Federal tyranny in that same "Old Capitol" Prison :—

"Through the bars of a second-story window that fronted each turn of my tramp, I saw—this: a slight figure, in the freshest summer-toilette of cool pink muslin; close braids of dark hair shading clear, pale cheeks; eyes that were made to sparkle, though the look in them was very sad; and the languid bowing down of the small head told of something worse than weariness.

"Truly a pretty picture, though framed in such a rude setting; but almost startling, at first, as the apparition of the fair witch in the forest to Christabelle. . . . .

" No need to ask what her crime had been: aid and abetment of the South suggested itself before you detected the ensign of the South that the *démoiselle* still wore undauntedly—a pearl *solitaire*, fashioned as a Single

Star. I may not deny that my gloomy 'con-
stitutional' seemed thenceforward a shade or
two less dreary; but, though community of
suffering does much to abridge ceremony, it
was some days before I interchanged with the
fair captive any sign beyond the mechanical
lifting of my cap, when I entered and left her
presence, duly acknowledged from above. One
evening I chanced to be loitering almost under
the window. A low, significant cough made
me look up; I saw the flash of a gold bracelet,
and the wave of a white hand; and there fell
at my feet a fragrant, pearly rose-bud, nestling
in fresh green leaves. My thanks were, per-
force, confined to a gesture and a dozen hurried
words; but I would the prison-beauty could
believe that fair Jane Beaufort's rose was not
more prized than hers, though the first was a
love-token to a king, the last only a graceful
gift to an unlucky stranger. I suppose that
most men, whose past is not utterly barren
of romance, are weak enough to keep some
withered flowers till they have lived memory
down; and I pretend not to be wiser than my

fellows. Other fragrant messengers followed in their season; but if ever I 'win hame to my ain countrie,' I make mine avow to enshrine that first rose-bud in my *reliquaire* with all honor and solemnity, there to abide till one of us shall be dust."

With this explanatory introduction, I have now only to commend "*La Belle Rebelle*" to the kindly sympathies of her readers—not as an authoress (to this she makes no pretensions); nor as a partisan soldier, although as such she has done good service in the cause; nor even as a freed bird from the "Old Capitol" cage; but simply as a woman—a warm-hearted, impulsive, heroic woman of the South, who, maddened by the wrongs and cruelties inflicted upon her people, and exalted, by the love she bore them, above the common cares and considerations of life, dashed into the field, bearing more than a woman's part in her country's struggle for liberty.

Like the flashing of the plume in the helmet of Navarre, the glancing of the Con-

federate ensign, when waved by a woman's
hand, has never failed to fire the soldier's
heart to "lofty deeds and daring high;" and
on more than a hundred Southern battle-fields
that proud banner, consecrated by prayers and
kisses, baptized in tears and blood, has been
greeted by the closing eyes of its dying de-
fenders as the oriflamme of victory.   Though
lost for the moment in clouds and darkness,
prophetic Hope, the last solace of the unfortunate, still waits and watches for its re-
appearance as the harbinger of Southern
liberty and independence :—

> "For the battle to the strong
>   Is not given,
> While the Judge of Right and Wrong
>   Sits in heaven!
> And the God of David still
> Guides the pebble with his will.
> There are giants yet to kill,
>   Wrongs unshriven!"

Since the above was written, the Southern
people have suffered a heavy calamity in the
assassination of the President of the United
States.   Not that Mr. Lincoln was their friend:

on the contrary, every man and woman in the South, and every child born within the last four years, regarded him as the official head and personal embodiment of all their enemies. But, by the removal of the Commander-in-Chief of the great army and navy with which they were contending, a far more vindictive and unrelenting man is invested with the supreme power of the nation. Abraham Lincoln, with all his faults and fanaticism, his angularities of character and vulgarities of manner, had a sunny side to his nature; and there is every reason to believe that, with his idol Union once nominally restored, he would have adopted an indulgent, humane policy towards the brave and vanquished South, believing, with the great poet, that

> "Earthly power doth then show likest God's,
> When mercy seasons justice."

The suspicion which has been officially and wickedly thrown upon an honorable and heroic people, touching "the deep damnation of his taking off," is sufficiently answered by

the universal regret expressed throughout the
Confederacy at President Lincoln's death, the
public denunciation of his murderer, and the
horror everywhere felt at the idea of being
"ruled with a rod of iron" by such an un-
principled demagogue as Andrew Johnson!
It is usual, in cases of murder, to look for the
criminal among those who expect to be benefited
by the crime.   In the death of Lincoln, his
immediate successor in office alone receives
"the benefit of his dying."   ·

While deploring the event which places the
reins of power in the hands of one as unfit to
control the destinies of a great nation as was
the reckless youth to guide the chariot of the
Sun, there can be no injustice in alluding to
the fact, that the Northern Powers and the
Northern Press have much to answer for on the
head of assassination. I have yet to learn that
the written programme of Colonel Dahlgren,
which designed the burning of Richmond, the
ravaging of its women, and the murder of
President Davis and all his cabinet, has ever
been disavowed or denounced by the Washing-

ton Government, or by the newspapers that support it. Philosophy and religion alike teach us that, while *crime* only belongs to the *act*, the *sin* of murder consists in the *intent*. In the light of this judgment, faint in comparison with that "awful light" yet to be thrown, not only upon all human actions, but upon "the very thoughts and intents of the heart," both North and South, friend and foe, rebel and loyalist, the victim and the victor, the living and the dead, must all be tried and sentenced by ONE who "judgeth not as man judgeth."

In the mean time, let us pray, and hope, and labor for liberty, love, and peace.

LONDON, *May 17th*, 1865.

BELLE BOYD.

CHAPTER I.

Home—Glimpse at Washington City.

My English readers, who love their own hearths and homes so dearly, will pardon an exile if she commences the narrative of her adventures with a brief reminiscence of her far-distant birthplace—

> "Loved to the last, whatever intervenes
> Between us and our childhood's sympathy,
> Which still reverts to what first caught the eye."

There is, perhaps, no tract of country in the world more lovely than the Valley of the Shenandoah. There is, or rather, I should say, there was, no prettier or more peaceful little

village than Martinsburg, where I was born
in 1844.

All those charms with which the fancy of
Goldsmith invested the Irish hamlet in the
days of its prosperity were realized in my
native village. Alas! Martinsburg has met a
more cruel fate than that of " sweet Auburn."
The one, at least, still lives in song, and will
continue to be a household word as long as
the English language shall be spoken : the
other was destined to be the first and fairest
offering upon the altar of Confederate freedom ; but no poet has arisen from her ruins
to perpetuate her name.

While America was yet at peace within
itself, while the States were yet united, many
very beautiful residences were erected in the
vicinity of Martinsburg, which may be said
to have attained some degree of importance
as a town, when the large machinery buildings
were raised, at a vast outlay, by the Baltimore
and Ohio Railway Company. They were not
destined to repay those who designed them.

While they were yet in course of construction, their doom was silently but rapidly approaching. They were destroyed, as the only means of averting their capture by the advancing Yankees, by that undaunted hero, that true apostle of Freedom, "Stonewall" Jackson.

Reader, I must once again revert to my home, which was so soon to be the prey of the spoiler.

Imagine a bright warm sun shining upon a pretty two-storied house, the walls of which are completely hidden by roses and honeysuckle in most luxuriant bloom. At a short distance in front of it flows a broad, clear, rapid stream: around it the silver maples wave their graceful branches in the perfume-laden air of the South.

Even at this distance of time and space, as I write in my dull London lodging, I can hardly restrain my tears when I recall the sweet scene of my early days, such as it was before the unsparing hand of a ruthless enemy had defaced its loveliness. I frequently indulge in a fond soliloquy, and say, or rather think, "Do my English readers ever bestow a thought upon that cruel fate which has overtaken so many of their lineal descendants, whose only crime has been that love of freedom which the Pilgrim Fathers could not leave behind them when they left their island home? Do they bestow any pity, any sympathy, upon us homeless, ruined, exiled Confederates? Do they ever pause to reflect what would be their own feelings if, far and wide throughout their country, the ancestral hall, the farmer's homestead, and the laborer's cot were giving shelter to the licentious soldiers of an invader or crackling in incendiary flames? With what emotions would the citizens of London watch the camp-fires of a besieging army?

> " ' Say with what eye along the distant down
> Would flying burghers mark the blazing town—
> How view the column of ascending flames
> Shake his red shadow o'er the startled Thames.' "

Much has lately been written of the comfort of our Southern homesteads; and now, though so many of them are things of the past, while those that remain are no longer what they were, I may safely say, that not even English homes were more comfortable, in the true sense of the word, than ours; while for hospitality we have never been surpassed.

I passed my childhood as all happy children usually do, petted and caressed by a father and mother, loving and beloved by my brothers and sisters. The peculiarly sad circumstances that attended my father's death will be found recorded at a future page. Where my mother is hiding her head, I know not: doubtless she is equally ignorant of my fate. My brothers and sisters are dispersed God knows where.

But to return to my narrative. I believe I shall not be contradicted in affirming that nowhere could be found more pleasant society than that of Virginia. In this respect the neighborhood of Martinsburg was remarkably fortunate, populated as it was by some of the best and most respectable families of "the Old Dominion" — respectable, I mean, both in reputation and in point of antiquity — de-

3

scendants of such ancestors as the Fairfaxes
and Warringtons, upon whom Mr. Thackeray
has lately conferred immortality.

According to the custom of my country, I
was sent at twelve years of age to Mount
Washington College, of which Mr. Staley, of
whom I cherish a most grateful recollection,
was then principal. At sixteen my education
was supposed to be completed, and I made
my *entrée* into the world in Washington City
with all the high hopes and thoughtless joy
natural to my time of life. I did not then
dream how soon my youth was to be "blasted
with a curse"—the worst that can befall man
or woman—the curse of civil war.

Washington is so well known to English
people that I need not pause to describe the
city, its gayeties and pleasures. In the winter
of 1860-1, when I made my first acquaintance
with it, the season was pre-eminently brilliant.
The Senate and Congress halls were nightly
dignified by the presence of our ablest orators
and statesmen; the *salons* of the wealthy and
the talented were filled to overflowing; the

theatres were crowded to excess, and for the last time for many years to come the daughters of the North and the South commingled in sisterly love and friendship.

I am inclined to think that at the time of which I speak the City of Washington must have very nearly resembled that of Paris during those few years which immediately preceded 1789, while the elements of a stupendous revolution were yet hidden beneath a tranquil and deceitful surface. Like the Parisians of that memorable epoch, we were wilfully or fatally blind to the signs of the times; we ate and drank, we dined and danced, we went in and came out, we married and were given in marriage, without a thought of the volcano that was seething beneath our feet.

Who can predict what will be the end and issue of our revolution, when we consider that the effects of that which burst forth seventy-five years ago, wrapped all Europe in flames, and hurled kings from their thrones, are even now but partially developed ? How many thousands of our sons have fallen in battle, against oppressors who would not confess that our freedom was beyond their power! How many hapless women and children have perished miserably, or been driven forth to beg their bread in foreign countries, before enemies who with heavy hands have sought to rivet our chains —enemies who could not discern the truth of the Irish orator's memorable axiom, and acknowledge that the genius of liberty is universal and irresistible!

CHAPTER II.

Political Contest.—Commencement of the Great Struggle in
America.—Secession of the Southern States.—We hear
of the Fall of Fort Sumter.—Call for Troops.—The Stars
and Bars.—Volunteers.—Enlistment of my Father.—
Patriotism of the Southern Women.—Harper's Ferry.—
Visit to Camp.—Picnics, Balls, &c., &c.

THE gayeties of Washington, to which I
alluded in my first chapter, were soon
eclipsed by the clouds that gathered in the
political horizon.

The contest for the Presidentship was
over, and the men of the South could no
longer hide it from themselves, that the issue
of the struggle must determine their fate.

The secession of the Southern States, indi-
vidually or in the aggregate, was the certain
consequence of Mr. Lincoln's election. His

accession to a power supreme and almost unparalleled was an unequivocal declaration, by the merchants of New England, that they had resolved to exclude the landed proprietors of the South from all participation in the legislation of their common country.

I will not attempt to defend the institution of slavery, the very name of which is abhorred in England; but it will be admitted that the emancipation of the negro was not the object of Northern ambition; that is, of the faction which grasps exclusive power in contempt of general rights. Slavery, like all other imperfect forms of society, will have its day; but the time for its final extinction in the Confederate States of America has not yet arrived. Can it be urged that a race which prefers servitude to freedom has reached that adolescent period of existence which fits it for the latter condition? Meanwhile, which stands in the better position, the helot of the South, or the "free" negro of the North—the willing slave of a Confederate master, or the reluctant victim of Federal conscription?

And here I must take leave to ask a question of two great authors, both formerly advocates of an instantaneous abolition of slavery. Is the ghost of Uncle Tom laid? Has the slave dreamed his last dream? Will Mrs. H. B. Stowe and Mr. Longfellow admit that in either instance the hero owes his reputation for martydom to a creative genius and to an exquisite fancy? or will they still contend that the negro slave of the Confederate States is, physically and morally, a real object of commiseration?

The first champion of freedom—I speak advisedly, and in defiance of a seeming paradox—was South Carolina. She was a slave-holding State, but she flung down the gauntlet in the name and for the cause of liberty. Her bold example was soon followed; State after State seceded, and the Union was dissolved. It was now that we heard of the fall of Fort Sumter and Mr. Lincoln's demand upon the State of Virginia. He called upon her to furnish her quota of 75,000 recruits, to engage in battle with her sister States. He sowed the dragon's teeth, and he soon reaped the only harvest that could spring from such seed.

Virginia promptly answered to the call, and produced the required soldiers; but they did not rally under the Stars and Stripes. It was to the Stars and Bars, the emblem of the South, that Mr. Lincoln's Virginia soldiers tendered the oath of military allegiance. The flag of the once loved, but now dishonored Union, was lowered, and the colors of the Confederacy were raised in its place.

Since that memorable epoch, those colors have been baptized with the blood of thousands, to whose death, in a cause so righteous, the honor and reverence that wait upon martyrdom have been justly awarded:—

"Oh, if there be in this earthly sphere
A boon, an offering, Heaven holds dear,
It is the libation that Liberty draws
From the heart that bleeds and breaks in her cause."

The enthusiasm of the enlistment was adequate to the occasion. Old men, with gray hairs and stooping forms, young boys, just able to shoulder a musket, strong and weak, rich and poor, rallied round our new standard, actuated by a stern sense of duty, and eager for death or victory. It was at this exciting crisis that I returned to Martinsburg; and, oh! what a striking contrast my native village presented to the scenes I had just left behind me at Washington! My winter had been cheered by every kind of amusement and every form of pleasure: my summer was about to be darkened by constant anxiety and heart-rending affliction.

My father was one of the first to volunteer. He was offered that grade in the army to which his social position entitled him; but, like many of our Virginian gentlemen, he preferred to enlist in the ranks, thereby leaving the pay and emoluments of an officer's commission to some other, whose means were not so ample, and whose family might be straitened in his absence from home, an absence that must, of course, interfere with his avocation or profession.

The 2nd Virginian was the regiment to which my father attached himself. It was

3*

armed and equipped by means of a subscription raised by myself and other ladies of the Valley. On the colors were inscribed these words, so full of pathos and inspiration:—

"Our God, our country, and our women."

The corps was commanded by Colonel Nadenbush, and belonged to that section of the Southern army afterwards known as "the Stonewall Brigade." "The Stonewall Brigade!"—the very name now bears with it traditions of surpassing glory; and I seize this opportunity of assuring English readers that it is with pride we Confederates acknowledge that our heroes caught their inspiration from the example of their English ancestors. When our descendants shall read the story of General Jackson and his men, they will be insensibly attracted to those earlier pages of history which record the exploits of Wellington's Light Division.

My father's regiment was hardly formed when it was ordered to Harper's Ferry; for the sacred soil of Virginia was threatened with invasion, and it was thought possible to make a stand at this lovely spot, to see which is "worth a voyage across the Atlantic." At the outbreak of the war Harper's Ferry could boast of one of the largest and best arsenals in America, and of a magnificent bridge, which latter, spanning the broad stream of the Potomac, connected Maryland with Virginia. Both arsenal and bridge were blown up in July, 1861, by the Confederate forces, when the Federals, pressing upon them in overwhelming numbers, compelled a retreat.

My home had now become desolate and lonely: the excitement caused by our exertions to equip our father for the field had ceased, and the reaction of feeling had set in. A general sadness and depression prevailed throughout our household. My mother's face began to wear an anxious, careworn expression. Our nights were not passed in sleep, but in thinking painfully of the loved one who was exposed to the dangers and privations of war.

My mother, the daughter of an old officer, was left an orphan when very young; she had married my father just as she entered upon her sixteenth year; and now, almost for the first time, they were parted, under circumstances which made the separation bitter indeed. For myself, I endeavored to while away the long hours of those summer days by the aid of my books, and in making up different kinds of portable provisions for the use of my father, to whom I knew they would, in his novel position, be a luxury.

But, notwithstanding all the restrictions I laid upon myself, and all the self-control I endeavored to exert, I soon found these employments too tame and monotonous to satisfy my temperament, and I made up my mind to pay a visit to the camp, *coûte qui coûte*. I had no difficulty in prevailing upon some of my friends to accompany me in an expedition to head-quarters. Like myself, they had friends and relations to whom they felt their occasional presence would be a source of encouragement and solace; and we all knew that such a good-

ly company as we formed could return safely
to Martinsburg at almost any hour of the day
or night.

The camp at Harper's Ferry was at this
time an animated scene. Officers and men
were as gay and joyous as though no bloody
strife awaited them. The ladies, married and
single, in the society of husbands, brothers,
sons, and lovers, cast their cares to the winds,
and seemed, one and all, resolved that whatever calamity the future might have in store
for them, it should not mar the transient
pleasures of the hour. Since then I have had
occasion to observe that such a state of feeling
is not unnatural or unusual in the minds of
men standing, as it were, on the brink of a
precipice, or walking, as it were, over the
surface of a mine. "Perils commonly ask to
be paid in pleasures," and the payment is
doubly sweet when it is taken in anticipation
of the debt.

I fear that at this time many fond vows
were exchanged and many true hearts pledged
between the girls of the neighborhood and

the occupants of the camp; but it may be pardoned to beauty and innocence if they are not insensible to the virtues of courage and patriotism.

A true woman always loves a real soldier. In the earliest ages poets and philosophers foretold that the Goddess of Love and Beauty would ever move in the same orbit and in close conjunction with the God of Battles, and the experience of ages has confirmed the judg· ment of antiquity. Alas! the loves of Har· per's Ferry were in but too many instances buried in a bloody grave. The soldier who plighted his faith to his lady-love was not tried in a long probation, but canonized by an early death. War will exact its victims of both sexes, and claims the hearts of women no less than the bodies of men.

To return from this digression. Our *insouciance* was not of long duration. The advance of a Federal army was reported; and General Jackson, with a force amounting to five thousand men, marched out to recon· noitre, and, if possible, to check their aggressive movement. Our people encamped at "Falling Waters," a romantic spot, eight miles from Martinsburg and four from Williamsport; for at this point of the river, it was rumored, the Yankees had resolved to force a passage.

It was early in the morning of the 3d July that we "gude folks" of dear Martinsburg were startled by the roar of artillery and the rattle of musketry; and the intelligence was presently circulated that the Yankees were advancing upon us in force, under the command of Generals Patterson and Cadwallader. It turned out, however, that, at the moment of which I speak, their advanced guard only was in motion; but the skirmish between our people and the enemy was sustained during nearly five hours. On both sides some fell, and besides the casualties of the Federals in killed and wounded, we took about fifty of them prisoners.

About ten o'clock, General Jackson's army, in admirable array, marched through Martinsburg. They were in full retreat, their object being to effect a junction with the main body, under General J. E. Johnston, who had evacuated Harper's Ferry, and was falling back, by way of Charlestown, upon Winchester.

Jackson's retreat was covered by a few horsemen under the gallant Colonel Ashby; and scarcely were these latter disengaged from the streets of the town, when the shrill notes of the fife and the roll of the drum announced the approach of the Federal army, which proved to be twenty-five thousand strong.

It was to us a sad, but an imposing sight. On they came (their colors streaming to the breeze, their bayonets glittering in the sunlight), with all the "pomp and circumstance of glorious war." We could see from afar the dancing plumes of the cavalry—

> "the glittering files,
> O'er whose gay trappings stern Bellona smiles!"

we could before long hear the rumbling of the gun-carriages, and, worse than this, the hellish shouts with which the infuriated and undisciplined soldiers poured into the town.

At the time of their entry, I was in the

hospital, with my negro maid and some ladies of my acquaintance, in attendance upon two of our Southern soldiers, who had been stricken down with fever, and were lying side by side. These were the sole tenants of the hospital: all the others had been borne off by the retreating army.

I was standing close by the side of one of these poor men, who was just then raving in a violent fit of delirium, when I was startled by the sound of heavy footsteps behind me; and turning round, I confronted a captain of Federal infantry, accompanied by two private soldiers. He held in his hand a Federal flag, which he proceeded to wave over the bed of the sick men, at the same time calling them " ——— rebels."

I immediately said, with all the scorn I could convey into my looks, " Sir, these men are as helpless as babies, and have, as you may see, no power to reply to your insults."

" And pray," said he, "who may you be, Miss ?"

I did not deign to reply; but my negro maid answered him, "A rebel lady."

Hereupon he turned upon his heel and retired, with the courteous remark, that "I was a —— independent one, at all events."

I hope my readers will pardon my quoting his exact words: without such strict accuracy, I should fail to do justice to his gallantry.

Notwithstanding this interruption to our "woman's mission," the ladies to whom I have before alluded and myself were not discouraged; and, before long, we contrived to get our patients moved to more comfortable quarters. They were taken away on litters; and, while they were in this defenceless condition, a condition which would have awakened the sympathy and secured the protection of a brave enemy, the Federal soldiers crowded round and threatened to bayonet them!

Their gesticulations and language grew so violent; their countenances, inflamed by drink and hatred, were so frightful, that I nerved myself to seek out an officer and appeal to his sense of military honor, even if the voice of mercy were silent in his breast. Let me do him the justice to say, he restrained his turbulent men from further molestation, and I had the unspeakable satisfaction of conveying my sick men to a place of safety. The satisfaction was immeasurable; for I never for one moment forgot that insults such as I had just seen offered to defenceless men might at any moment be heaped upon my own father.

CHAPTER III.

Fourth of July.—The Yankee Flag is hoisted in Martinsburg.—Great Excitement.—My First Adventure.—An
Article of War is read to me.—Miss Sophia B.'s Walk.

THE morning of the 4th of July dawned
brightly.

I need hardly say, for it is well known,
that the anniversary of the Declaration of
Independence has, in each succeeding year
from that of its birth, been hailed with triumphant acclamations by a nation still too
young to moderate its transports and lend its
ear to the voice of reason rather than to the
impulse of passion.

The Yankees were in undisputed possession
of Martinsburg; the village was at their
mercy, and consequently entitled to their forbearance; and it would at least have been

more dignified in them had they been content to enjoy their almost bloodless conquest with moderation; but, whatever might have been the intentions of the officers, they had not the inclination, or they lacked the authority, to control the turbulence of their men.

The severance of the North from the South had now become in feeling so complete, that we Martinsburg girls saw the Union flag streaming from the windows of the houses with emotions akin to those with which the ladies of England would gaze upon the tricolor of France or the eagle of Russia floating above the keep of Windsor Castle. Those hateful strains of "Yankee Doodle" resounded in every street, with an accompaniment of cheers, shouts, and imprecations.

Whiskey now began to flow freely; for, amid the motley crowd of Americans, Dutchmen, and other nations, the Irish element predominated. The sprigs of shillelahs were soon at work, and the "sons of Erin" proved that they could use their sticks with no less effect in an American town than at an Irish fair. They set at defiance the authority of those among their officers who vainly interposed to quell the tumult and restrain the lawless violence that was offered to defenceless citizens and women.

The doors of our houses were dashed in; our rooms were forcibly entered by soldiers who might literally be termed "mad drunk," for I can think of no other expression so applicable to their condition. Glass and fragile property of all kinds was wantonly destroyed. They found our homes scenes of comfort, in some cases even of luxury; they left them mere wrecks, utterly despoiled and mutilated. Shots were fired through the windows; chairs and tables were hurled into the street.

In some instances a trembling lady would make a timid appeal to that honor which should be the attribute of every soldier, or, with streaming eyes and passionate accents, plead for some cherished object—the portrait, probably, of a dead father, or the miniature her lover placed in her hand when he left her to fight for his freedom and hers—upon which many a secret kiss had been pressed, many a silent tear had fallen, before which many an earnest prayer had been breathed.

To such applications the reply was invariably a volley of blasphemous curses and horrid imprecations. Words from which the mind recoils with horror, which no man with one spark of feeling would utter in the presence even of the most abandoned woman, were shouted in the ears of innocent, shrinking girls; and the soldiers of the Union showed a malignant, a fiendish delight in destroying the effigies of enemies whom they had not yet dared to meet upon equal terms in an open field of battle.

Surely it is not strange that cruelties such as I have attempted to describe have exasperated our women no less than our men, and inspired them with sterner feelings than those which inflame the bosoms of ladies who know nothing of invasion but its name, who have never at their own firesides shuddered at the oaths and threats of a robber disguised in the garb of a soldier.

Shall I be ashamed to confess that I recall without one shadow of remorse the act by which I saved my mother from insult, perhaps from death—that the blood I then shed has left no stain on my soul, imposed no burden upon my conscience?

The encounter to which I refer was brought about as follows:—A party of soldiers, conspicuous, even on that day, for violence, broke into our house and commenced their depredations; this occupation, however, they presently discontinued, for the purpose of hunting for "rebel flags," with which they had been informed my room was decorated. Fortunately for us, although without my orders, my negro maid promptly rushed up-stairs, tore down the obnoxious emblem, and before our enemies could get possession of it, burned it.

They had brought with them a large Federal flag, which they were now preparing to hoist over our roof in token of our submission to their authority; but to this my mother would not consent. Stepping forward with a firm step, she said, very quietly, but resolutely,

"Men, every member of my household will die before that flag shall be raised over us."

Upon this, one of the soldiers, thrusting himself forward, addressed my mother and myself in language as offensive as it is possible to conceive. I could stand it no longer; my indignation was roused beyond control; my blood was literally boiling in my veins; I drew out my pistol* and shot him. He was carried away mortally wounded, and soon after expired.

Our persecutors now left the house, and we were in hopes we had got rid of them, when one of the servants, rushing in, cried out—

"Oh, missus, missus, dere gwine to burn de house down; dere pilin' de stuff ag'in it! Oh, if massa were back!"

The prospect of being burned alive naturally terrified us, and, as a last resource, I contrived to get a message conveyed to the Federal officer in command. He exerted him-

* All our male relatives being with the army, we ladies were obliged to go armed in order to protect ourselves as best we might from insult and outrage.

4

self with effect, and had the incendiaries arrested before they could execute their horrible purpose.

In the mean time it had been reported at head-quarters that I had shot a Yankee soldier, and great was the indignation at first felt and expressed against me. Soon, however, the commanding officer, with several of his staff, called at our house to investigate the affair. He examined the witnesses, and inquired into all the circumstances with strict impartiality, and finally said I had "done perfectly right." He immediately sent for a guard to head-quarters, where the *élite* of the army was stationed, and a tolerable state of discipline preserved.

Sentries were now placed around the house, and Federal officers called every day to inquire if we had any complaint to make of their behavior. It was in this way that I became acquainted with so many of them; an acquaintance "the rebel spy" did not fail to turn to account on more than one occasion.

When the news reached the Confederate

camp at Darksville, seven miles from Martinsburg, on the Valley Road, that I had shot a
Yankee soldier in self-defence, together with
the false report that for so doing I had been
thrown into the town jail, the soldiers with
one accord volunteered to storm the prison
and rescue me, or die to a man in the attempt.
It is with pride and gratitude that I record
this proof of their esteem and respect for what
I had done. It is with no less pleasure I
reflect that their devotion was not put to the
test, and that no blood was shed on my account.

And now, for seven consecutive days, General Jo. Johnston sent in a flag of truce offering battle to General Patterson: this challenge
Patterson persistently declined. I am not so
ignorant of warfare as not to know that *stra-
tegic* reasons justify the most daring general
in refusing battle whenever and wherever he
pleases.

" If thou art a great soldier, come and fight."
" If thou art a great soldier, make me come and
fight."

But, though the Federal commander had a perfect right to choose his own battle-field, he had, in my opinion, no right to couple his refusal of the challenge with a threat that, as soon as Johnston should think fit to make an aggressive movement, he would at once shell Martinsburg, which sheltered the non-combatants, the women and the children, the sick and the infirm.

Meanwhile, my residence within the Federal lines, and my acquaintance with so many of the officers, the origin of which I have already mentioned, enabled me to gain much important information as to the position and designs of the enemy. Whatever I heard I regularly and carefully committed to paper, and whenever an opportunity offered I sent my secret dispatch by a trusty messenger to General J. E. B. Stuart, or some brave officer in command of the Confederate troops. Through accident or by treachery one of these missives fell into the Yankees' hands. It was not written in cipher, and, moreover, my handwriting was identified. I was immediately summoned to appear before some colonel, whose name I have forgotten; but I remember it was Captain Gwyne who escorted me to head-quarters. There I was alternately threatened and reprimanded, and finally the following "Article of War" was read to me in a most emphatic manner, and with the caution that it would be carried out in the spirit and the letter:—

"ARTICLE OF WAR.

"Whoever shall give food, ammunition, information to, or aid* and abet the enemies of the United States Government in any manner whatever, shall suffer death, or whatever penalty the honorable members of the court-martial shall see fit to inflict."

I was not frightened, for I felt within me the spirit of the Douglas, from whom I am descended. I listened quietly to the recital of the doom which was to be my reward for ad-

* I had been confiscating and concealing their pistols and swords on every possible occasion, and many an officer, looking about everywhere for his missing weapons, little dreamed who it was that had taken them, or that they had been smuggled away to the Confederate camp, and were actually in the hands of their enemies, to be used against themselves.

hering to the traditions of my youth and the cause of my country, made a low bow, and, with a sarcastic "Thank you, gentlemen of the Jury," I departed; not in peace, however, for my little "rebel" heart was on fire, and I indulged in thoughts and plans of vengeance.

From this hour I was a "suspect," and all the mischief done to the Federal cause was laid to my charge; and it is with unfeigned joy and true pride I confess that the suspicions of the enemy were far from being unfounded.

On one occasion a friend of mine, Miss Sophia B——, of Martinsburg, a lovely girl, slipped away with a *lettre de cachet*, walked seven miles to the camp of Stonewall Jackson, and handed him important information, which was productive of much good. She, like myself, had brothers enrolled in that band of heroes.

CHAPTER IV.

Battle of Manassas—Establishment of a Hospital at Front Royal (Virginia)—A Runaway Excursion—Capture of Federal Officers.

THROUGHOUT the North the utmost confidence was felt that the subjugation of the rebels would be rapid and complete. "Ninety days!" "On, on to Richmond!" was the cry; but the shout was changed to a wail, on Manassas plains, where the first great battle of the war was fought.

The action was precipitated by Patterson's attempt to prevent Johnston from effecting a junction with Beauregard at Manassas. In this he failed, and the result of the movements and counter-movements was the battle of "Bull Run." * This great Confederate

* Here it was that the Stonewall Brigade acquired its name. The fire was very hot, and the —th South Carolina Regiment

victory has become an historical fact; I shall therefore pass it by in silence, and proceed to the narrative of my own personal adventures.

At the time in question I was at Front Royal (Virginia), on a visit to my uncle and aunt, Mr. and Mrs. S——. I wish it were in my power to give my readers some faint idea of this picturesque village, which nestles in the bosom of the surrounding mountains, and reminds one of a young bird in its nest. A rivulet, which sometimes steals round the obstacles to its course, sometimes bounds over them with headlong leap, at last finds its way to the valley beneath, and glides by the village in peace and beauty.

---

of Infantry, thrown into confusion, wavered, and was upon the point of breaking.

"Steady, men, steady," shouted Colonel Bartow, in a loud voice. "Look at General Jackson's brigade; they stand firm and immovable as a stone wall. The —th, animated by the voice and gesture of their gallant commander, and by the example of Jackson's men, rallied; and Colonel Bartow, taking advantage of the enthusiasm he had kindled, led his regiment at once to the charge, when he fell covered with wounds and honor.

The scene is far beyond my powers of description. It is worthy of the pencil of Salvator Rosa, or the pen of the author of "Gertrude of Wyoming," and I only wish the great landscape-painter had been given to our age and had wandered to the hills and valleys of Virginia.

To this romantic retreat my uncle and aunt had fled, as deer fly for safety to the hills. They had resided in Washington, but their Southern sympathies were too strong and too openly expressed to allow of their remaining unmolested in the Northern capital. They left a magnificent house, replete with handsome furniture, a prey to the Yankees, who converted it into barracks.

Orders now came from the battle-field of Bull Run to the effect that the General in command had fixed upon Front Royal for the site of an extensive hospital, for the wounded Confederate soldiers. Every one in the village and the neighborhood showed the greatest alacrity—I should say, enthusiasm—in preparing, in the shortest possible time, all that

4*

our suffering heroes could require. I bore my part, and, before long, was duly installed one of the "matrons."

My office was a very laborious one, and my duties were painful in the extreme; but then, as always, I allowed but one thought to keep possession of my mind — the thought that I was doing all a woman could do in her country's cause. The motto of my father's regiment was engraven on my heart, and I trust that I have always shown by my actions that I understand its significance.

After six or eight weeks spent in incessant nursing, I was forced to return to my home at Martinsburg, in order to recruit my health, which had suffered severely; and I leave my readers to imagine with what joy I heard my dear mother's praises of actions which she, in her fond affection, styled heroic.

In October my mother and myself resolved upon a short visit to my father at Manassas. We stayed at a large house, situated in the very centre of the camp. This tenement was then the temporary abode of several other ladies, wives and daughters of officers.

During this period I had frequently the honor of acting the part of courier between General Beauregard, General Jackson, and their subordinates.

This was a happy time, but it did not last long; and, after a few weeks spent as above described, my mother and I returned to Martinsburg. The winter passed very quietly, and brought me but a single adventure worth recording.

"I was riding out one evening with two young officers,* one a cousin and the other a friend, when my horse, a young and high-spirited creature, took fright, and ran away with me. Notwithstanding all my efforts, I failed to stop him until he had carried me within the Federal lines, a goal to which my companions could not venture to follow me.

I felt rather uncomfortable, not knowing

* My English readers may deem it strange that a young girl should ride alone with young gentlemen, but the practice is not in America considered a breach of decorum.

exactly how to act; but I soon made up my mind that, for this once, at all events, valor would be the better part of discretion, if not prudence itself; so, riding straight up to the officer in command of the picket, I said—

"I beg your pardon—you must know that I have been taking a ride with some of my friends; my horse ran away with me, and has carried me within your lines. I am your captive, but I beg you will permit me to return."

"We are exceedingly proud of our beautiful captive," replied one of the officers, with a bow, "but of course we cannot think of detaining you." Then, after a moment's pause, he added—

"May we have the honor of escorting you beyond our lines and restoring you to the custody of your friends? I suppose there is no fear of those cowardly rebels taking us prisoners?"

"I had scarcely hoped," I replied, "for such an honor. I thought you would probably have given me a pass; but since you are so kind as to offer your services in person, I cannot do otherwise than accept them. Have no fear, gentlemen, of the 'cowardly rebels.'"

They little thought how those words, "cowardly rebels," rankled in my heart.

Off we started; and imagine their blank looks when, soon after they had escorted me beyond their lines, my Confederate friends, who had been anxiously waiting for me, rode out from their ambush and joined the party. All four looked surprised and embarrassed. I broke the general silence, by saying, with a laugh, to the Confederates, "Here are two prisoners that I have brought you."

Then turning to the Federal officers, I said—

"Here are two of the 'cowardly rebels' whom you hoped there was no danger of meeting!"

They looked doubtfully and inquiringly at me, and, after a short pause, exclaimed almost simultaneously—

"And who, pray, is the lady?"

"Belle Boyd, at your service," I replied.

"Good God! the rebel spy!"

"So be it, since your journals have honored me with that title."

After this short colloquy we escorted them, without any attempt at resistance on their part, to head-quarters, and related all the circumstances of the adventure to the officer in command, who ordered them to be detained.

The Yankees reproached us bitterly with our treachery; but when it is considered that their release followed their capture within an hour, that they had in the first instance stigmatized the rebels, when none were near, as cowards, that they had immediately afterwards yielded without a blow to an equal number of these self-same cowards, I think my readers will admit their spirit of bravado well merited a slight humiliation. Let us hope they have profited by the lesson. I consoled myself that " all was fair in love and war."

Although Bull Run had been fought, and I had witnessed the outrages of July 4th at Martinsburg, we had hardly yet realized the horrors of war, or, to speak more correctly, we did not allow ourselves to believe in their continuance. We hoped that enough had been done to pave the way for reconciliation. Winter set in and closed the campaign, and, with a cessation of active hostilities, our apprehensions for the future were forgotten in our enjoyment of the present.

It was only when spring returned, and brought with it no sign of a dove from the ark, that we realized how far the waters of the deluge were from subsiding. Balls and sleighs, mirth and laughter, vanished with the last snows of winter; and it was with sad and sickening hearts we saw Colonel Ashby and his cavalry evacuate the town.

But a very few years since, Henry, afterwards Colonel Ashby, was one of those young men whose characters have been so often imagined by writers of romance, but are so rarely met with in real life. He united in himself all those qualifications which justly recommend their possessor to the love of the one sex and to the esteem of the other. At once tender and respectful, manly and accom-

plished, animated and handsome, he won
without an effort the hearts of women.
Brave and good-humored, he combined sim-
plicity with talents of the highest order. He
entertained a strict sense of honor, and never
forgot what was due to himself; and he was
ever wont to forget an injury, and even to
pardon an insult, upon the first overture of
the offender.

Endowed with such qualities, it is not
surprising he was a universal favorite; and,
indeed, it was commonly said the spirit of
Admirable Crichton had revisited the world in
the person of Henry Ashby.

Such a man was sure to be among the
first to draw his sword in the cause of independence.

At an early period of the war he was
appointed to the command of a regiment of
cavalry, in which capacity he displayed an
unusual degree of vigilance and alacrity in the
arduous service of outpost duty.

On one occasion his regiment was drawn
up at some distance from a railroad which

passed directly across his front.' On the farther
side was broken ground, well calculated to
conceal a large body of men. Colonel Ashby,
therefore, ordered out a small party to reconnoitre, putting them under command of his
younger brother, between whom and himself
there subsisted an affection warm, genuine,
almost romantic.

Unfortunately "Dick Ashby's" impetuosity overlaid his judgment, and, exceeding the
instructions he had received from his brother,
he passed some distance beyond the railway,
and suddenly found himself in presence of a
large body of the enemy.

He retreated in admirable order; but the
Yankees pressed hard upon him, and he and
his little band were overtaken upon the railroad.

Here a fatal accident befell poor Dick
Ashby. His horse stumbled and fell at one
of the cuts.* In this defenceless condition he

* These cuts are large drains, or rather tunnels, cut
transversely through the lines of American railways, at short
intervals. They serve to carry off such a rush of water as
would otherwise inundate the line after a heavy fall of rain

was set upon without mercy, without even quarter being offered, by five Yankees at once.

In spite of these odds, and the disadvantage at which he was taken, he sold his life so dearly that his five assailants were all killed or wounded.   By this time Colonel Ashby, leading on his regiment at a gallop, had reached the scene of action, and, the contest being now pretty equal, the Federals soon fled, and were pursued as far as the nature of the ground would permit.   The victors then returned to the railway, and hastily dug a shallow grave, into which all that remained of Dick Ashby was consigned.

Colonel Ashby dismounted, and, kneeling by the mutilated body, gently disengaged the sword from his dead brother's hand; then breaking it into pieces, he cast them into the grave, and on that solemn spot vowed to avenge his brother's murder and to consecrate the remainder of his life to the service of his country.

or the overflow of a river.   They are of course covered, and the trains pass over them.

This vow he faithfully kept. His character underwent a change as instantaneous and enduring as that of Colonel Gardiner. All his gayety and high spirits forsook him. In society he was rarely heard to speak, never seen to smile, and, after a brief but glorious career, he fell in an unequal and desperate struggle, cheering on his men with his dying breath.

> "The bravest are the tenderest:
> The gentle are the daring."

I shall conclude this chapter with another short episode, which proves how suddenly national disorders discover the hidden force of individual character.

Miss D., at the outbreak of the war, was a lovely, fragile-looking girl of nineteen, remarkable for the sweetness of her temper and the gentleness of her disposition.

A few days before the battle of Bull Run, a country market-cart stopped in the Confederate lines, at the door of General Bonham's tent. A peasant-girl alighted from the cart and begged for an immediate interview with the General.

It was granted.

"General Bonham, I believe?" said the young lady, in tones which betrayed her superiority to the disguise she had assumed. Then, tearing down her long, black hair, she took from its folds a note, small, damp, and crumpled; but it was by acting upon this informal dispatch that General Beauregard won the victory of Bull Run.

Miss D. had passed through the whole of the Federal army. I dare not now publish her name; but, if ever these pages meet her eye, she will not fail to recognize her own portrait, nor will she be displeased to find that her exiled countrywoman cherishes the remembrance of her intrepidity and devotion.

CHAPTER V.

Advance of the Federal Army—I leave Home with my
Father—Battle of Kearnstown—I am Arrested and
carried Prisoner to Baltimore—Released and sent to
Martinsburg—I attempt to go South to Richmond—
Shields's Army at Front Royal—Incidents, &c., &c.

WITH the first genial days of spring, the
Federal troops broke up their winter-quarters,
and advanced again upon the devastated
village of Martinsburg, which had been held
during the winter by the Confederates. Martinsburg, situated as it was on the border of
the State, was incessantly a bone of contention,
and its capture and recapture were of frequent
recurrence.

My father, who had been at home on sick-
leave for several weeks, was now able to resume
his military duties, and he decided upon removing me farther south, as our home was in

constant peril, and I had gained a notoriety which would hardly recommend me to the favorable notice of the Federals in the event of their shortly reoccupying Martinsburg, which seemed only too probable.

Accordingly, I was again sent to Front Royal, there to remain until our home should once more be secure.

A few days after my arrival at Front Royal a battle was fought close by, at Kearnstown. The Confederates, vastly overmatched in numbers, were forced to retreat, and Front Royal became the prize of the conquerors. Thus, to use a homely adage, "out of the frying-pan into the fire" had been my fate.

Upon the approach of the enemy, my uncle and aunt, taking with them one daughter, quitted home with the intention of reaching Richmond, leaving their other daughter, Alice S——, a beautiful girl about my own age, our grandmamma, Mrs. Glynn and myself, to take charge of the house and servants, and act in all contingencies to the best of our ability.

When I found that the Confederate forces

were retreating so far down the Valley, and reflected that my father was with them, I became very anxious to return to my mother; and, as no tie of duty bound me to Front Royal, I resolved upon the attempt at all hazards.

I started in company with my maid, and had got safely without adventure of any kind as far as Winchester, when some unknown enemy or some malicious neutral denounced me to the authorities as a Confederate spy.

Before, however, this act of hostility or malice had been perpetrated, I had taken the precaution of procuring a pass from General Shields; and I fondly hoped that this would, under all circumstances, secure me from molestation and arrest; for I was not aware that, while I was in the very act of receiving my bill of "moral health," an order was being issued by the Provost-Marshal which forbade me to leave the town.

When the hour which I had fixed for my departure arrived, I stepped into the railway-cars, and was congratulating myself with the thought that I should ere long be at home once more, and in the society of those I loved, when a Federal officer, Captain Bannon, appeared. He was in charge of some Confederate prisoners, who, under his command, were *en route* to the Baltimore prison.

I was more surprised than pleased when, handing over the prisoners to a subordinate, he walked straight up to me, and said :—

"Is this Miss Belle Boyd?"

"Yes."

"I am the Assistant-Provost, and I regret to say, orders have been issued for your detention, and it is my duty to inform you that you cannot proceed until your case has been investigated; so you will, if you please, get out, as the train is on the point of starting."

"Sir," I replied, presenting him General Shields's pass, "here is a pass which I beg you will examine. You will find that it authorizes my maid and myself to pass or any road to Martinsburg."

He reflected for some time, and at last said :—

"Well, I scarcely know how to act in your case. Orders have been issued for your arrest, and yet you have a pass from the General allowing you to return home. However, I shall take the responsibility upon my shoulders, convey you with the other prisoners to Baltimore, and hand you over to General Dix."

I played my *rôle* of submission as gracefully as I could; for where resistance is impossible, it is still left to the vanquished to yield with dignity.

The train by which we travelled was the first that had been run through from Wheeling to Baltimore since the damage done to the permanent way by the Confederates had been repaired.

We had not proceeded far when I observed an old friend of mine, Mr. M., of Baltimore, a gentleman whose sympathies were strongly enlisted on the side of the South. At my request, he took a seat beside me, and, after we had conversed for some time upon different topics, he told me, in a whisper,

5

that he had a small Confederate flag concealed about his person.

"Manage to give it me," I said; "I am already a prisoner; besides, free or in chains, I shall always glory in the possession of the emblem."

Mr. M. watched his opportunity, and, when all eyes were turned from us, he stealthily and quickly drew the little flag from his bosom, and placed it in my hand.

We had eluded the vigilance of the officer under whose surveillance I was travelling; and I leave my readers to imagine his surprise when I drew it forth from my pocket, and, with a laugh, waved it over our heads with a gesture of triumph. It was a daring action, but my captivity had, I think, superadded the courage of despair to the hardihood I had already acquired in my country's service.

The first emotions of the Federal officer and his men were those of indignation; but better feelings succeeded, and they allowed it was an excellent joke, that a convoy of Confederate prisoners should be brought in under a Confederate flag, and that flag raised by a lady.

Upon our arrival at Baltimore, I was taken to the Eutaw House, one of the largest and best hotels in the city, where, I must in justice say, I was treated with all possible courtesy and consideration, and permission to see my friends was at once and spontaneously granted.

As soon as it was known that I was in Baltimore, a prisoner and alone, I was visited, not merely by my personal friends, but by those who knew me by reputation only; for Baltimore is Confederate to its heart's core.

I remained a prisoner in the Eutaw House about a week; at the expiration of which time, General Dix, the officer in command, having heard nothing against me, decided to send me home. I arrived safely at Martinsburg, which is now occupied in force by the Federal troops.

Here I was placed under a strict surveillance, and forbidden to leave the town. I

was incessantly watched and persecuted; and
at last the restrictions imposed upon me became
so irksome and vexatious, that my mother
resolved to intercede with Major Walker,
the Provost-Marshal, on my behalf. The
result of this intercession was, that he granted
us both a pass, by way of Winchester, to
Front Royal, with a view to my being sent on
to join my relations at Richmond.

Upon arriving at Winchester, we had
much difficulty in getting permission to proceed; for General Shields had just occupied
Front Royal, and had prohibited all intercourse between that place and Winchester.
However, Lieutenant-Colonel Fillebrowne, of
the Tenth Maine Regiment, who was acting
as Provost-Marshal, at length relented, and
allowed us to go on our way.

It was almost twilight when we arrived at
the Shenandoah River. We found that the
bridges had been destroyed, and no means of
transport left but a ferry-boat, which the
Yankees monopolized for their own exclusive
purposes.

Here we should have been subjected to much inconvenience and delay, had it not been for the courtesy and kindness of Captain Everhart, through whose intervention we were enabled to cross at once.

It was quite dark when we reached the village, and, to our great surprise, we found the family domiciled in a little cottage in the court-yard, the residence having been appropriated by General Shields and his staff.

However, we were glad enough to find ourselves at our journey's end, and to sit down to a comfortable dinner, for which fatigue and a long fast had sharpened our appetite. As soon as we had satisfied our hunger, I sent in my card to General Shields, who promptly returned my missive in person. He was an Irishman, and endowed with all those graces of manner for which the better class of his countrymen are justly famous; nor was he devoid of the humor for which they are no less notorious.

To my application for leave to pass *instanter* through his lines, *en route* for Richmond, he replied, that old Jackson's army was so demoralized that he dared not trust me to their tender mercies; but that they would be annihilated within a few days, and, after such a desirable consummation, I might wander whither I would.

This, of course, was mere badinage on his part; but I am convinced he felt confident of immediate and complete success, or he would not have allowed some expressions to escape him which I turned to account. In short, he was completely off his guard, and forgot that a woman can sometimes listen and remember.

General Shields introduced me to the officers of his staff, two of whom were young Irishmen; and to one of these, Captain K., I am indebted for some very remarkable effusions, some withered flowers, and last, not least, for a great deal of very important information, which was carefully transmitted to my countrymen. I must avow the flowers and the poetry were comparatively valueless in my eyes; but let Captain K. be consoled: these were days of war, not of love, and there are still other ladies in the world besides the "rebel spy."

The night before the departure of General Shields, who was about, as he informed us, to "whip" Jackson, a council of war was held in what had formerly been my aunt's drawing-room. Immediately above this was a bed-chamber, containing a closet, through the floor of which I observed a hole had been bored, whether with a view to espionage or not I have never been able to ascertain. It occurred to me, however, that I might turn the discovery to account; and as soon as the council of war had assembled, I stole softly up stairs, and lying down on the floor of the closet, applied my ear to the hole, and found, to my great joy, I could distinctly hear the conversation that was passing below.

The council prolonged their discussion for some hours; but I remained motionless and silent until the proceedings were brought to a conclusion, at one o'clock in the morning. As soon as the coast was clear I crossed the court-yard, and made the best of my way to

my own room, and took down in cipher
every-thing I had heard which seemed to me
of any importance.

I felt convinced that to rouse a servant, or
make any disturbance at that hour, would
excite the suspicions of the Federals by whom
I was surrounded; accordingly I went straight
to the stables myself, saddled my horse, and
galloped away in the direction of the mountains.

Fortunately I had about me some passes
which I had from time to time procured for
Confederate soldiers returning south, and
which, owing to various circumstances, had
never been put in requisition. They now,
however, proved invaluable; for I was twice
brought to a stand-still by the challenge of
the Federal sentries, and who would inevita-
bly have put a period to my adventurous
career had they not been beguiled by my
false passport. Once clear of the chain of
sentries, I dashed on unquestioned across
fields and along roads, through fens and
marshes, until, after a scamper of about fifteen

miles, I found myself at the door of Mr. M.'s house. All was still and quiet: not a light was to be seen. I did not lose a moment in springing from my horse; and, running up the steps, I knocked at the door with such vehemence that the house re-echoed with the sound.

It was not until I had repeated my summons, at intervals of a few seconds, for some time, that I heard the response, "Who is there?" given in a sharp voice from a window above.

"It is I."

"But who are you? What is your name?"

"Belle Boyd. I have important intelligence to communicate to Colonel Ashby: is he here?"

"No; but wait a minute: I will come down."

The door was opened, and Mrs. M. drew me in, and exclaimed in a tone of astonishment—

"My dear, where did you come from? and how on earth did you get here?"

5*

"Oh, I forced the sentries," I replied, "and here I am; but I have no time to tell you the how, and the why, and the wherefore. I must see Colonel Ashby without the loss of a minute : tell me where he is to be found."

Upon hearing that his party was a quarter of a mile farther up the wood, I turned to depart in search of them, and was in the very act of remounting when a door on my right was thrown open, and revealed Colonel Ashby himself, who could not conceal his surprise at seeing me standing before him.

"Good God! Miss Belle, is this you? Where did you come from? Have you dropped from the clouds? or am I dreaming?"

I first convinced him he was wide awake, and that my presence was substantial and of the earth—not a visionary emanation from the world of spirits—then, without further circumlocution, I proceeded to narrate all I had overheard in the closet, of which I have before made mention. I gave him the cipher, and started on my return.

I arrived safely at my aunt's house, after a two hours' ride, in the course of which I "ran the blockade" of a sleeping sentry, who awoke to the sound of my horse's hoofs just in time to see me disappear round an abrupt turning, which shielded me from the bullet he was about to send after me. Upon getting home, I unsaddled my horse and "turned in"—if I may be permitted the expression, which is certainly expressive rather than refined—just as Aurora, springing from the rosy bed of Tithonus, began her pursuit of the flying hour; in plain English, just as day began to break.

A few days afterwards General Shields marched south, laying a trap, as he supposed, to catch "poor old Jackson and his demoralized army," leaving behind him, to occupy Front Royal, one squadron of cavalry, one field battery, and the 1st Maryland Regiment of Infantry, under command of Colonel Kenly; Major Tyndale, of Philadelphia, being appointed Provost-Marshal.

My mother returned home, and it was arranged that I should remain with my grandmother until an opportunity of travelling south in safety should present itself. Within a few days after my mother's departure, my Cousin Alice and I applied to Major Tyndale for a pass to Winchester. He at first declined to comply with our request, but afterwards relented, and promised to let us have the necessary passport on the following day. Accordingly, next morning, May 21st, my cousin, one of the servants, and myself were up betimes, and equipped for the journey, the carriage was at the door, but no passes made their appearance; and when we sent to inquire for the Major, we were informed he had gone " out on a scout," and would probably not be back until late at night. We were, of course, in great perplexity, when, to our relief, Lieutenant H., belonging to the squadron of cavalry stationed in the village, made his appearance and asked what was the matter.

I explained our case, and said—

" Now, Lieutenant H., I know you have permission to go to Winchester, and you profess to be a great friend of mine : prove it by assisting me out of this dilemma, and pass us through the pickets."

This I knew he could easily manage, as they were furnished from his own troop.

After a few moments' hesitation, Lieutenant H. consented, little thinking of the consequences that were to ensue. He mounted the box, my cousin, myself, and the servant got inside, and off we set. Shortly before we got to Winchester, Lieutenant H. got down from his seat with the intention of walking the rest of the way, as he had some business at the camp, which was close to the town.

Finding we could not return the same day, we agreed to remain all night with some friends.

Early the next morning a gentleman of high social position came to the house at which we were staying, and handed me two packages of letters, with these words:—

"Miss Boyd, will you take these letters and send them through the lines to the Confederate army? This package," he added, pointing to one of them, "is of great importance: the

other is trifling in comparison. This also," he
went on to say, pointing to what appeared to
be a little note, "is a very important paper: try
to send it carefully and safely to Jackson, or
some other responsible Confederate officer. Do
you understand?"

"I do, and will obey your orders promptly
and implicitly," I replied.

As soon as the gentleman had left me I concealed the most important documents about
the person of my negro servant, as I knew
that "intelligent contrabands"—*i. e.*, ladies and
gentlemen of color—were "non-suspects," and
had *carte blanche* to do what they pleased, and
to go where they liked, without hindrance or
molestation on the part of the Yankee authorities. The less important package I placed in
a little basket, and unguardedly wrote upon
the back of it the words, "Kindness of Lieu-
tenam H."

The small note upon which so much stress
had been laid I resolved to carry with my own
hands; and, knowing Colonel Fillebrowne was
never displeased by a little flattery and a few

delicate attentions, I went to the florist and chose a very handsome bouquet, which I sent to him with my compliments, and with a request that he would be so kind as to permit me to return to Front Royal.*

The Colonel's answer was in accordance with the politeness of his nature. He thanked the "dear lady for so sweet a compliment," and enclosed the much-coveted pass. Lieutenant H., having finished his business at the camp, rejoined our party, and we all set out on our return. Nothing happened until we reached

---

* My readers must bear in mind that, in time of war, it is almost impossible to travel the slightest distance without a pass signed by some official. On one occasion, when a picket was stationed between our farm-yard and the dairy, the dairy-maid was not allowed to milk the cows without a pass signed by the officer of the day. This was a decided nuisance, and I hit upon the following plan to get rid of it. I wrote the following pass and got it duly signed: "These cows have permission to pass to and from the yard and dairy for the purpose of being milked twice a day, until further orders." This pass I pasted between the horns of one of the cows; and I was gratified to find that it had the desired effect, for they were not again stopped on their harmless errand; and whenever my pass came off the head of the cow I took care to replace it by another in the same style.

the picket-lines, when two repulsive-looking fellows, who proved to be detectives, rode up, one on each side of the carriage.

" We have orders to arrest you," said one of them, looking in at the window, and addressing himself to me.

".For what ?" I asked.

" Upon suspicion of having letters," he replied ; and then turning to the coachman, he ordered him to drive back forthwith to Colonel Beale's head-quarters. Upon arriving there we were desired to get out and walk into the office.

My cousin trembled like a poor bird caught in a snare ; and, to tell the truth, I felt very much discomposed myself, although I did not for a moment lose my presence of mind, upon the preservation of which I well knew our only hopes rested. The negress, almost paralyzed by fear, followed my cousin and myself, and it was in this order we were ushered into the awful presence of our inquisitor and judge.

The first question asked was, had I any letters. I knew that if I said No, our persons would be immediately searched, and my false-hood detected: I therefore drew out from the bottom of the basket the package I had placed there, and which, it will be remembered, was of minor importance, and handed it, with a bow, to the Colonel.

"What!" exclaimed he, in an angry tone—"what is this? 'Kindness of Lieutenant H.!' what does this mean? Is this all you have?"

"Look for yourself," I replied, turning the basket upside down, and emptying its contents upon the floor.

"As to this scribbling on the letter," I continued, "it means nothing; it was a thought-less act of mine. I assure you Lieutenant H. knew nothing about the letter, or that it was in my possession."

The Lieutenant turned very pale, for it sud-denly occurred to him that he had in his pocket a little package which I had asked him to carry for me.

He immediately drew it out and threw it upon the table, when, to his consternation, and to the surprise of the Colonel, it was found to

be inscribed with the very identical words—
"Kindness of Lieutenant H."—which had already excited the suspicions of the Federal
commander.

This made matters worse; and when the
package, upon being opened, disclosed a copy
of that decidedly rebel newspaper, *The Maryland News-sheet*, the Colonel entertained no
further doubt of Lieutenant H.'s complicity
and guilt.

It was in vain I asserted his innocence, and
repeated again and again that it was impossible he could know that a folded packet contained an obnoxious journal, and that it was
highly improbable, to say the least of it, he
could be an accomplice in my possession of the
letter.

"What is that you have in your hand?"
was the only reply to my remonstrances and
expostulations on behalf of the unfortunate
officer I had so unintentionally betrayed.

"What—this little scrap of paper? You
can have it if you wish: it is nothing. Here
it is;" and I approached nearer to him, with

the seeming intention of placing it in his hand; but I had taken the resolution of following the example set by Harvey Birch, in Cooper's well-known novel of "The Spy," in the event of my being positively commanded to "stand and deliver."

Fortunately, however, for me, the Colonel's wrath was diverted from the guilty to the guiltless: he was so incensed with Lieutenant H., that he forgot the very existence of Belle Boyd, and the precious note was left in my possession.

We were then and there dismissed, Colonel Beale contenting himself with giving a hurried order to the effect that I was to be closely watched. He then proceeded to the investigation of Lieutenant H.'s case. Bare suspicion was the worst that could be urged against him, yet, upon this doubtful evidence, or rather in the absence of any thing like evidence, a court-martial, composed of officers of the Federal army, dismissed him from the service.

Some time after the adventure I have just related the secret of our arrest transpired.

A servant had observed the gentleman to whom I have alluded give me the letter in my friend's house at Winchester. He gave information, and the result was, a telegram was sent to Major Tyndale, who was already incensed against me for having slipped through the pickets and got to Winchester without his pass. He communicated at once with Colonel Beale, and our arrest followed as I have described.

Had it not been for the curious manner in which Lieutenant H. was involved in the affair, and in which that unoffending officer was so unjustly treated, very much to my regret, I should not have escaped so easily.

CHAPTER VI.

My Prisoner—Battle of 23rd May—My Share in the Action—
The Federals Fire upon me—The Little Note once more
—The Confederates are Victorious—Letter from General
Stonewall Jackson.

AMONG the Federals who then occupied
Front Royal was one Mr. Clark, a reporter to
the *New York Herald*, and, although an Irishman, by no means a gentleman.

He was domiciled at head-quarters, which
were established, as I have before mentioned,
at my aunt's residence ; and thus it was that
I saw him daily, for we could not possibly get
into the street without crossing the court-
yard and passing through the hall-way.

This Mr. Clark endeavored upon several
occasions to intrude his society upon me; and,
although I told him plainly his advances were
extremely distasteful, he persevered so far

that I was forced more than once to bolt the door of the room in which my cousin and myself were seated, in his face.

These rebuffs he never forgave, and from an intrusive friend he became an inveterate enemy. It is to him I am indebted for the first violent, undisguised abuse with which my name was coupled in any Federal journal; but I must do the editors of the Yankee newspapers the justice to admit they were not slow to follow the example set them by Mr. Clark. They seemed to think that to insult an innocent young girl was to prove their manhood and evince their patriotism. I think my English readers will neither admire their taste nor applaud their spirit.

On the evening of the 23rd May I was sitting at the window of our room, reading to my grandmother and cousin, when one of the servants rushed in, and shouted, or rather shrieked—

"Oh, Miss Belle, I t'inks de revels am a-comin', for de Yankees are a-makin' orful fuss in de street."

I immediately sprang from my seat and went to the door, and I then found that the servant's report was true. The streets were thronged with Yankee soldiers, hurrying about in every direction in the greatest confusion.

I asked a Federal officer, who just then happened to be passing by, what was the matter. He answered that the Confederates were approaching the town in force, under Generals Jackson and Ewell, that they had surprised and captured the outside pickets, and had actually advanced within a mile of the town without the attack being even suspected.

"Now," he added, "we are endeavoring to get the ordnance and the quartermaster's stores out of their reach."

"But what will you do," I asked, "with the stores in the large dépôt?"

"Burn them, of course!"

"But suppose the rebels come upon you too quickly?"

"Then we will fight as long as we can by any possibility show a front, and in the event of defeat make good our retreat upon Winchester, burning the bridges as soon as we cross them, and finally effect a junction with General Banks's force."

I parted with the Federal officer, and returning to the house, I began to walk quietly up-stairs, when suddenly I heard the report of a rifle, and almost at the same moment I encountered Mr. Clark, who, in his rapid descent from his room, very nearly knocked me down.

"Great heavens! what is the matter?" he ejaculated, as soon as he had regained his breath, which the concussion and fright had deprived him of.

"Nothing to speak of," said I; "only the rebels are coming, and you had best prepare yourself for a visit to Libby Prison."

He answered not a word, but rushed back to his room and commenced compressing into as small a compass as possible all the manuscripts upon which he so much plumed himself, and upon which he relied for fame and credit with the illustrious journal to which he was contributor. It was his intention to collect and secure these inestimable treasures, and then to skedaddle.*

I immediately went for my opera-glasses, and, on my way to the balcony in front of the house, from which position I intended to reconnoitre, I was obliged to pass Mr. Clark's door. It was open, but the key was on the outside. The temptation of making a Yankee prisoner was too strong to be resisted, and, yielding to the impulse, I quietly locked in the "Special Correspondent" of the *New York Herald.*

After this feat I hurried to the balcony, and, by the aid of my glasses, descried the advance-guard of the Confederates at the distance of about three-quarters of a mile, marching rapidly upon the town.

* This American cant term is exactly rendered into English by the phrase "to hook it." Slang is now so well understood that I apprehend few of my readers require to be told that "to hook it" signifies to make off, to run away. Our Transatlantic expression can boast, I believe, of the earlier derivation. The meaning of Σκεδάννῦμι, the root of which is *skeda*, was, I am told, understood in that early age in which were recorded the wrath of Achilles and the patriotism of Hector.

To add to my anxiety, my father, who was at that time upon General Garnett's staff, was with them. My heart beat alternately with hope and fear. I was not ignorant of the trap the Yankees had set for my friends. I was in possession of much important information, which, if I could only contrive to convey to General Jackson, I knew our victory would be secure. Without it I had every reason to anticipate defeat and disaster.

The intelligence I was in possession of instructed me that General Banks was at Strasbourg with four thousand men, that the small force at Winchester could be readily re-einforced by General White, who was at Harper's Ferry, and that Generals Shields and Geary were a short distance below Front Royal, while Fremont was beyond the Valley; further, and this was the vital point, that it had been decided all these separate divisions should co-operate against General Jackson.

I again went down to the door, and this time I observed, standing about in groups, several men who had always professed attachment to the cause of the South. I demanded if there was one among them who would venture to carry to General Jackson the information I possessed. They all with one accord said, " No, no. You go."

I did not stop to reflect. My heart, though beating fast, was not appalled. I put on a white sun-bonnet, and started at a run down the street, which was thronged with Federal officers and men. I soon cleared the town and gained the open fields, which I traversed with unabated speed, hoping to escape observation until such time as I could make good my way to the Confederate line, which was still rapidly advancing.

I had on a dark-blue dress,* with a little fancy white apron over it; and this contrast of colors, being visible at a great distance, made me far more conspicuous than was just then agreeable. The skirmishing between the outposts was sharp. The main forces of the opposing armies were disposed as follows:—

* This dress was afterwards cut up into two shirts for two wounded Confederate soldiers.

The Federals had placed their artillery on a lofty eminence, which commanded the road by which the Confederates were advancing. Their infantry occupied in force the hospital buildings, which were of great size, and sheltered, by which they kept up an incessant fire.

The Confederates were in line, directly in front of the hospital, into which their artillerymen were throwing shells with deadly precision; for the Yankees had taken this as a shelter, and were firing upon the Confederate troops from the windows.

At this moment, the Federal pickets, who were rapidly falling back, perceived me still running as fast as I was able, and immediately fired upon me.

My escape was most providential; for, although I was not hit, the rifle-balls flew thick and fast about me, and more than one struck the ground so near my feet as to throw the dust in my eyes. Nor was this all: the Federals in the hospital, seeing in what direction the shots of their pickets were aimed, followed the example and also opened fire upon me.

Upon this occasion my life was spared by what seemed to me then, and seems still, little short of a miracle; for, besides the numerous bullets that whistled by my ears, several actually pierced different parts of my clothing, but not one reached my body. Besides all this, I was exposed to a cross-fire from the Federal and Confederate artillery, whose shot and shell flew whistling and hissing over my head.

At length a Federal shell struck the ground within twenty yards of my feet; and the explosion, of course, sent the fragments flying in every direction around me. I had, however, just time to throw myself flat upon the ground before the deadly engine burst; and again Providence spared my life.

Springing up when the danger was passed, I pursued my career, still under a heavy fire. I shall never run again as I ran on that, to me memorable day. Hope, fear, the love of life, and the determination to serve my country to the last, conspired to fill my heart with more than feminine courage, and to lend preternatural strength and swiftness to my limbs.

I often marvel, and even shudder, when I reflect how I cleared the fields, and bounded over the fences with the agility of a deer.

As I neared our line I waved my bonnet to our soldiers, to intimate that they should press forward, upon which one regiment, the First Maryland "rebel" Infantry, and Hay's Louisiana Brigade, gave me a loud cheer, and, without waiting for further orders, dashed upon the town at a rapid pace.

They did not then know who I was, and they were naturally surprised to see a woman on the battle-field, and on a spot, too, where the fire was so hot. Their shouts of approbation and triumph rang in my ears for many a day afterwards, and I still hear them not unfrequently in my dreams.

At this juncture the main body of the Confederates was hidden from my view by a slight elevation which intervened between me and them. My heart almost ceased to beat within me; for the dreadful thought arose in my mind, that our force must be too weak to be any match for the Federals, and that the gal-

lant men who had just been applauding me
were rushing upon a certain and fruitless
death. I accused myself of having urged
them to their fate; and now, quite overcome
by fatigue, and by the feelings which tor-
mented me, I sank upon my knees and offered
a short but earnest prayer to God.

Then I felt as if my supplication was
answered, and that I was inspired with fresh
spirits and a new life. Not only despair, but
fear also forsook me; and I had again no
thought but how to fulfil the mission I had
already pursued so far.

I arose from my kneeling posture, and had
proceeded but a short distance, when, to my
unspeakable, indescribable joy, I caught sight
of the main body fast approaching; and soon
an old friend and connection of mine, Major
Harry Douglas, rode up, and, recognizing me,
cried out, while he seized my hand—

"Good God, Belle, you here! what is it?"

"Oh, Harry," I gasped out, "give me time
to recover my breath."

For some seconds I could say no more;

but, as soon as I had sufficiently recovered myself, I produced the "little note," and told him all, urging him to hurry on the cavalry, with orders to them to seize the bridges before the retreating Federals should have time to destroy them.

He instantly galloped off to report to General Jackson, who immediately rode for ward, and asked me if I would have an escort and a horse wherewith to return to the village I thanked him, and said, "No; I would go as I came;" and then, acting upon the information I had been spared to convey, the Confederates gained a most complete victory.

Though the dépôt building had been fired, and was burning, our cavalry reached the bridges barely in time to save them from destruction: the retreating Federals had just crossed, and were actually upon the point of lighting the slow match which, communicating with the bursting charge, would have riven the arches in pieces. So hasty was their retreat that they left all their killed and wounded in our hands.

Although we lost many of our best and bravest—among others the gallant Captain Sheetes, of Ashby's cavalry, who fell leading a brilliant and successful charge upon the Federal infantry—the day was ours; and I had the heartfelt satisfaction to know that it was in consequence of the information I had conveyed at such risk to myself General Jackson made the flank movement which led to such fortunate results.

And here let me pause a moment to do justice to the memory of a brave enemy, Colonel Kenly, who commanded the Federals, and who fought at their head with the courage of desperation, until he fell mortally wounded.

The Confederates, following up their victory, crossed the river by the still standing bridges, and pushed on by the road which led to Winchester.

General Banks was startled from his lair at Strasbourg, and leaving everything but his own head and a handful of cavalry behind him, with the victorious Confederates in hot pursuit, rushed through Winchester and Martinsburg,

6*

and finally crossed the river at Williamsport, Maryland; and it is said that he and his command have never stopped running since.

During this hasty flight General Banks halted for a few minutes to take breath in the main street of Martinsburg. Upon the sidewalk were standing many children and young girls, among whom was my little sister.

One of these girls, recognizing General Banks's aide-de-camp, walked up to him and said—

"Captain, how long are you going to stay here?"

"Until Gabriel blows his horn," replied he.

To this mistimed vaunt my sister quietly rejoined, looking full in his face as she spoke—

"Ah, Captain, if you were to hear Jackson's horn just outside the town, you would not wait for Gabriel's."

Nor did they wait; for the echo of the Confederate General's bugles had little less terror for them than the sound of the archangel's trump.

When I first returned from the battle-field,

tired, or, to say the truth, utterly enervated and exhausted, the Confederates were filing through the town, and the enthusiastic hurrahs with which they greeted me did more than any thing else could have done to revive my drooping spirits and restore my failing powers. The dead and wounded were now being brought in, and our house soon became a hospital.

Notwithstanding my fatigue, I contrived to render some assistance in dressing the wounds and alleviating the sufferings of our poor soldiers, who consoled themselves in their agonies with the reflection that they had done their duty nobly, and that their pangs were not imbittered by the sting and remorse with which defeat always torments a true soldier.

Among the dead who were brought next day to our house for interment were Captains Sheetes, Baxter, and Thaxter, all of Ashby's cavalry, and Major Davis, of Louisiana.

To my great joy my father came safe out of the battle, with but a very slight wound in the leg.

All the Federals left in Front Royal were captured; among them my particular friend, Mr. Clark, who, upon endeavoring to leave his room unseen during the confusion, found himself locked in.

I afterwards heard an amusing account of the manner in which he extricated himself, by letting himself down from the window; this, however, was unfortunately a work of time, and the delay was the cause of his capture. He was being escorted a prisoner down the street when, catching sight of me as I stood upon the door-step, he shouted out—

"I'll make you rue this: it's your doing that I am a prisoner here."

During the battle, and while Colonel Fille-browne was preparing to remove his effects from Winchester, a gentleman of high social position and Southern proclivities stepped into his office and said, "Colonel, how on earth did you get into such a trap? Did you know nothing of the advance of the Confederates?" Colonel Fillebrowne turned, and, pointing to the bouquet I had sent him only a day or two before, he said, "That bouquet did all the mischief: the donor of that gift is responsible *for all* this misfortune."

I could not but be aware that I had been of some service to my country; and I had the further satisfaction of feeling that neither a desire of fame nor notoriety had been my motive for enacting the *rôle* I did in this sad drama. I was not prepared, however, for that recognition of my services which was received on the very day they were rendered, and which I here transcribe:—

"May 23d, 1862.

"Miss Belle Boyd,

"I thank you, for myself and for the army, for the immense service that you have rendered your country to-day.

"Hastily, I am your friend,

"T. J. Jackson, C. S. A."

This short note, which was written at Mr. Richards's house, very near Front Royal, was brought to me by a courier, and I am free to confess, I value it far beyond any thing I possess in the world.

The object General Jackson had in view

was too important to admit of his leaving behind him an adequate force for the protection
of Front Royal; one regiment, the Twelfth
Georgia Infantry, was all that could be
spared; and thus Front Royal was retaken
by the Federals, just one week after its brilliant capture by our troops.

During our short possession of the town,
there was, among the prisoners taken in the
pursuit beyond the river and sent back into
our custody, a woman who represented herself
to be the wife of a soldier belonging to the
Michigan cavalry. She was handed over to
me, and I furnished her with clothing, and did
all that lay in my power to make her comfortable and happy.

Upon the arrival of the Federels under
General Geary, most of the Twelfth Georgia
were taken prisoners, together with all the
sick and wounded.

The woman of whom I have just spoken
was of course liberated; and the first use she
made of her freedom was to report me to
General Kimball as a most dangerous rebel,

and a malignant enemy to the Federal Government.

The General immediately placed me under arrest, and surrounded our house with sentries, so that to escape was actually impossible. Within a few hours, however, after my incarceration, General Shields arrived; and, being senior in the service to General Kimball, naturally superseded him in the command of the army. He at once released me, and I thank him for his urbanity and kindness.

Rumors soon reached us to the effect that the Confederate army was retreating up the Valley, and once more all this portion of the country fell into the hands of the Yankees.

CHAPTER VII.

Tone of the Northern Press towards me—General Banks refuses to pass me South—How I procure Passes—The two
Confederate Soldiers—I write to "Stonewall Jackson"—
Novel Method of conveying Information—My Letter is Intercepted—I am warned to depart South without delay—I
prepare to leave.

THE Northern journals vied with one another in publishing the most extravagant and
improbable accounts of my exploits, as they
were pleased to term them, on the battle-field
of the 23d May.

One ascribed to "Belle Boyd" the honor
of having directed the fire of the Confederate
artillery throughout the action; another represented her as having, by the force of her
genius, sustained the wavering counsels of the
Southern generals; while a third described
her as having, sword in hand, led on the

whole of the attacking line to the capture of Front Royal; but as I believe that the veracity of the Yankee press is pretty well known and appreciated, I shall give no more extracts from their eloquent pages.

At the conclusion of the last chapter, I mentioned that General Shields released me from the arrest under which General Kimball had placed me, upon the report of the ungrateful *ci-devant* prisoner; and, after a short time, finding no further persecution was resorted to, I thought the opportunity favorable for making an attempt to get south.

Meanwhile, General Banks had returned, and encamped close to the town, making my aunt's house his head-quarters.

It was to him, therefore, I applied for permission to depart.

"Where do you wish to go?" he asked.

"To Louisiana, where my aunt resides."

"But what will Virginia do without you?"

"What do you mean, General?"

"We always miss our bravest and most

illustrious, and how can your native State do
without you ?"

I laughingly thanked him for the compli
ment, and he conversed with the utmost good-
nature and pleasantry upon the part that I
had taken in his recent defeat. Though a
rabid Abolitionist, the General was certainly
one of the most affable gentlemen I have ever
met.

Several weeks passed by in peace and
quiet, unmarked by any incident worthy of
record, and at the expiration of this period,
Front Royal was again evacuated by the
Federal troops, with the exception of the
Third Delaware Infantry, which corps was
left in garrison. Their colonel was a very
large, coarse man, with the manners and appearance of a butcher rather than of an officer.

On the other hand, Major McEnnis and
Lieutenant Preston, who officiated severally as
Provost and Assistant Provost-Marshal, were
upon all occasions not only courteous, but
kind, the natural consequence of which be-

havior was, that they were both highly respected and esteemed by us " rebels."

In the court-yard of the General's headquarters, and at a few yards only from our cottage, they had pitched a flag-tent, which served the purposes of their office, and here it was that all passes for the South were granted or refused, as the case might be. How many of these were procured upon false pretences and transferred to recruits on their way to join the Southern army, or by whom this ingenious *ruse* was practised, *I* shall not here say.

I was one morning sitting in the drawing-room, when I noticed two men, dressed as Confederate soldiers, standing near the Provost-Marshal's tent. At my request, my grandmother sent for the Major, who obeyed her summons without loss of time.

We asked him who the men were. He told us they were paroled Confederate soldiers procuring passes to go south. We then asked if they might be permitted to dine with us, and received a ready assent. In the mean time they had disappeared; but one of them shortly reappearing, I accosted him thus :—

"Won't you dine with us? the Major says you may."

"With pleasure, if you dine shortly; I have only two or three hours allowed me to get beyond the pickets."

"Poor fellow!" said I; "but I am glad that you will soon be free. Won't you take a letter from me to General Jackson?"

Upon his assenting to this request, I went off towards my own room to write my dispatch; but, as I was passing by the kitchen-door, one of the servants stopped me suddenly, and exclaimed :—

"Miss Belle! who's dat man yose a-talkin' to?"

"I know no more about him than that he is a paroled rebel soldier, going south."

"Miss Belle, dat man ain't no rebel; I seen him 'mong de Yankees in de street. If he has got secesh clothes on, he ain't no secesh. Can't fool Betsy dat way. Dat man's a spy— dat man's a spy. Please God, he am."

I, however, entertained a different opinion from that of the negro woman, so I persevered in my intention, and wrote a long friendly letter to General Jackson. At the same time, I introduced a great deal of valuable information concerning the Yankees, the state of their army, their movements and doings, and matters of a like nature.

Disregarding the warning voice of my sable Cassandra, I fancied the man was true and might be safely trusted; so as soon as dinner was finished, I called him aside and confided the letter to him with these words:—

"Will you promise me faithfully, upon the honor of a soldier, to take the utmost care of this, and deliver it safe to General Jackson? They tell me you are a spy, but I do not believe it."

He, of course, denied the soft impeachment, and swore, by all the host of heaven, to execute my commission with fidelity and dispatch.

Reader, conceive my feelings when, shortly after this man's departure, one of the officers came in and informed me that he was a spy, and was on his way to the Confederate lines at Harrisburg.

I immediately set about to rectify my unfortunate error, and, after some reflection, I decided upon the following expedient:—

I sat down and wrote Major Harry Gilmore, of the Confederate cavalry, a few lines, giving an accurate account of the man's personal appearance, and explaining the motive and circumstances of his journey south, and by what means I had been entrapped into trusting him with a letter for General Jackson. This note I dispatched by a conveyance, to which we rebels had given the name of "the underground railway."

The locomotive on this railway was an old negro, and the mail-car was an enormous silver watch from which the works had been extracted. I sent off my train, with orders that if, in passing the pickets, any one should inquire the time of day, the answer must be that the imposing-looking time-piece was out of order, and had ceased to mark the hours and minutes.

Our friend the spy, however, went neither to Harrisburg nor to General Jackson, but made his way straight to the Federal General Sigel and gave him my letter. The General, in his turn, forwarded it to Stanton, the Secretary-at-War, who, I make no doubt, still retains it in his possession.

The fate of the spy, like that of so many of his fraternity, was tragic. He was soon after detected in the pursuit of his calling on the Rappahannock, and hanged. My readers, perhaps, may think I ought to congratulate myself upon having hitherto escaped a similar fate.

Shortly after this adventure an officer came and told me that further misconduct on my part might bring down upon me the severest punishment, and hinted that the Yankees, once thoroughly incensed, would not hesitate at the perpetration of any atrocity.

Entertaining these views, he recommended my immediate departure; and this kind advice meeting with the approval of my grandmother, I gave my consent, and immediately my maid had orders to prepare for a journey to Richmond. It was on a Tuesday that the officer promised to get a pass, and we were to be sent through the lines on the next ensuing Thursday. But fate had ordained otherwise.

CHAPTER VIII.

I am Arrested by Order of Mr. Stanton, Federal Secretary of
War—My Room and Trunks are closely Searched—
Yankee Disregard for the Rights of Personal Property—
My Departure for Washington—My Escort—I arrive at
General White's Head-Quarters in Winchester.

It was on a lovely Wednesday evening that
our firm and valued friend Lieutenant Preston,
my Cousin Alice, and myself were standing on
the balcony, watching the last rays of the setting sun as it sank behind the western hills.

Our conversation turned upon the divided
and unhappy state of our country. We recalled the peaceful scenes and joyous days of
the past, which were so painfully contrasted
by the present, and we were forced to agree
that we had nothing to expect from the future
but a continuance, if not an augmentation, of
our calamities.

7

In such gloomy forebodings, and in the interchange of apprehensions and regrets, we passed some time, and the twilight was fast deepening into gloom, when we heard the sound of horses' hoofs; and, straining our eyes through the darkness, we discerned a large body of cavalry approaching the house.

I immediately conceived the idea that it was a scouting-party on their way to the mountains with the design of surprising Major Harry Gilmore's cavalry, and feared that their enterprise would prove successful unless the Confederate officer should have timely notice of his danger. I ran at once to my room and wrote a hasty note, in which I communicated my suspicions to Major Gilmore, and warned him to be on his guard.

This note I transmitted in the manner I have described in a previous chapter, by my "underground railway." After this feat I retired to bed, and slept quietly, undisturbed by any dream or vision of my approaching captivity.

Next morning I rose early, and soon after

breakfast I went to the cottage door, where I daily spent much of my time, watching the movements of the persons who, for various purposes, frequented head-quarters. I had not been long at my post when I observed several Yankee soldiers go into the coach-house. They immediately proceeded to drag out the carriage, and pull it up at the door of head-quarters, where they put to the horses.

There was nothing very extraordinary in all this; but in these anxious days the minds of all were in a perpetual state of tension, and a slight incident was sufficient to cause alarm.

This may account for the strange feeling that came over me—an irrepressible desire to ascertain who was to be the occupant of the carriage, which was on the point of starting for a destination of which I was ignorant.

I walked out upon the balcony; and, looking up and down the street, I saw that it was thronged with cavalry, the men dismounted, lounging about, and conversing with each other, in groups of twos and threes, evidently waiting for the expected order to mount.

While I stood looking at this scene, not without interest and curiosity, one of the servants came to me and said—

"Miss Belle, de Provo' wishes to see you in de drawing-room, and dere's two oder men wid him."

I immediately went down-stairs, and, upon entering the room, I found the Major, whose face wore an expression of excitement and nervousness. There were, as the servant had said, two other men in the room with him: one, a tall, fine-looking man, was introduced to me by the name and title of Major Sherman, of the 12th Illinois cavalry; the other was low in stature, coarse in appearance, with a mean, vile expression of countenance, and a grizzly beard, which, it was evident, had not made the acquaintance of water or a comb for weeks at least. His small, restless eyes glanced here and there, with an expression of incessant watchfulness and suspicion. All his features were repulsive in the extreme, denoting a mixture of cowardice, ferocity, and cunning. In a word, his mien was unmistakably that of a finished villain, who was capable of per-petrating any act, however atrocious, when stimulated by the promise of a reward in money.

This man was a good type of his order: he was one of Secretary Stanton's minions—a detective belonging to, and employed and paid by, that honorable branch of Mr. Lincoln's Government, the secret Service Department.

I had not been in the room more than a few moments when Major McEnnis turned to me and said—

" Miss Boyd, Major Sherman has come to arrest you."

" Impossible! For what?" I cried.

Major Sherman here interposed, and speak-ing in a very kind manner, assured me that, although the duty he had to perform was painful to his feelings, he was, nevertheless, forced to execute the orders of the Secretary of War, Mr. Stanton; and, as he finished speak-ing, the detective produced from his pocket the document, which I transcribe as nearly as I can recollect:—

> "WAR DEPARTMENT.
>
> "SIR:—You will proceed immediately to Front Royal, Virginia, and arrest, if found there, Miss Belle Boyd, and bring her at once to Washington.
>
> "I am, respectfully,
>
> "Your obedient servant,
>
> "E. M. STANTON."

Such was the curt order that made me a prisoner; and, as remonstrance would have been idle and resistance vain, nothing was left for me but quiet, unconditional obedience.

The detective then informed me that it was his duty to examine all my luggage.

To this I could not do otherwise than assent, and only begged that a few minutes might be granted, to enable my servant to prepare my room, which was in great confusion, and that I might also be permitted to retire. I made this request to the detective, for it had not escaped my notice that Major Sherman was acting a subordinate part, and was virtually at the disposal and under the orders of the former.

As no answer was returned to my question, I took it for granted I had tacit permission to withdraw; but my disgust was great when, turning round upon the stairs, I saw my persecutor silently following at my heels.

I stopped short, and said—

"Sir, will not you wait until I see if my room is in a suitable condition for you to enter?"

The reply was characteristic, though not urbane.

"No, yer don't: I'm agoin' with yer. Yer got some papers yer want to get rid on;" and, with these words, he pushed violently past me, and hastily entered my room.

My clothes were first seized, and searched with the utmost scrutiny. My dresses were examined closely, and, after being turned inside out, and distorted into all sorts of fantastic shapes, were flung in a pile upon the floor, much to the horror and amazement of my maid, who had employed a great part of the previous night in packing them safely and neatly, and who was at a loss to understand the meaning of such treatment, which appeared to her, naturally enough, so strange and unseemly.

My under-clothing next underwent an ordeal precisely similar to that which my upper garments had passed through; and, finally, my desk and portfolio were discovered; but here, very fortunately, my devoted servant came to the rescue with the promptitude and courage of a heroine.

She well knew the value I attached to the contents of my portfolio, and made a shrewd guess as to how far they would compromise me with my captor and his employers. Acting upon a sudden impulse, she made a swoop upon the repository of the greatest part of the evidence that could be adduced against me; and, rushing at headlong speed down-stairs, she gained the kitchen in time to burn all the papers it contained. But some important papers were, unfortunately, in my writing-desk, and these fell into the possession of the detective, who also, much to my regret, made prize of a handsome pistol, with belt and equipments complete, which had been presented to me, on the 4th of July, by a Federal officer on the staff, as a token, he was pleased to say, of his admiration of the spirit I had shown in defence of my mother and my home.

It had always been my hope to have some day an opportunity of begging General Stonewall Jackson's acceptance of a present made to me, under very trying circumstances, by a gallant and generous enemy; but this could not be done. The pistol now occupies a conspicuous place in the War Department at Washington, and is entered in the catalogue of spoils in the following words :—

" A trophy captured from the celebrated rebel Belle Boyd."

Not contented with the seizure of my own papers, the emissary of Mr. Stanton proceeded to break open the private *escritoire* of my uncle, who was a lawyer, and who had left it in my room for safe-keeping during his absence from Front Royal.

The detective, bundling up the law-papers with mine, bade me, in the roughest manner,

7*

and in the most offensive language, be prepared
to start within half an hour.

I asked permission to be indulged with the
attendance of my maid; but this request was
refused, with imprecations, and she was only
allowed to pack one trunk with apparel absolutely necessary to comfort, if not to decency.
Brief time was granted for the packing; and,
before many minutes, my solitary trunk was
strapped to the back of the carriage.

I then nerved myself, and walking into
the drawing-room, announced, in firm, unbroken
accents, that I was ready to start.

I preserved my composure unshaken;
although it was a hard trial for me to see
my grandmother and cousin weeping piteously, and beseeching Major Sherman, in the most
moving terms, to spare me. Their supplications
were vain; and the detective, stepping up
close to my side, ordered me to get into the
carriage forthwith.

Then came the final parting—bitter enough,
God knows; for I was being dragged from
those to whom I was endeared by the associa-

tions of my happy youth, no less than by the ties of nature, and consigned to the safe-keeping of a man whose countenance alone would have immediately convicted him of any crime of which he might anywhere have been accused.

My negro maid clasped her arms round my knees, and passionately implored permission to attend me. She was torn from me, and I was hurried into the carriage without any opportunity of further expostulation on the part of myself or my relations.

The news of my arrest had spread quickly, and the streets were by this time filled with soldiers and citizens of the town. As I stepped into the carriage, which for aught I knew was my funeral car, I cast a rapid but comprehensive glance upon the crowd collected to witness my departure and the demeanor I should sustain under such a trial.

Upon many, nay, upon most of the faces that met my gaze, sorrow and sympathy were written in unmistakable characters; but there were, nevertheless, some looks the expression of which was that of exultation and malignant triumph.

I knew how closely I was watched by friend and foe, and I resolved neither to make myself an object of derision to the one, nor of pity to the other. Though my heart was throbbing, my eyes were dry; not a muscle of my face quivered; no outward sign betrayed the conflicting emotions that raged within.

I could not guess what fate was in store for me; but I felt that, if I might judge of the clemency of my captors by the bearing of their delegate, it would be the part of wisdom to steel my mind against the worst that could ensue.

I was seated in the back of the carriage, and, just as we started, my evil genius mounted the driver's seat. In his hand he clutched a tin case, which held the papers he had taken from my room; and, as he turned his ugly features round from time to time to scrutinize my looks, my imagination pictured him to me as the ill-omened incarnation of Satan himself. I could not help associating him

with the idea of Edgar Poe's raven, and asking
myself if the fancy of the poet was to be
realized in my case, and the companionship of
the bird was to cease only with my life.

That these were the visions of a disturbed
mind, I am now quite willing to allow; but, if
my readers will bear in mind that I was
young; that I had just been torn from my
friends; that a long captivity appeared certain,
and death not improbable; that while either
fate was in abeyance, I was in the custody of a
man whose character was clearly adapted to
his odious calling—they will not be surprised
that during a few hours my reason tottered,
and horrible imaginings got the better of my
fortitude.

My escort consisted of four hundred and
fifty cavalry, the officer in command of whom
observed all the regular precautions prescribed
by military law for a march through an
enemy's country. In addition to the ordinary
advance and rear-guards, fifty scouts were
detached in skirmishing order, to protect our
right from surprise, and an equal number to

guard our left; and in this order we advanced until about half our march was performed, and we reached an eminence which commanded a view of the country for several miles round.

Here, at a dreary spot, the cavalcade was brought to a halt. Field-glasses and signal-whistles were brought into requisition, and many other, to me, mysterious forms were gone through.

I had not yet shaken off my terrors, and I now resolved to collect my thoughts, and devote what I believed to be my last moments to prayer: for I could not then penetrate the motives which actuated the, to me, strange behavior of my escort, and I fully and firmly believed I should soon be dragged from the carriage and hanged from the bough of the maple-tree, the leaves of which were rustling over the carriage.

I afterwards ascertained that it was from fear of a rescue by Ashby's cavalry that all the precautions which alarmed me so much were taken; and I make no doubt but that that gallant Confederate, had he known of my situation, would have brought me off, or perished in the attempt.

After a long pause, the word "Forward" was given, and our march was resumed at a walk.

In due course, we gained the outskirts of Winchester, and were met by the remainder of the regiment by which I was escorted. The whole, amounting to five hundred and fifty sabres, some in front, some in rear of the carriage, marched in solemn procession down the main street of the town; and I believe the citizens, who rushed to the windows and doors, at first supposed that the carriage which conveyed my small but living person was the funeral-car of a general officer, bearing the warrior to his place of interment.

It was about six o'clock in the evening when I was brought to General White's headquarters, which were fixed about a quarter of a mile beyond the town.

I was immediately ordered to alight, and, without a minute's delay, I was ushered into his presence.

He received me with a graceful bow, and bade me welcome with marked courtesy.

I returned his salutation with as much ease as I could assume, and asked what he intended doing with me.

"To-morrow," replied he, "I shall send you on to the commanding officer at Martinsburg. He can best inform you what is to be done with you. You will rest here after your journey, for the night."

"But surely," I interceded, "you will at least allow me to remain with my friends in the village until the morning?"

"No, no," he rejoined, rather pettishly; "I cannot consent to that. It would take a whole regiment to guard you; for, though the rebel cavalry should not enter the town to attempt your rescue, I make no doubt that the citizens themselves would try it."

"But surely," I then pleaded, "you do not mean that I am to sleep here, defenceless and alone in a tent, at the mercy of your brigade? I never yet slept in a tent when I was present with our army, and how can I endure such a penance in the camp of my enemies?"

"My own tent," replied the General, with a low bow, "has been properly prepared for the reception of a lady. Whenever you wish to retire you can follow your inclinations; and you may rest assured you shall sleep in perfect security."

Supper was then brought in; and it did not escape my notice that the table was decorated with a dazzling display of rich silver plate, which I more than suspected had formerly been the property of some of our dear old Virginian families; and the thought that the rightful owners were at that moment miserable outcasts, probably in want of the bread my Federal lords despised, effectually destroyed any appetite my sufferings might have left me.

I said not a word until supper was finished, then, rising quietly from my camp-stool, I begged permission to retire to the tent which I had been informed was to be my dormitory.

The General rang a small bell, which was quickly answered by an "intelligent contraband," bearing two very massive silver candlesticks, which, like the spoons and forks, were doubtless the spoils of my native province, probably once the property of an intimate friend.

"Show this lady to the tent that has been prepared for her reception;" and these words, with the accompaniment of a bow, were all I had in exchange for the prayers and blessings I had been accustomed to carry with me to my bed.

No sooner had I entered the tent than the negro left me to sleep or to my own reflections.

For some time I listened to the tramp of the sentries as they paced to and fro outside; then I tried to distract my thoughts and forget my grief, in attempting to guess how many Yankee soldiers were told off to guard a single Confederate girl. But all would not do: for the time being I was conquered in body and spirit; my burden seemed heavier than I could bear. I sat down upon my camp-stool, and pressed my hands upon my aching brow, and before long the fatigue and anxiety I had undergone stood me in stead, and I fell asleep.

CHAPTER IX.

A False Alarm—Arrival at Martinsburg—My Mother and
Family visit me—Departure for Washington—My Recep-
tion at the Dépôt—The "Old Capitol"—My Prison
Room—My Treatment—Interview with the Chief of
Detectives—Offers of Liberty—My Reply—A Pleasing
Reminiscence of my Captivity.

ABOUT half-past three the following morning I was suddenly aroused from my comfortless
slumbers by the beating of the long roll, and
by the reports of several muskets fired in quick
succession.   Officers half dressed sprang to
arms, rushed to their horses, and rode off to
the outposts.   Meanwhile, I had lighted my
candle, my heart beating high with hope ; for
I persuaded myself that the alarm was caused
by an attempt on the part of the Confederates
to effect my rescue.   I sat down anxiously
awaiting the result, when one of the officers,

who was rushing to the front, stopped opposite my tent and shouted, or rather roared out—

"Put out that light: it is some signal to the rebels. Do you hear me?"

I of course obeyed the mandate, and a few minutes afterwards I heard the retreat beat; upon which one of the sentries explained the meaning of what had happened, and how it came to pass that the camp had been thrown into such a state of confusion. It appeared that an obtuse cow had strayed from a neighboring field, and, not understanding the challenge of the sentry, had disregarded the order to halt, although twice repeated. Hereupon the sentry, who could not make out the outline of the cow in the darkness, fired, and the other sentries on his right and left, taking the hint, fired also, though at what they aimed it would be difficult to say. However, fire they did at random, as is the custom of undisciplined troops everywhere, and thus all my hopes of a rescue were extinguished by a cow.

Dawn was hardly breaking when I was

ordered to get ready once more, as I was to be taken directly to Martinsburg.

My preparations were soon made, and with two hundred for my escort I set forward. At eight o'clock we came to a halt at a small farm-house standing by the road-side. Here break-fast had been prepared, and I was informed the refreshment was at my disposal. No sooner was my appetite satisfied—a consummation which was easy and rapid—than we resumed our journey to Martinsburg, at which bourne I arrived about one in the afternoon, tired and exhausted with the fatigue and anxiety I had undergone.

Major Sherman, compassionating my for-lorn condition, very kindly stayed behind the cavalcade and prevailed upon his wife to accompany me to the camp, which was pitched at a short distance on the north side of the town.

I was forthwith conducted to the tent of the commanding officer. My head was now almost bursting with pain; and I implored him to have me taken to my home, which was close

by in a suburb of the village, there to rest
and refresh myself for a few hours, as I understood I was to start for Washington at two
o'clock next morning. I make no doubt my
petition would have been granted had not the
detective here interposed and informed the
Federal Colonel that Mr. Secretary Stanton
would probably take exception to such an
indulgence, which would give me an opportunity of holding communication with persons
inimical to the United States Government.

"After putting this "spoke in my wheel,"
so to speak, my amiable custodian went himself to my home and ransacked all my father's
private papers, under pretence of hunting for
"communications" from myself to my mother.
Fortunately, however, he found none, and his
unwelcome visit was not crowned with the
success he had anticipated.

To return to myself.

I was sitting on the camp-stool in my tent,
gazing listlessly about me, when my attention
was suddenly attracted to a carriage which
was driving into the encampment. It stopped,

and a lady rapidly alighted. She was dressed in deep mourning; a thick veil entirely concealed her face. But I recognized her at once, in spite of her disguise.

The feverish intelligence which accompanies danger and suffering was superadded to that natural instinct which, though no one can explain, all have experienced; and I *felt*, for I could not see, that the visitor was my mother.

I sprang from my seat, and rushed into her arms, with a cry of joy I have no power to repress.

" My poor, dear child!" she said, or rather gasped, and then sank fainting at my feet.

They carried her into the tent, and the first use she made of restored consciousness was to implore the Colonel, in the most moving terms, to allow her to carry me home. She begged him to trust to the evidence of his own senses, and to read in my haggard looks the bodily prostration to which I was reduced, no less than the mental anguish which was consuming me; and in very truth the iron had entered into my soul, and my sufferings were almost greater than I could bear.

The Colonel politely but firmly refused to grant my mother's prayer; and I am willing to believe that in this refusal he was actuated by a stern sense of duty, for his feelings so far prevailed as to induce him to authorize my removal to Raemer's Hotel, which is contiguous to the station from which the trains for Washington start. No sooner had I, a young girl, weak and ill, accompanied by my mother and Mrs. Sherman, set foot in the hotel, than the building was girdled by a cordon of sentries, twenty-seven in number, in addition to whom, three were posted in the passage leading to my room, and one more was stationed just outside my door; and then, with these material guarantees for my security and good behavior, my little sister, my brothers, and my mother, were allowed to visit me.

It had been arranged that the detective who arrested me should be my escort as far as Washington; but I so loathed the sight of this man, that I sent for Colonel Holt, and

8

implored him to substitute for the odious rep-
tile any one of his officers who could be spared,
and upon whom he could rely for my safe-
conduct.

. Colonel Holt kindly granted my request,
and detailed Lieutenant Steele, of the Twelfth
Illinois Cavalry, for " escort duty."

As the time for my arrival approached, my
feelings overpowered my self-control, and, for
once, I yielded to a passionate burst of grief.
Nor was I without an excuse for my weakness.
My nearest and dearest were lamenting around
me, and within a few minutes I was to be torn
from their arms and consigned to the doubtful
mercies of strangers and enemies. My strength,
too, failed me; and, just as the fatal moment
drew near, I sank down in a stupor, from
which I was suddenly and painfully awakened
by the ominous screech of the railway engine.
I nerved myself by a vigorous effort, and
within a few seconds I found myself seated in
the train. I say found myself, for I have
never been able distinctly to recall how I
reached the station—whether I walked or was

carried, I know not. I was soon, however, conscious that Lieutenant Steele was by my side, and that Washington was my destination. I felt grateful for the presence of an officer to whom I might reasonably look for protection, and the reflection that, come what would, I had escaped the clutches of the detective, roused my drooping spirits.

Alas! this infatuation was soon dispelled, for, upon looking about me, I was horrified to see my "evil genius" occupying the left seat of the carriage.

The image of Edgar Poe's raven arose in my mind, and my disturbed imagination whispered that I was doomed to the perpetual companionship of an incarnate fiend.

It afterwards transpired that this able minion of Mr. Stanton had telegraphed to the chief of detectives at Washington to meet us at the dépôt.*

Mr. Steele, who had no idea I was to be thrown into prison, observed that, upon our arrival at Washington, I should go to Wil-

* In America, a railway terminus is called a dépôt.

lard's Hotel, and, after a short rest, proceed to the office of the Secretary-at-War. This plan, however, was by no means in accordance with the programme drawn up by the detective. He was one of Mr. Stanton's chosen and trusted agents. He, doubtless, well knew what was in store for me, and he did not scruple to presume upon his position, and use very sharp words to Lieutenant Steele.

It was about nine o'clock in the evening when we arrived at Washington; but, notwithstanding the lateness of the hour, a very large concourse of people had assembled in and about the dépôt, in order to catch a glimpse of "the wonderful rebel;" for the news of my arrest had preceded my arrival.

As I stepped upon the platform, the chief of the detectives, another kindred spirit of Mr. Stanton's, seized me roughly by the arm, and, in a gruff voice, shouted out—

"Come on; I'll attend to you."

He was then proceeding to push me through the crowd, when Lieutenant Steele, thrusting himself forward, protested vehe-

mently against such usage, and declared that
I should not be treated in so barbarous a
manner; that I was a lady, and that my
character and position should be respected.

The torrent of abuse that was poured upon
him for thus endeavoring to take my part, was
conveyed in words too horrible to bear repe-
tition; and at that moment I would gladly
have lain down and died, for the thought
flashed across my mind—

"My God! if this is the beginning, what
will the end be?"

Amongst the crowd I had many sympathizers; but they dared not interfere. At
Washington might was indeed right; and I
will venture to say, that the arbitrary exercise
of power by the United States Government
has cast into the shade all that we read of
the Spanish Inquisition, and all that we hear
of Russian domination in Poland. A word of
encouragement, nay, a whisper of condolence,
would have been sufficient to introduce an
imprudent friend to that receptacle which was
awaiting me—a prison cell.

I was thrust into a carriage; and the order, "Drive to the Old Capitol," was promptly given; but, before it could be obeyed, Lieutenant Steele, who had been very unceremoniously dismissed from further attendance upon me, stepped up and politely begged permission to wait upon me to prison. To a gruff refusal he firmly rejoined—

"I am determined to see her out of your hands, at least."

The carriage was driven at a rapid pace, and we soon came within sight of my future home—a vast brick building, like all prisons, sombre, chilling, and repulsive.

Its dull, damp walls look out upon the street: its narrow windows are further darkened by heavy iron stanchions, through which the miserable inmates may soothe their captivity by gazing upon those who are still free, but whose freedom hangs but by a slender thread.

Such is the calm retreat provided by a free and enlightened community for those of its citizens who have the audacity to express their disapproval of the policy adopted by the Government of the hour.

In the days of old France the victims of royal indignation were seized under cover of night, and buried with secrecy and dispatch in the impenetrable recesses of the Bastille; the most jealous care, the most unceasing vigilance, was observed, in order that the mystery of their doom should never be elucidated; the *lettre de cachet*, which was the implement of their destruction, was in its very nature a proof that such acts of violence and injustice were a source of fear and shame even to the despot who committed them.

Many a dark deed has been perpetrated within the old walls of the Tower of London; its stones have more than once been stained with the blood of the innocent; but here, again, tortures and death were studiously concealed, and, when detected, amply avenged.

The autocrat of Russia does not exhibit to the world the instruments with which he chastises his naughty children; the clank of

Siberian chains is not heard in any other quarter of the globe.

It has been reserved for the Government of the United States of America, the Apostles of Liberty, the tender-hearted emancipators, who shudder at the bare idea of the African's wrongs, to cast into a dungeon in open day, without accusation or form of trial, any one of their fellow-countrymen and countrywomen whom they may suspect of disaffection to the clique which retains them in power and office.

One of the greatest authors, ancient or modern, when speaking of our forefathers, said—

"They left their native land in search of freedom, and found it in a desert."

Could "Nominis Umbra," wrapped in his old veil of mystery, revisit our world, he would be appalled to find how completely the men of this generation have parted with that freedom without receiving so much as a mess of pottage in exchange for their glorious birthright.

To return to my narrative.

Upon my arrival at the prison, I was ushered into a small office. A clerk, who was writing at a desk, looked up for a moment, and informed me the superintendent would attend to my business immediately. The words were hardly uttered when Mr. Wood entered the room, and I was aware of the presence of a man of middle height, powerfully built, with brown hair, fair complexion, and keen, bluish-gray eyes.

Mr. Wood prides himself, I believe, upon his plebeian extraction; but I can safely aver that beneath his rough exterior there beats a warm and generous heart.

"And so this is the celebrated rebel spy," said he. "I am very glad to see you, and will endeavor to make you as comfortable as possible; so whatever you wish for, ask for it and you shall have it. I am glad I have so distinguished a personage for my guest. Come, let me show you to your room."

We traversed the hall, ascended a flight of stairs, and found ourselves in a short, narrow

8*

passage, up and down which a sentry paced, and into which several doors opened. One of these doors, No. 6, was thrown open; and behold my prison cell!

Mr. Wood, after repeating his injunction to me to ask for whatever I might wish, and with the promise that he would send me a servant, and that I should not be locked in as long as I "behaved myself," withdrew, and left me to my reflections.

At the moment I did not quite understand the meaning of the last indulgence, but within a few minutes I was given a copy of the rules and regulations of the prison, which set forth that if I held any communication whatever with the other prisoners, I should be punished by having my door locked.

There was nothing remarkable in the shape or size of my apartment, except that two very large windows took up nearly the whole of one side of the wall.

Upon taking an inventory of my effects, I found them to be as follows:—A washing-stand, a looking-glass, an iron bedstead, a table, and some chairs.

From the windows I had a view of part of Pennsylvania Avenue, and far away in the country the residence of General Floyd, ex-United States Secretary of War, where I had formerly passed many happy hours.

At first I could not help indulging in reminiscences of my last visit to Washington, and contrasting it with my present forlorn condition; but rousing myself from my reverie, I bethought myself of the indulgence promised me, and asked for a rocking-chair and a fire; not that I required the latter, for the room was already very warm, but I fancied a bright blaze would make it look more cheerful.

My trunk, after being subjected to a thorough scrutiny, was sent up to me, and, having plenty of time at my disposal, I unpacked it leisurely.

Upon each floor of the prison were posted sentries within sight and call of each other. The sentry before my door was No. 6, and when I had occasion for my servant I had to request him to summon the corporal of the guard. My attendant was an "intelligent contraband," who was extremely useful to me during my enforced residence in the Old Capitol.

I had not unpacked my trunk, when dinner was served; and here I shall do plain justice by transcribing the bill of fare; and it will be allowed I claim no commiseration on the plea of bread-and-water diet, though such had been ordered for me by Mr. Stanton :—

BILL OF FARE.

Soup — Beef Steak — Chicken — Boiled Corn — Tomatoes —
Irish Stew—Potatoes—Bread and Butter—Cantelopes—
Peaches—Pears—Grapes.

This, with but little variety, constituted my dinner every day until released.

At eight o'clock, Mr. Wood came to my room, accompanied by the chief of the detectives, who desired an interview with me on the part of the Secretary-at-War.

I begged this worthy to be seated—a request he immediately complied with; and he then delivered the following graceful exhortation, which I transcribe verbatim :—

" Ain't you pretty tired of your prison a'ready? I've come to get you to make a free confession now of what you've did agin our cause; and, as we've got plenty of proof agin you, you might as well acknowledge at once."

" Sir," I replied, " I do not understand you; and, furthermore, I have nothing to say. When you have informed me on what grounds I have been arrested, and given me a copy of the charges preferred against me, I will make my statement; but I shall not now commit myself." Thereupon the oath of allegiance was proffered, and I was harangued at some length upon the enormity of my offence, and given to understand the cause of the South was hopeless.

" Say, now, won't you take the oath of allegiance? Remember, Mr. Stanton will hear of all this. He sent me here."

To this peroration I replied—

" Tell Mr. Stanton from me, I hope that

when I commence the oath of allegiance to the United States Government, my tongue may cleave to the roof of my mouth; and that if ever I sign one line that will show to the world that I owe the United States Government the slightest allegiance, I hope my arm may fall paralyzed by my side."

This speech of mine he immediately took down in his note-book, and, growing very angry at my determination, he called out—

"Well, if this is your resolution, you'll have to lay here and die; and serve you right."

"Sir," I retorted, "if it is a crime to love the South, its cause, and its President, then I am a criminal. I am in your power; do with me as you please. But I fear you not. I would rather lie down in this prison and die, than leave it owing allegiance to such a government as yours. Now leave the room; for so thoroughly am I disgusted with your conduct towards me, that I cannot endure your presence longer."

Scarcely had I finished my defiance, which

I confess was spoken in a loud tone of voice, when cheers and cries of "Bravo!" reached my ears. Until that moment, I was not aware that the rooms on the floor with my own were occupied; for, having kept my door shut all day, I had no means of noticing what was passing around me.

My door, however, had been left open during my interview with the detective, consequently my neighbors, whom I afterwards ascertained to be Confederate officers and Englishmen, had overheard our whole conversation, and hailed with applause the firmness with which I had rejected Mr. Stanton's overtures of liberty, conditional as they were upon my renunciation of the Confederacy and on my allegiance to the Federal Government. And now Mr. Wood, taking pity upon me, withdrew the detective, saying—

"Come, we had better go: the lady is tired."

Within a few minutes of their departure, I heard a low, significant cough, and, as I turned in the direction from whence it proceeded, something small and white fell at my feet. I picked it up, and found that it was a minute nut-shell basket, upon which were painted miniature Confederate flags. Round it was wrapped a small piece of paper, upon which were traced a few words expressive of sympathy with my misfortunes. I afterwards found out that the author of this short communication was an Englishman; and I can assure him that his kindness was like a ray of light from heaven breaking into the cell of a condemned prisoner. I wrote a hasty reply, and, watching my opportunity, threw it to him. I then lay down on my bed in a tranquil—I had almost said a happy—frame of mind; and I closed my first day in a dungeon by repeating to myself, more than once—

> "Stone walls do not a prison make,
> Nor iron bars a cage:
> A free and quiet mind can take
> These for a hermitage."

CHAPTER X.

MY FIRST NIGHT IN PRISON.

THE first night in a convent forms the subject of a melancholy, but beautiful picture. My first night in a prison must be painted in dark colors, unrelieved by the radiance that plays upon the features of the sleeping devotee, who has of her own free will cast aside the world, exulting in the belief that the voluntary sacrifice of youth, love, and all the ties of nature, will be more than recompensed by an immortality of bliss.

Her dreams are of paradise: enthusiasm comes to the aid of religion, and gives her a foretaste of eternity.*

"Her soul is gone before her dust to heaven."

Prophets, angels, and saints people her silent cell; a vision of glory streams in through her narrow window; and the first night in the convent is the night of ecstasy

I said, at the conclusion of my last chapter, that I was comforted by the spontaneous proof of sympathy given by my unknown correspondent; but my situation was too painful to admit of real, lasting consolation. The medicine administered was at best but a momentary stimulant; the reaction soon set in; and, as my fatigue gained ground, the sense of my miserable condition prevailed against my bodily energies.

I rose from my bed and walked to the window. The moon was shining brightly. How I longed that it were in my power to spring through the iron bars that caught and scattered her beams around the room!

The city was asleep, but to my disordered imagination its sleep appeared feverish and perturbed. Far away the open country, visible in the clear night, looked the express image of peace and repose.

"God made the country, and man made the town," I thought, as I contrasted the close atmosphere of my city prison with the clear air of the fields beyond.

What would I not have given to exchange the sound of the sentry's measured tread for the wild shriek of the owl and the drowsy flight of the bat!

The room which was appropriated to me had formerly been the committee-room of the old Congress, and had been repeatedly tenanted by Clay, Webster, Calhoun, and other statesmen of their age and mark.

A thousand strange fancies filled my brain, and nearly drove me mad. The phantoms of the past rose up before me, and I fancied I could hear the voices of the departed orators as they declaimed against the abuses and errors of the day, and gave their powerful aid to the cause of general liberty. They never dreamed that the very walls which re-echoed the eloquence of freedom would ere long confine the victims of an oligarchy. Theirs was the bright day—ours is the dark morrow, of which the evil is more than sufficient. Those great men (for great they unquestionably were) lacked not the gift of prophecy, for they did not fail to discern the little cloud, then no bigger than a man's hand, which was gathering in the horizon—that dark speck which was so soon to generate a tempest far blacker than that from which the chariot of Ahab made haste to escape.

Throughout that long dreary night I stood at the window watching, thinking, and praying. It seemed to me that morning would never come.

> " Methought that streak of dawning gray
>   Would never dapple into day,
>   So heavily it rolled away
>   Before the eastern flame."

But the morning came at last—the herald,

let me hope, from a brighter world of another morrow to us. No sooner did the first faint light find its way through the windows, than I threw myself again upon my bed, and almost immediately sank into a deep sleep.

It was about nine o'clock, I believe, when I was aroused by a loud knocking at my door.

"What is it?" I cried, springing up.

"The officer calling the roll, to ascertain that no one has escaped."

"You do not expect me to get through these iron bars, do you?"

"No, indeed," was the chuckling rejoinder; and immediately afterwards I heard the officer's retreating footsteps as he passed on in the execution of his duty.

Soon after the servant who had been assigned to me came to make preparations for breakfast; and, as my morning meal was no less ample and choice than my dinner of the preceding evening, I will not detain my readers with a second prison bill of fare.

It was but a few minutes after breakfast

when the sentry directly outside my door was relieved.

I listened attentively to catch the orders given to the relief. They were—

"You will not allow this lady to come outside her door or talk to any of those fellows in the room opposite; and if she wants any thing, call the corporal of the guard. Now don't let these —— rebels skear yer."

There was no more information to be gained for the moment; so I sat down and amused myself with the morning papers, which had been brought to me with my breakfast.

They all contained an account of my capture, and a summary of my career. The subject-matter was, of course, personally interesting, although in every instance my motives were misconstrued, and my character was aspersed. I must, however, admit that many of the most bitter calumnies then published of me were contradicted not many days afterwards in the very same journals which had originally circulated them.

There was a narrow space behind the

prison which was reserved for the prisoners' exercise—an indulgence they were granted at stated hours. On their way to their play-ground most of them had to pass my door, and in the procession I recognized, on the second day of my imprisonment, several of my old friends and acquaintances who had formerly belonged to the army of Virginia.

The tedious day wore on, and a shudder passed over me as I recalled the hideous thoughts which had banished sleep throughout the previous night.

Late in the evening, when my servant came with my tea, she told me that many prisoners had been brought in during the day, and that two of the newly-arrived captives had been consigned to the room adjoining mine.

By this time it had become known through-out the length and breadth of the prison-house that I was no other than that persecuted young lady, "Belle Boyd."

Acting upon this knowledge, my neigh-bors, who were the friends of happier days, devised a scheme by means of which they

were enabled to make themselves known to
me.

At about eleven o'clock I sat down and
opened my Bible. I selected a chapter, the
promises contained in which are peculiarly
consoling to the captive; but I had not read
more than two or three verses when my attention was distracted by a knock against the
wall. I listened with attention, and presently
felt sure that the next sound which reached
my ears was that made by a knife scooping out
the plaster of the wall.

Within a few minutes the point of a long
case-knife was visible; and I was not slow to
co-operate with those pioneers of free communication—the inmates of the next room.

I made use of the knife that remained on
my supper-tray; and before long the two
knives had conjointly made an aperture large
enough to admit of the transmission of notes
rolled tight and of the circumference of a
man's forefinger. The clandestine correspondence that was thus carried on was, on either

side of the wall, a source of much pleasure, and served to beguile many a tedious hour.

In the room immediately above mine, and in which Mrs. Greenhow had been incarcerated and suffered so much for five long, weary months, were confined some gentlemen of Fredericksburg. They had contrived to loosen a plank in the floor, and to make an aperture through which the occupant of the room beneath them might receive and return letters.

Whenever I desired to communicate with the prisoners whose rooms were on the opposite side of the passage, I adopted the expedient of wrapping my note round a marble, which I rolled across, taking care that the sentry's back was turned when my missive was started on its voyage of discovery.

I have described how I established a post between my room and the room on my right; the same system was applied, with equal success, to the one on the left, which was then the abode of Major Fitzhugh, of Stuart's staff, and Major Morse, of Ewell's. This room,

9

which joined with many others, became a medium of communication with all; and we were soon enabled to transmit intelligence to each other throughout the prison.

It was on the fourth morning of my imprisonment, as I was watching from my door the prisoners going down to breakfast, that a little Frenchman handed me, unobserved, a half-length portrait of Jefferson Davis. This I forthwith hung up in my room over the mantel-piece, with this inscription below it—

"Three cheers for Jeff. Davis and the Southern Confederacy!"

One of the prison officials, Lieutenant Holmes, passing by my door, caught sight of the hostile President's likeness, and the words with which I had decorated it. Rushing like a madman into my room, he tore it down with many violent oaths. "For this," he said, " you shall be locked in ;" and he was as good as his word, for he turned the key in the door as he left the room.

My offence was severely punished. I was kept a close prisoner; and so little air was stirring in the sultry month of July that I grew very ill and faint, and at times I really thought I should have died from the oppressive heat of the room; and this misery I had to endure for several weeks. At last Mr. Wood paid me a visit, and, observing how pale and ill I had become under such rigorous treatment, took pity upon me, and gave orders that my door should be once more left open. Soon after I was granted the further indulgence of half an hour's walk daily in that portion of the prison yard which had been assigned to ladies for exercise.

One day, whilst standing in the doorway, my attention was attracted to an old gentleman almost bent double with age; his long white hair hung down to his shoulders, whilst his beard, gray with the heavy touch of old Father Time's fingers, reached nearly to his waist.

A feeling of pity took possession of my soul, and I could not but help thinking, as I gazed upon him, "Poor old man! what an unfit place for you; even I, the delicate girl, can better stand the hardships of this dreary, comfortless place, than you." And what was his crime? This—he was designated a traitor to the Northern Government because he firmly believed that the Constitution as it was should remain unaltered. I afterwards learnt that he was Mr. Mahony, the editor of the *Dubuque* (Iowa) *Crescent*, and who, when released, published a book, "The Prisoner of State," which was, however, suppressed by the Secretary of War, Stanton.

The rules of the prison, of course, interdicted all intercourse between the prisoners, but, alas! I was on one occasion taken so completely by surprise as to obey my first impulse and commit a flagrant breach of orders.

I was walking up and down my "seven feet by nine" promenade, when I suddenly recognized one of my cousins, John Stephenson, a young officer in Mosby's cavalry. So glad was I to see him that I never thought of consequences, but rushed up to exchange a few words with him. The charged bayonet of the sentry soon checked my impetuosity, and I was summarily sent back to my room, although "play-time" had not expired. My unfortunate cousin was at once removed to the guard-room.

It was late one evening, and I was sitting reading at my open door, when Mr. Wood came down the stairs exclaiming—

"All you rebels get ready; you are going to 'Dixie' to-morrow, and Miss Belle is going with you."

At this joyful news all the prisoners within hearing of the tidings of their approaching liberation joined in three hearty cheers. For my part, I actually screamed for joy, so suddenly had my return to freedom been announced.

The next day all the prisoners whose turn for exchange had come were drawn up in line in the prison yard.

Soldiers were stationed from the door of the prison half-way across the street, which was thronged by a dense crowd, brought together by curiosity to witness the departure of the rebel prisoners.

Two hundred captives, inclusive of the officers and myself, were then passed beyond the prison walls, and formed in line on the opposite side of the street.

I stepped into an open carriage, followed by Major Fitzhugh, who had been "told off" to convey me to Richmond.

I carried concealed about me two gold sabre-knots, one of which was intended for General Jackson, the other for General Joe Johnston.

As we drove off, the Confederate prisoners cheered us loudly; their acclamations were taken up by the crowd, so that the whole street and square resounded with applause. When we arrived at the wharf, we were sent on board the steamer *Juanita*, which lay at her moorings all that night.

I shall conclude this chapter with two or three prison reminiscences, which will, I hope, give my reader some idea of the *ménage* of the "Old Capitol."

On one occasion my servant had just brought me a loaf of sugar, when it occurred to me that the Confederate officers in the opposite room across the passage were in want of this very luxury. Accordingly I asked the sentry's permission to pass it over to them, and received from him an unequivocal consent in these plain words—"I have no objection."

This, I thought, was sufficient; and it will hardly be believed that, while I was in the very act of placing the sugar in the hand of one of the officers, the sentry struck my left hand with the butt-end of his musket, and with such violence was the blow delivered that my thumb was actually broken. The attack was so unexpected, and the pain so excruciating, that I could not refrain from bursting into tears.

As soon as I could master my feelings, I demanded of the sentry that he should summon the corporal of the guard; and upon his refusing my just demand, I stepped forward with the intention of exercising my undoubted right *in propriâ personâ*.

But my tyrant was now infuriated; he charged bayonets, and actually pinned me to the wall by my dress, his weapon inflicting a flesh-wound on my arm.

At this moment, fortunately for me, the corporal of the guard came rushing up the stairs to ascertain the cause of the disturbance. The sentry was taken off his post, and, unless I am grievously mistaken, a short confinement in the guard-room was considered sufficient punishment for such outrageous conduct.

Not long after this adventure, my aunt called to see me. Permission was given to me to pass down-stairs for the purpose of an interview with my relation, and I was proceeding on my way, when one of the sentries, with a volley of oaths, commanded me to "halt."

"But I have permission to go down and see my relation."

"Go back, or I'll break every bone in your body;" and a bayonet was presented to my breast.

I produced the certificate which authorized me to pass him; and I think, from his manner, he would have relented in his intentions towards me, and returned to a sense of his own duty, but he was encouraged in his mutinous behavior by the cheers of a roomful of Federal deserters, who called upon him to bayonet me. In this predicament I was saved by Major Moore, of the Confederate States Army, and the timely arrival of Captain Higgins and Lieutenant Holmes, two prison authorities, who secured me from further molestation.

This man's crime, which was neither more nor less than open mutiny, was visited by a slight reprimand. This leniency was perhaps intended for a personal compliment to me. If so, let me assure the Yankee officers, I duly appreciate both its force and delicacy.

Mr. Wood, the superintendent, will, I am sure, forgive me for relating one characteristic anecdote of him.

It was Sunday morning when he came stalking down the passage into which my room opened, proclaiming in the tones and with the gestures of a town-crier—

9*

"All you who want to hear the Word of God preached according to 'Jeff. Davis' go down into the yard; and all you who want to hear it preached according to 'Abe Lincoln' go into No. 16."

This was the way in which he separated the goats from the sheep. I need not say which party was considered the goats within the walls of the Old Capitol.

CHAPTER XI.

Arrival at Fortress Monroe—Passage up the James River—
Arrival at Richmond—"Home Again"—Interview with
General "Stonewall" Jackson—A Refugee once more—
Review of the Confederate Army under General Lee—
I receive my Commission—Flying Visit to my Home—
Letter. from "Stonewall" Jackson—My Reception by
the People of Knoxville—I hear of the Death of General
Jackson—Battle of Winchester—At Home once more.

AT early dawn, the *Juanita* cast off from her
moorings, and late in the evening of the same
day we dropped anchor at the mouth of the
Potomac, where we passed that night. Next
day, about 4 A. M., we proceeded on our way
up the river, arriving at Fortress Monroe late
in the evening; and here we were boarded
by Lieutenant Darling, of General Dix's staff.
On each side of us lay General McClellan's
transports, filled with soldiers; about half a

mile distant was the "Rip Raps," a fort quite
equal to Sumter in strength. Notwithstanding our position, which was exposed to the
fire of this splendid fort, our people indulged
their feelings by singing from time to time
"the songs of the sunny South," and these
they interspersed with loud cheers for Jeff.
Davis.

At one time a Yankee officer on board one
of the transports, irritated evidently by these
repeated expressions of animosity to his
Government, hailed us with the words—

"Three cheers for the Devil!"

"It is only natural you should cheer for
the advocate of your cause," was the ready
retort; "and we will cheer for ours." And
so these shouts and counter-shouts were kept
up until we got under way again, and steamed
up the muddy waters of the James River.

As we rounded a bend in the stream we
caught sight of the glorious flag of our country, the Stars and Bars. It was waving in the
evening breeze from a window in the house
of Mr. Aikens.

Until that well-known and beloved emblem met my eyes again, I had but imperfectly realized my freedom. Now it was present and visible in its chosen symbol. If our men had cheered before, their shouts, when surrounded by the transports and under the guns of the fort, were as nothing to those with which they hailed the emblem of "Dixie's" resolution to uphold its independence, defend its natural rights, and resist force with force.

At the wharf we were met by Colonel Ould, who held the office of Commissioner of Exchange at Richmond. He was attended by his assistant, Mr. Watson; and it was under the supervision and by the direction of these gentlemen that the exchanged soldiers were marched on shore. I passed that night very agreeably under Mr. Aikens's hospitable roof, and enjoyed myself thoroughly in his society and that of his family. Next morning Colonel Allen sent his carriage and horses from Richmond, to convey me at my ease into the city. I decided, without hesitation, to drive to the Ballard House, where, in fact, I had been informed rooms were prepared for my reception. My route lay close by the encampment of the Richmond Blues; and I confess to the mixed feeling of pride and pleasure I derived from the high compliment paid me by them. The company was drawn up in review order, and presented arms as I drove by. In the evening I was serenaded by the city band; in short, my reception at the hands of all classes was flattering in the extreme.

After a sojourn of ten days at the Ballard House, I removed to Mrs. W.'s boarding-house in Grace Street, where I enjoyed the delightful society of many old and warm friends.

At the period of which I speak not a few of the notorieties of Richmond were assembled at Mrs. W.'s excellent establishment; among others, General and Mrs. Joe Johnston, General Wigfall and his family, and Mrs. C., that celebrated leader of *ton* at Washington, equally and justly renowned for her wit and charms. Her conversation attracted around her, where-ever she appeared, crowds of admiring listeners; and I feel sure that many of my American readers will recognize the fair lady to whose name I have, for obvious reasons, placed the initial letter only.

I was engaged one evening in a desultory conversation, when an officer who had been one of my fellow-captives in Washington came up to me and placed in my hands a note and small box. Upon opening the latter I found that it contained a gold watch and châtelaine, both handsomely enamelled, and richly set with diamonds; and upon reading the note I discovered that the beautiful and useful ornament was offered to my acceptance "in token of the affection and esteem of my fellow-prisoners in the Old Capitol."

For a few moments I could not find words to thank their delegate, so overpowered was I by this striking and unexpected mark of the feelings entertained for me by my countrymen.

I had been in Richmond but a short time, when my father came to take me home. The

battle of Antietam had been fought, and Mar
tinsburg was once more in the hands of the
Confederates.

The very day after my return home I rode
out to the encampment, escorted by a friend of
my family, in order to pay a visit to General
Jackson. As I dismounted at the door of his
tent, he came out, and, gently placing his
hands upon my head, assured me of the pleasure he felt at seeing me once more well and
free. Our interview was of necessity short, for
the demands upon his valuable time were incessant; but his fervent "God bless you, my
child," will never be obliterated from my
memory, as long as Providence shall be
pleased to allow it to retain its power.

In the course of our conversation the General kindly warned me that, in the event of
his troops being forced to retreat, it would be
expedient that I should leave my home again,
as the evacuation of Martinsburg by the Confederates would, as on former occasions, be
rapidly followed by its occupation by our enemies, and that it would be unwise and unsafe

for me to expose myself to the caprice or resentment of the Yankees, and run the risk of another imprisonment. He added that he would give me timely notice of his movements, by which my plans must be regulated.

Very shortly after the interview I have just noticed the General rode into the village and took tea with us, and on the very day after his visit I received from him a message to the effect that the troops under his command were preparing for a retrograde movement upon Winchester, and that he could spare me an ambulance, by aid of which I should be enabled to precede the retreat of the army, and thus keep my friends between my enemies and myself.

I must here explain that, when we had occasion to retire from the border, we were forced to look to the army for the means of transportation, it being the invariable practice of the Yankees, when they evacuated any place, to take with them every horse and mule, without the slightest discrimination between public and private property; and, should circumstances compel them to leave any animal behind, it was in these instances wantonly destroyed.

Acting upon General Jackson's advice, I removed to Winchester; and it was there and then that I received my commission as Captain and honorary Aide-de-camp to "Stone-wall" Jackson; and thenceforth I enjoyed the respect paid to an officer by soldiers.

Upon the occasion of the review of the troops in presence of Lord Hartingdon and Colonel Leslie, and again, when General Wilcox's division was inspected by Generals Lee and Longstreet, I had the honor to attend on horseback, and to be associated with the staff officers of the several commanders.

While General Wade Hampton held possession of Martinsburg I seized the opportunity of paying many visits to my home, and upon one of these expeditions I narrowly escaped being again captured.

The party that accompanied me was a large one; and, upon our arrival at Martinsburg, we improvised a dance. We were informed that the Yankees were advancing, but we had suffered a similar alarm to disperse us without cause more than once before. We therefore easily persuaded ourselves it was only the old cry of "Wolf! wolf!" This time, however, the warning voice was a true one; and we were barely off when heavy skirmishing commenced at no great distance from us—in fact, at the very outskirts of the town. This was the last opportunity I had of seeing my mother for nearly a year.

The Yankees were advancing by way of Culpepper Court-House, and our people, leaving the valley, crossed the mountains to intercept them.

As the small-pox was raging fearfully at Stanton, it was, of course, dangerous even to enter that town. Accordingly I, in company with several officers' wives, among whom were Mrs. G., Mrs. W., Mrs. F., and others, avoided the pestilential spot, and adopted a different route.

We were well in advance of the army, but our servants were with our baggage, which was transported in the ordnance wagons of General W.'s division. Passing through Flint Hill—the inhabitants of which gave me a cordial reception—I went on to Charlottesville, where I remained some time.

At last, feeling very anxious to rejoin my mother, I determined to write to General Jackson and ask his opinion upon the step I so longed to take. I was prepared to run almost any risk; but, at the same time, I resolved to abide by the General's decision.

It was pronounced in the following note, which I transcribe verbatim, as there is a kind of satisfaction in noting down the words of a truly great man, however trivial the subject that may have called them forth:—

> " Head-Quarters, Army of Virginia,
>   " Near Culpepper Court-House,
>   " January 29th, 1862.
>
> " MY DEAR CHILD,
>
> " I received your letter asking my advice regarding your returning to your home, which is now in the Federal lines. As you have asked for my advice, I can but candidly give it. I think that it is not safe; and therefore do not attempt it until it is, for you know the consequences. You would doubtless be imprisoned, and possibly might not be

released so soon again. You had better go to your relatives in Tennessee, and there remain until you can go with safety. God bless you.

"Truly your friend,
"T. J. JACKSON."

I lost no time in acting upon this sound and friendly advice, and was soon "on the road" once more.

Upon arriving at Knoxville, I was received with every mark of kindness and hospitality. The second night after my arrival I was serenaded by the band, and the people congregated in vast numbers to get a glimpse of the "rebel spy;" for I had accepted the *sobriquet* given me by the Yankees, and I was now known throughout North and South by the same cognomen.

After one or two appropriate airs had been played, the people in the streets took it into their heads to call for my appearance on the balcony. I rather dreaded the publicity that would attend a compliance with their wishes, and I begged General J. to be my substitute and thank them in my name. But they would not be satisfied without a look at me; so I

steadied my nerves and stepped forth from
the window. Hereupon the shouts were
redoubled, and I took the opportunity of con-
cocting a pretty speech; but it did not please
me, and I felt morally convinced I should
break down were I to attempt any thing like
an oration. So soon, therefore, as silence was
restored, I addressed my kind-hearted audience
in the following words, which contain an allu-
sion to an expression once made use of in
public by General Joe Johnston :—

"Like General Joe Johnston, 'I can fight,
but I cannot make speeches.' But, my good
friends, I no less feel and appreciate the kind
compliment you have paid me this night."

I confess that I felt relieved when this
harangue, brief and plain as it was, was over.
It was followed by "Dixie's Land" and
"Good Night." After which national airs the
band marched off and the people dispersed.

Next morning the newspapers gave circumstantial accounts of the whole affair, in highly
complimentary language, and, instead of being
described as the "rebel spy," I was designated

" the Virginian heroine." I now became the guest of my relative, Judge Samuel Boyd; and pleasant indeed was my visit to Knoxville. The city at this period was gay and animated beyond description. Party succeeded party, ball followed ball, concert came upon concert, and I took no thought of time.

When spring came round I made up my mind to make a tour through the South, and then return to Virginia.

I have said so much of the various receptions which I met with at different places that I almost fear I shall be accused of egotism rather than given credit for gratitude; but it should be borne in mind that the period of which I write had its perils and its pleasures, its griefs and its joys, exciting enough to justify outbreaks of feeling in a people naturally warm-hearted and sensitive. But, whatever criticism I expose myself to, I cannot refrain from expressing my warm thanks to that large body of my countrymen whose incessant kindness towards me made my progress through the Southern States one long ovation. My advent was anticipated by telegrams at each town through which I passed. Invitations of the most hospitable and delicate nature poured in upon me. Offers of assistance and assurances of regard and affection were innumerable. I accepted as many invitations as my time would permit, and was rejoiced at the opportunities I enjoyed of going over the famous and productive cotton plantations of Alabama.

After a long and delightful stay in Montgomery, I made the best of my way to Mobile, a city I had always wished to see, and one which existing circumstances made doubly interesting to all true Southern hearts.

Before arriving at the last-named port, a rumor had reached me that General Jackson had been wounded at the battle of Chancellorsville, but the rumor also affirmed that the wound was very trifling—so slight, indeed, as to be of no consequence. Conceive then the shock I experienced when this fatal telegram was put into my hand:—

"Battle House, Mobile, Alabama.

"Miss Belle Boyd,

"General Jackson now lies in state at the Governor's mansion.

"T. Bassett French,

"A. D. C. to the Governor."

And this was all. These few words were the funeral oration of a man who, for a rare combination of the best and the greatest qualities, has seldom or never been surpassed.

It is not for me to trace the career and paint the virtues of "Stonewall" Jackson: that task is reserved for an abler pen; but I may be permitted to record my poignant grief for the loss of him who had condescended to be my friend.

The sorrow of the South is unmitigated and inextinguishable.

When Nelson fell, at the crowning victory of Trafalgar, it was given to England to engrave that thrilling epitaph—

"Hoste devicto requievit,"

upon the tomb of her darling hero, whom she
10

justly loved and reverenced beyond all the great sons that Providence had sent her with so lavish a hand.

Alas! it was not General Jackson's destiny to deliver his country; but future ages will not measure his fame by the shortness of his career.

"The lightning that lighteneth out of the one part under heaven shineth unto the other part under heaven." Yet no sooner do men see its brightness than it vanishes.

And such was the glory of Jackson. It had neither dawn nor twilight. It rose and set in meridian splendor.

During the next thirty days—the space of time allotted for the outward and visible sign of a soldier's sorrow—I wore a crape band on my left arm; then leaving Mobile with a heavy heart, I proceeded to Charleston, South Carolina, where I remained one day only. I found time, however, to accept an invitation to go on board the two gunboats which lay in the harbor, and from their decks, by the aid of glasses, I could make out nearly all the ships of the Yankee blockading squadron.

In the evening I dined on shore with General Beauregard and several of the officers of his staff; and shortly after dinner one of the officers kindly presented me with a large supply of fresh fruit, which was part of the cargo of a blockade-runner which had just run in safe and sound from Nassau. Besides the oranges, pine apples, and bananas, which were most acceptable, my kind friend gave me a very handsome parrot, which I contrived to take home with me.

When I made good my return to Richmond, I learnt, on the best authority, that the Confederate troops were making a second advance down the valley, their object being the recapture of Winchester. Being now very anxious to get home, I followed close upon the rear of our army, and when the attack upon Winchester commenced I was but four miles distant from the scene of action.

When the artillery on both sides opened fire, the familiar sound reminded me of my own adventures on a former battle-field, and I resolved to be at least a spectatress of this. I joined a wounded officer, who, though disabled from taking an active part in the fight, where, by his crippled condition, he would but have hindered his men, was yet able to accompany me some way.

Accordingly we rode together to an eminence which commanded an uninterrupted view of the combat. Here we sat some short time, absorbed in the struggle that was going on beneath us.

> "The broken billows of the war,
>   And pluméd crests of chieftains brave,
>   Floating like foam upon the wave."

But this calm feeling was not of long duration. I was mounted upon a white horse, which was quite conspicuous to the artillery-men of a Yankee battery which had been pushed up to within three-quarters of a mile of the spot that we had selected for our watch-tower. A foolish report had been circulated through their army that in battle I rode a white horse, and was "invariably at General Jackson's side." Acting upon this mistaken idea, the guns of the battery were turned upon us.

By this time the officer of whom I have spoken and myself had been joined by several citizens, ladies and gentlemen, who were attracted by curiosity and anxiety to witness the fight. They were for the most part mounted on emaciated horses and mules which had been overlooked by the Yankees when they retired, and they one and all seemed to consider me as perfect security for themselves.

I shall never forget the stampede that was made when a shell came suddenly hissing and shrieking in among us. I joined, *con amore*, in the general flight; for I had seen enough of fighting to prefer declining with honor the part of a living target, when exposure, being quite useless, becomes an act of madness.

The battle was not of long duration. The terms were too equal to leave the issue long in doubt.

Milroy's "skedaddle" was even more disgraceful than that of Banks. The victorious Confederates, led on by General Lee, pressed hard upon the flying Yankees, of whom they killed many, and took more prisoners. The pursuit was not abated until the enemy were again in Maryland.

My father, whose health had been broken by the severe hardships of the campaign, was at home on leave; and I had the double pleasure of being welcomed by both my parents to poor Martinsburg.

CHAPTER XII.

ELATED by their continued successes, the Confederates, under General Lee, marched on into
Pennsylvania. A panic seized the people of
the North; for they knew of the depredations
that they had been committing in the South,
and of course could not expect much mercy from
the invading army. General Lee, however, issued an order to the officers under him not to
allow their men to burn, pillage, or destroy any
property; if they did, they were to be punished.

Though the hearts of the sympathizers with the South beat high with hope—for rumor said that Baltimore and Washington were to be attacked—their hopes were blighted. The battle of Gettysburg was fought. And, oh! how many of those brave and noble fellows who went forward proudly to the front, eager to avenge the wrongs the South had suffered, who had left the beautiful shores of Virginia to defend their native soil, found a soldier's grave! Or, perchance, they were not even buried, their bodies lying upon the battle-field where they fell, with no covering save the blue canopy of heaven, their bones left to bleach in the sunlight, or gleaming ghastly white in the moon's pale beams.

Martinsburg soon became one vast hospital; for, as fast as they could be brought to the rear, the Confederate wounded of the great battle were sent back southward. There was no established hospital in my native village, it being too near the border; so that the churches and many of the public buildings were obliged to be used temporarily for that purpose. My time was constantly occupied in attending to the poor soldiers with whom our house was filled. Mrs. Judge McM., of Georgia, who had come to seek the dead body of her son, having heard of his untimely end, was also staying at my mother's.

Upon the retreat of the Southern army, after the battle of Gettysburg, they marched through Martinsburg, leaving the border again in the possession of the Confederate cavalry under General B., as General Wade Hampton had been severely wounded.

I had been from home so long, and my mother and father were so anxious that I should remain with them, that I hoped, by keeping quiet, to be allowed to do so. My mother was taken very ill just as the Confederates evacuated the town, it being found that they could no longer retain it in their possession, and for a short time all was quiet.

My little baby-sister was but three days old when, as I sat in my mother's room, I heard the servants exclaim, " Oh, here comes de Yankees trou' de town !" I went to the

10*

window, and, looking out, saw that a whole
brigade had halted in front of my home. In
a short time two officers approached the door,
and one of them rang the bell. My father,
who had gone to meet them, sent me word
that Major Goff and Lieutenant —— wished
to see me. I descended to the drawing-room
and was introducd to them, when the Major
said—

"Miss Boyd, General Kelly commanded me
to call and see if you really had remained at
home, such a report having reached head-
quarters; but he did not credit it, so I have
come to ascertain the truth."

To this I answered—

"Major Goff, what is there so peculiarly
strange in my remaining in my own home
with my parents?" feigning perfect ignorance,
as I spoke, that there was any danger to be
apprehended from my so doing. He replied—

"But do you not think it rather dangerous? Are you then really not afraid of being
arrested?"

"Oh no! for I don't know why they should do so. I am no criminal!"

"Yes, true," said he; "but you are a rebel, and will do more harm to our cause than half the men could do."

"But there are other rebels besides myself."

"Yes," he answered; "but then not so dangerous as yourself."

After a few moments' longer conversation he withdrew, bidding us "Good morning," as he left.

For some days we saw nothing of him, and began to hope that I should not be further annoyed. But, alas! my hopes were doomed to disappointment; for scarce four days had passed by before an order was issued for my arrest. My mother was very ill when they came to take me, and, fearing that if I were removed it might prove fatal to her in her delicate state of health, my father begged that they would let me stay at home, at least until she became convalescent. We hoped thus to gain time, and, through private influence, to

procure my release from the department at
Washington. To be just, although an avowed
enemy of the Federal cause, I will state that
they obligingly complied with this request,
and placed me on parole, but at the same time
stationed guards around the house; watching
me so strictly that I was not even allowed to
go out upon the front balcony.

It was amusing to hear the orders given to
the sentries; for instance, "that they must
not let me come near them, for I might give
them chloroform, or send a dagger through
their hearts."

This was in July; and, between my mother's illness, the warm weather, and my being
a prisoner, I scarcely knew what to do. Without the necessary pass no one was allowed to
go in or come out of our house. On one occasion, desiring to take a walk, I got a special
permit from the commanding officer, which
read as follows:—

"*Miss Belle Boyd has permission to walk
out for half an hour, at 5 o'clock this* A. M.,
giving her word of honor that she will use

nothing which she may see or hear to the disadvantage of the U. S. troops."

I had gone only a few blocks from home when I was arrested and sent back, with a guard on each side of me, their muskets loaded. In about an hour's time I received a note from the head-quarters of the general, informing me that, although on parole, "*I was not allowed to promenade freely in Martinsburg.*" Vexatious and insulting to my feelings as this was, my troubles were not at an end.

Nearly a month passed away, during which period I was kept in a state of anxious suspense as to what would eventually be my fate. At last, one day, when we were all hoping that I should soon be at liberty to do and act as I pleased, Major Walker, the Provost-Marshal, called, with a detective, and informed me that I must get ready to go to Washington City; that the Secretary of War, Mr. Stanton, had so ordered it; and that I was to take my departure from home at eleven A. M. the next day.

There was no hope of escape for me, as the house was vigilantly guarded by the sentries. My poor mother, but just recovered from her grave illness, became seriously worse at the bare idea of my being again thrown into prison. My father, who was always so good and kind to me, determined that I should not go unaccompanied, trusting myself to the tender mercies of a detective. So, next day, when the time came for us to leave, I was attended by my fond parent; and, after bidding a tearful adieu to my poor mother, brothers, and sisters, who wept bitterly, we started once more for Washington City.

I shall pass over my dreary journey of one hundred miles. There was little of interest to commend it to the attention of my readers; for they can readily imagine the sad, tearful girl, and the father vainly attempting to comfort her.

When I arrived in Washington, tired and worn, I was immediately taken, not to my former quarters, but to the Carroll Prison. This large, unpretending brick building, situ-

ate near the Old Capitol, was formerly used
as a hotel, under the name of Carroll Place,
and belonged to a Mr. Duff Green, a resident
in the city. But, since my first taste of prison
life, it had been converted into a receptacle for
rebels, prisoners of state, hostages, blockade-
runners, smugglers, desperadoes, spies, crimi-
nals under sentence of death, and, lastly, a
large number of Federal officers convicted of
defrauding the Government. Many of these
last were army-contractors and quartermasters,
of whom I shall merely observe that they
seemed to care very little about their ultimate
fate, and evidently enjoyed the, to them, pre-
posterous notion, suggested in the journals of
the day, that Mr. Lincoln was Napoleonic in
his idea of punishing them for their misdeeds.

At the guarded gates of this Yankee Bastile, I bade adieu to my father; and, once
more, iron bars shut me off from the outer
world, and from all that is dear in this life. I
was conducted to what was termed the "room
for distinguished guests"—the best room
which this place boasts, except some offices

attached to the building. In this apartment
had been held, though not for a long period of
time, Miss Antonia F., Nannie T., with her
aged mother, and many other ladies belonging
to our best families in the South. Again my
monotonous prison routine began. It seemed
to me that the world would never go round
on its axis; for the days and nights were in-
terminably long, and many, many were the
hours that I spent gazing forth through the
bars of my grated windows with an apathetic
listlessness. Yet there were times when I
wished that my soul were but free to soar
away from those who held me captive.

Friends who chanced to pass the Carroll
would frequently stop and nod in kindly recognition of some familiar face at the windows; unconscious that, in so doing, they
violated prison regulations. When noticed by
the sentries, these good Samaritans were immediately "halted;" and, if riding or driving,
were often made to dismount by the officious
and impudent corporal of the guard, and
forced to enter the bureau of the prison—

there to remain until such time as it should please their tormentors to let them depart. Can it be doubted that many went away with the unalterable opinion that a sterner despotism than existed in the United States was nowhere to be found? Defenceless women were not permitted to pass unscathed, because a drunken and brutal set, vested with a "little brief authority," saw fit to vent their spleen upon the weak.

A few days after my arrival at the prison, I heard the "old familiar sound" of a grating instrument against the wall, apparently coming from the room adjoining mine. Whilst engaged in watching to see the exact portion of the wall whence it came, I observed the plaster give way, and next instant the point of a knife-blade was perceptible. I immediately set to work on my side, and soon, to my unspeakable joy, had formed a hole large enough for the passing of tightly-rolled notes.

Ascertaining my unfortunate neighbors to be, beyond a doubt, "sympathizers," I was greatly relieved; for our prison was not with-

out its system of espionage to trap the in-
cautious. These neighbors were Messrs.
Brookes, Warren, Stuart, and Williams; and
from them I learnt that they had been here
for nine months, having been captured whilst
attempting to get South and join the Southern
army.

But soon, alas! this little paper correspondence, that enlivened, whilst it lasted, a portion
of my heavy time, was put a stop to by Mr.
Lockwood, the officer of the keys, whose duty
it was to secure our rooms, and who was always prying about when not otherwise engaged. Although it was well concealed on
both sides, our impromptu post-office could not
escape his Yankee cunning; and he at once
had the gentlemen removed into the room beyond, and the mural disturbance closed up
with plaster.

Several days subsequently I learned that I
was to have a companion in a Miss Ida P.,
arrested on the charge of being a rebel mail-
carrier. I was allowed to speak with and
visit her as soon as she arrived, and she was

placed in the room that had been occupied by the above-mentioned gentlemen.

Now, between her room and that to which the gentlemen had been removed, there was a door. This the workmen nailed up, and then boarded over; but I watched very attentively which plank was placed over the key-hole, and pointed it out to the new-comer. We then held a council of war as to the best way of getting the board off the key-hole. We tried several times, but our combined efforts produced no effect upon the stoutly nailed wood-work; and, having neither hatchet nor hammer, we were about to give it up, when I suddenly bethought me of the sentry outside. "Oh!" I said, "I will manage it!" and, going to the door, I bribed the sentinel with some oranges and apples, and, after talking to him for some time, asked him to "lend me his bayonet?" Pausing an instant, he finally unfixed it from his gun, then, with the whispered injunction of "Be quick, miss!" handed it to me. I ran into the room with it, and, whilst Miss Ida watched, I endeavored to wrench off the obstinate board.

But, at this critical juncture, the prison superintendent, Mr. Wood, came rushing up the stairway; and I only had time to thrust the bayonet under the camp bedstead when he entered the room. I was frightened, I will admit; for in a few minutes the sentries would be relieved, and of course the soldier would have to account for the loss of his bayonet. We wanted to free him from complicity in the affair; and woman's wit came to my assistance, as it had often done before.

I proposed that, my room being larger than Miss Ida's, we should go in there and sit down. Fortunately to this the superintendent agreed. After remaining for a short time, I said, "Oh! Miss Ida, I have forgotten my pocket-handkerchief!" and, running hastily into her room, I seized the bayonet, wrenched off the board, and returned the weapon to the scared sentinel.

Little did Mr. Wood imagine the part I had just played, as he sat glaring around him with his cat-like eyes, and boasting that "there warn't any thing going on in that prison that he didn't know of." For several days after this, Miss Ida and I whiled away our time by writing and receiving notes.

Miss P., however, did not remain here long, for, having given her parole that she would do nothing more against the Yankee Government, she was released.

CHAPTER XIII.

A very Romantic Way of Corresponding—The Prison Authorities for once are at a Loss—My Confederate Flags—
They wave over Washington in spite of Yankee Asser-
tions to the contrary—I become very ill—Mr. Stanton in
an unfavorable Light once more—My Prisoner of Front
Royal in her true Character—Sentence of Court-Martial
is announced to me—A Relapse of my former Illness—I
am banished—The Cry of "Murder" raised round the
Corner—Incidents in my Prison Life.

ONE evening, about nine o'clock, while seated
at my window, I was singing "Take me back
to my own sunny South," when quite a crowd
of people collected on the opposite side of the
street, listening. After I had ceased, they
passed on; and I could not help heaving a
sigh as I watched their retreating figures.
What would I not have given for liberty?
Rising from my chair, I approached the gas,
lowered it, then resumed my seat, and, leaning

my head against the bars, sank into deep
thought.

I was soon startled from this reverie by
hearing something whiz by my head into the
room and strike the wall beyond. At the
moment I was alarmed; for my first impression was that some hireling of the Yankee
Government, following the plan of Spanish
countries, had endeavored to put an end to
my life. I almost screamed with terror; and
it was some minutes before I regained sufficient
self-command to turn on the gas, so that, if
possible, I might discover what missile had
entered the room.

Glancing curiously round, I saw, to my
astonishment, that it was an arrow which had
struck the wall opposite my window; and
fastened to this arrow was a letter; I immediately tore it open, and found that it contained the following words:—

"Poor girl! you have the deepest sympathy of all the
best community in Washington City, and there are many who
would lay down their lives for you, but they are powerless to
act or aid you at present. *You have many very warm
friends;* and we daily watch the journals to see if there is

any news of you. If you will listen attentively to the instructions that I give you, you will be able to correspond with and hear from your friends outside.

"On Thursdays and Saturdays, in the evening, just after twilight, I will come into the square opposite the prison. When you hear some one whistling ''Twas within a mile of Edinbro' town,' if alone and all is safe, lower the gas as a signal and leave the window. I will then shoot an arrow into your room, as I have done this evening, with a letter attached. Do not be alarmed, as I am a good shot.

"The manner in which you will reply to these messages will be in this way: Procure a large india-rubber ball; open it, and place your communication within it, written on foreign paper; then sew it together. On Tuesdays I shall come, and you will know of my presence by the same signal. Then throw the ball, with as much force as you can exert, across the street into the square, and trust to me, I will get it.

"Do not be afraid. *I am really your friend.*

"O. H."

For a long time I was in doubt as to the propriety or safety of replying to this note; for I naturally reasoned that it was some Yankee who was seeking to gain evidence against me. But prudence at last yielded to my womanly delight at this really romantic way of corresponding with an unknown who vowed he was my friend; and I decided on replying.

It was an easy thing for me to procure an

india-rubber ball without subjecting myself
to the least suspicion; and by this means I
commenced a correspondence which I had no
reason to regret; for whoever the mysterious
personage may have been, he was, without
doubt, honorable and sincere in his profes-
sions of sympathy.

Through him I became possessed of much
valuable information regarding the movements of the Federals; and in this unique
style of correspondence I have again and
again received small Confederate flags, made
by the ladies of Washington City, with which
I was only too proud and happy to adorn my
chamber.

Little did the sentries below know of the
mischief that was brewing above their heads;
and where and how I had been enabled to
obtain Confederate flags was a subject of
much wonderment in the prison. It is almost
needless to remark that I took care to keep
the secret, though I must acknowledge that
there was rashness in displaying the tiny
Southern banners, and danger of subjecting

11

myself to insult from the brutes who guarded
me.   But I could not resist the temptation!

On several occasions I fastened one of
these ensigns to a broom-stick, in lieu of a
flag-staff, and then suspended it outside the
window, after which I retired to the back part
of the room, out of sight of the sentinel.   In a
short time this would attract his attention—
for, when on watch, the sentinels generally
were gazing heavenwards, the only time, I
really believe, that such was the case—and
he would roar out at the top of his voice some
such command as—

"Take in that —— flag, or I'll blow your
—— brains out!"

Of course I paid no attention to this, for I
was out of danger, when the command would
generally be followed up by the report of a
musket; and I have often heard the thud of
the Minié-ball as it struck the ceiling or wall
of my room.   Before the sentinel had time to
reload his piece, I would go to the window
and look out, seemingly as unconscious as

though nothing had occurred to disturb my equanimity.

Just after this episode of the "arrow-headed" correspondence—a green spot in my memory, to which I revert with pleasure—I was taken dangerously ill with typhoid fever. Can this be wondered at when I inform my readers that the room in which I was confined was low and fearfully warm, and that the air was fetid and rank with the fumes of an ill-ventilated Bastile?

In this same room Miss McDonough died (as will be seen by referring to my husband's journal). The poor child was under the treatment of Doctor F., the surgeon of the prison—the same who attended me for some time, but under whose awkward treatment I grew daily, nay, hourly, worse. Nor did I begin to recover until I met with the kind attendance of a Confederate surgeon, who was a prisoner, like myself, in the Old Capitol; and it is to him that I feel indebted for my final recovery.

Years may roll by, but my sufferings in

that prison, both mental and physical, can never be obliterated from my memory; and to attempt to describe them would be utterly impossible. There I was, far from home and friends—no soft hand to smooth my fevered brow, no gentle woman near me, save an humble negress, who nursed me through my illness as though she had been my own "black mammee." Relations and friends, who had heard of my attack of fever, as well as my immediate family, endeavored, time and again, to gain access to me; but they were referred, by his own orders, to Secretary Stanton, who, when application was made to him for me to be removed from the prison during my illness at least, would remark, ".No; she is a —— rebel; let her die there!"

At the expiration of three weeks, passed under the treatment of my new physician, I was pronounced convalescent; and at the end of the fourth I was able once more to walk about.

It was at this period of my imprisonment that, one day, Captain Mix, of whom I shall

have occasion to speak hereafter, came into
my room and said—

"A most beautiful woman has arrived
here to-day, and is in the room at the further
end of the passage below you."

At the time, I took no notice of the remark,
and had almost forgotten the incident, when,
one morning, whilst walking in the passage, I
saw our new inmate.   Judge of my astonishment on recognizing in her my prisoner at
Front Royal, who had requited my kindness
to her when there by informing the general
that I was a bitter enemy of the Yankees.
She proved to be—alas! that I should have
to write aught derogatory to one of my own
sex—not what she had represented herself, the
wife of a soldier, but a camp-follower, known
as "Miss Annie Jones."   She was said to
have been insane; but how far this report is
to be credited I know not.

Shortly after she was placed here, another
arrival, a Frenchwoman, came in, who was
charged with having sold her dispatches to
the Confederate States authorities, enacting

the " spy " for both sides. Neither of these women possessed that priceless jewel of womanhood—reputation. Yet it was with such that I was immured, though, thank Heaven! I was not thrown into immediate contact with them.

My trial by court-martial had meanwhile been progressing, under the fostering tenderness of the Judge-Advocate, L. C. Turner—as thoroughly unscrupulous a partisan as the United States Government possesses in its service.

One day Captain Mix came into the passage, and said to Miss Annie Jones, "Prepare yourself to go to the Lunatic Asylum to-morrow, as it is the Secretary of War's orders." She immediately commenced screaming hysterically, and rushed towards the spot where I was standing. I turned to leave, when he added, "Oh, you need not put on airs by getting out of the way, for you've got to go to Fitchburg Jail during the war. You have been sentenced to hard labor there."

Miss Jones's screams, coupled with this intelligence, completely unnerved me, and I fell fainting on the floor, whence I was conveyed to my room, only to suffer a relapse of the fever from which I had just recovered.

My father, who was in Martinsburg when he heard of my sentence and second illness, immediately came on to Washington, and, after untiring exertions in my behalf, succeeded in having the sentence commuted. What that commutation was he did not then know. It was "banishment to the South—never to return North again during the war."

Among the gentlemen who were retained as prisoners at the Carroll was Mr. Smithson, formerly one of the wealthiest bankers in Washington City. He was charged by the Yankees with holding correspondence with friends residing in the South, was arrested by the authorities, tried by court-martial, found guilty, and sentenced to five years' imprisonment in the Penitentiary at hard labor. All his property was confiscated, and his refined and delicate wife, with two little children, who had been reared in the lap of luxury, were obliged to see their residence taken from them and made into quarters for the Yankee officers. They were compelled to retire to a garret, with scarcely any of the necessaries of life whereon to support themselves.

Before leaving for the South, one of the imprisoned Confederate officers, Colonel ——, gave me letters of introduction to the Vice-President, the Honorable Alexander Stephens, and to the Honorable Bowling Baker, Chief Auditor of the Southern Treasury Department. In both of these letters he spoke of my untiring devotion to the Confederacy, of the zeal that I had shown to serve my country at all times, and of my kindness, as far as lay in my power, to my fellow-prisoners. The Colonel further commended me to his friends' "kind care and protection." These letters were, of course, contraband; and I intended, if I possibly could do so, to smuggle them through to Richmond.

It was agreed that I should leave for Fortress Monroe on the 1st day of December, 1863. My father was still in Washington, residing with his niece; but he was so ill that he could not visit me previous to my departure.

One evening, whilst I was looking out of my room-door, a significant cough attracted my attention, and, glancing in the direction whence it proceeded—the sentry's back being turned—I perceived a note, tightly rolled up, thrown towards me. I picked it up quickly, and, reading it, found that it was from Mr. K., of Virginia, begging me to aid himself and two friends to escape, and also asking for money to advance their object. I wrote, in reply, that I would do all that lay in my power, and, unobserved, I handed him forty dollars. By means of my india-rubber ball I arranged every thing, and the night when the attempt should be made was fixed.

Above Mr. K.'s room was a garret occupied by his two friends, who intended to escape with him; and it was so contrived that he should get into the garret with the others whilst returning from supper.

At one time I was afraid that this attempt would be frustrated, for the sentry, observing

11*

Mr. K. upon the garret staircase, commanded him to "Halt!" adding, "You don't belong there; so come down." Standing in the doorway of my chamber at the time, I quickly retorted, "Sentry, have you been so long here and don't know where the prisoners are quartered? Let him pass on to his room." Taking the hint, Mr. K. declared that he "knew what he was about," which it was very evident he did; and the sentinel, thinking that he had made a mistake, allowed him to proceed upstairs.

This part of the scheme being satisfactorily carried out, I wrote a note to the superintendent, informing him that I was desirous of seeing him for a few minutes. He accordingly came, and I managed to detain him by conversing upon various topics. Suddenly, from round the corner of the prison that faced on the street, arose a startling cry of "Murder! murder!" I know that my heart beat violently, but I kept the composure of my face as well as I was able; for this sudden cry was the commencement of a *ruse de guerre* which, if it should succeed, would liberate my friends from thraldom.

Mr. Wood had, at the first cry of "Murder!" rushed to one of the windows and flung it open to see what was the matter; and some soldiers, who were lounging outside, waiting for their turn of sentry duty, ran hurriedly to the spot from which the cries proceeded. Meanwhile, those in the room above were not idle. Removing in haste a portion of the roof, they scrambled out upon the eaves, descended by means of a lightning-conductor into the street below, and made off, sheltered by the darkness.

Of course, the next morning, when the roll was called, and the prisoners were mustered, Mr. K. and his companions were found to be missing. It was strongly suspected that I had connived at their escape, and knew more than I pretended about the affair; but as they could not prove any thing against me, I was not punished. I subsequently heard, to my great joy, that the fugitives had arrived safely in Richmond.

Shortly after my recovery from the severe

illness which had prostrated me, I wrote to
General Martindale (commandant at that time
of the forces in and around Washington), asking him to grant me the privilege of walking
for a while each day in the Capitol Square.
This square lies in front of the Carroll; and I
thought that a change, however slight, from
the close confinement of my room, would
greatly strengthen me. To my letter I received
a gracious answer, with permission to promenade in the square, on condition that I gave a
written promise that, on my word of honor as
a lady, I would hold communication with no
one, either by word of mouth or by letter.

I was glad to do any thing to get once more
a breath of pure air that did not come to me
through prison bars. So I signed the promise;
and every evening, when I felt so inclined, I
was permitted to walk for half an hour, from
five until half-past, in the square, followed by
a corporal and guard with loaded muskets.

Even this limited enjoyment was not of
long duration; for, when it became known in
Washington City, through the public journals,

that I walked in the square, Southern sympathizers — and their name was legion — both ladies and gentlemen, would congregate to see me; and often, when I passed, would they give utterance to pitying expressions on my account.

Intelligence of this eventually reached the ears of the authorities, through various channels, and ultimately led to an order from Mr. Stanton revoking the parole that had been granted. Thus my promenade became one of the things of the past, to which I often reverted with regret.

On one occasion a party of young girls, in passing me, dropped a square piece of Bristol board that had a Confederate battle-flag and my name worked upon it in worsted. The corporal detected the movement, and, before I could gain possession of this treasonable gift, picked it up himself. He commanded the whole group to "halt" immediately; and, had it not been for my earnest entreaties and supplications on their behalf, he would have arrested the entire party, who, terrified beyond measure at the turn affairs had assumed, added their appeals for mercy to mine. The corporal happening to possess that commodity, a heart, was merciful, and dismissed them with a slight reprimand.

Promising to say nothing that would implicate him should the flag ever be discovered upon me, I succeeded in procuring it from my guardian by a bribe of five dollars; and I wore it concealed long after I had left Washington for the South.

Had I been a queen, or a reigning princess, my every movement could not have been more faithfully chronicled at this period of my imprisonment. My health was bulletined for the gratification of the public; and if I walked or was indisposed, it was announced after the most approved fashion by the newspapers. Thus, from the force of circumstances, and not through any desire of my own, I became a celebrity.

CHAPTER XIV.

On the first day of December, early in the norning, I started for Fortress Monroe, under the charge of Captain Mix and an orderly-sergeant. It was my poor father's intention to have accompanied me as far as Baltimore, and beyond, if he could get the necessary permission. Just before I left, however, a message was brought to me stating that my

father, though not dangerously ill, was confined to the house by severe indisposition.

When I heard that I could not see my
fond parent, it distressed me greatly; but I
was powerless to act in the matter; and,
though I entreated them to let me go to him,
if but for a moment, it was refused.

After being subjected to the annoying and
ungentlemanly conduct of Captain Mix, who
seemed to exert himself especially to make
every thing as disagreeable as he possibly
could for me, I arrived in Fortress Monroe
about 9 A. M. on Wednesday morning. Captain Mix immediately went on shore to report
to Captain Cassels, the Provost-Marshal and
Aide-de-camp to Butler, to whose care I was
to be committed until the "exchange boat"
should start for Richmond.

Meanwhile all the passengers had landed,
and I was left in the charge of the orderly-
sergeant. Major (now General) Mulford, the
exchange officer, returned on board with Captain Mix, and was introduced to me. I found
him an elegant and courteous gentleman. In

a short time I was escorted from the boat to
the Provost-Marshal's office, passing between
a company of negro soldiers, who were filed
on each side. Thence I was taken into the
fortress, to Butler's head-quarters, and, after
waiting a short time, I was conducted into his
august presence.

He was seated near a table, and upon my
entrance, he looked up and said, "Ah, so this
is Miss Boyd, the famous rebel spy. Pray be
seated."

"Thank you, General Butler, but I prefer
to stand."

I was very much agitated, and trembled
greatly. This he noticed, and remarked,
"Pray be seated. But why do you tremble
so? Are you frightened?"

"No; ah! that is, yes, General Butler; I
must acknowledge that I do feel frightened in
the presence of a man of such world-wide
reputation as yourself."

This seemed to please him immensely,
and, rubbing his hands together and smiling
most benignly, he said, "Oh, pray do be

seated, Miss Boyd. But what do you mean when you say that I am widely known?"

"I mean, General Butler," I said, "that you are a man whose atrocious conduct and brutality, especially to Southern ladies, is so infamous that even the English Parliament commented upon it. I naturally feel alarmed at being in your presence."

He had evidently expected a compliment when I commenced to reply to his inquiry, but, at the close of my remarks, he rose, and, with rage depicted upon every lineament of his features, he ordered me out of his presence.

I was conducted to the hotel, and felt for the time being exceedingly uneasy lest, by my Parthian shot at an enemy whom I thoroughly detested, I should have laid myself open to his petty spirit of revenge. I feared that I should be remanded to a dreary prison cell: for General Butler was all-powerful in the North about this period.

Events have since clearly proved this man, even to the Yankees themselves, to be but a meretricious hero and a political charlatan. Like others who render themselves rather notorious than great, he first pleased a fickle populace. by his acts of brutality, then disgusted his contemporaries, who feared that he might become to America what Robespierre had been to France. The tyrant of New Orleans, having failed most signally at Wilmington, was discovered to be a coward, and suspected of being a rogue. Well might the baffled New England attorney exclaim, "*Facilis descensus Averni !*" In the hope of being styled a modern Cincinnatus, he retired to Lowell, to live upon the ill-gotten gains extorted by threats or force from Southern people.

But to resume the thread of my story. I was obliged to give my parole that I would not leave the house until permitted to do so. Here I found the Misses Lomax, sisters of the Confederate General Lomax, and a Miss Goldsborough, of Baltimore, who were to be sent South. These ladies, however, were not the only sympathizers in the hotel; there were others whose names I dare not mention.

On Wednesday evening the order came for Miss Goldsborough and myself to be in readiness to start that same night for Richmond. The Misses Lomax, for some reason, were not allowed to proceed, but were sent back to Baltimore. When the time arrived for our departure, we were taken back to the Provost-Marshal's office; and here I found my luggage, consisting of two Saratoga trunks and a bonnet-box. The keys were demanded of me, and I complied with the request.

A man and two women immediately set to work to ransack my boxes, although I assured them that they need not search, as I had just come from prison. This appeal, however, was ineffectual, and they still continued their examination. Imagine their astonishment and my chagrin when they pulled from the bottom of one of my trunks two suits of private clothes, a uniform for Major-General W——, a dozen linen shirts, &c. These things I had succeeded in smuggling into prison by means of an underground railway, of which Superintendent Wood, sharp as he imagined himself to be, was little aware. I was interrogated as to how I had obtained the articles in question, but they did dot succeed in eliciting any thing by their queries.

All the goods considered contraband, including several pairs of army gauntlets and felt hats, with a pair of field-glasses which had formerly belonged to General Jackson, and which I greatly prized, together with much clothing, were taken from me. I entreated them to let me retain the glasses; but this was flatly refused; and they were, to my mortification, given to General Butler.

When I saw how these Vandals were robbing me of nearly every thing, I strove in vain to restrain my tears; and my trunks having been thoroughly ransacked, I was informed that I must undergo a personal search. At this turn of affairs I began to feel very nervous, for I had concealed about me twenty thousand dollars in Confederate notes, five thousand in greenbacks, and nearly one thousand in gold, as well as the letters of introduction which I have previously mentioned.

I earnestly appealed to their forbearance assuring them that I had nothing contraband; for I did not consider my money contraband.

As it was getting late, the captain said, " Well, if you will take an oath to the effect that you have nothing contraband upon you —no letters or papers—you shall not be searched."

As this was impossible, I told him that I could not make such a declaration, handing him my letters at the same time. He then asked if I had any money about me. To this I replied by giving him a roll of two or three thousand dollars in Confederate money, which I had placed in my pocket. This he regarded as valueless, and sneeringly informed me that I might keep " that stuff."

Upon opening my letters and finding mention of " my immense services to my country," " my kindness towards prisoners," " my devotion to the Southern cause," &c., he became very angry, and said, " I shall send this to General Butler in the morning. I would do so now, but it is after office hours."

Miss Goldsborough sat by meanwhile, a quiet spectator of the whole affair, she having undergone the ordeal of search in the morning. We were then conducted to the wharf, placed on board a tug, and sent off to the exchange boat, the *City of New York*, which lay at anchor in the stream. Upon our arrival on board we were kindly received by Major Mulford, who conducted us to the saloon and introduced us to his wife, a very charming, lady-like woman. Here we remained all night, and next morning, about seven o'clock, got under way. Shortly afterwards we ran aground, and it was not until eight A. M. that we succeeded in getting the vessel off again. Then, under a full head of steam, we steered for City Point.

About this time the little steam-tug that had brought us alongside the *City of New York* quitted the wharf, apparently in chase of us. My heart sank, for I felt intuitively that this pursuit had something to do with me, and that General Butler must have given an order for my detention. But the larger

steamer had already waited so long that Major
Mulford, angry and impatient at the delay,
took no notice of our pursuers, and, to my
great joy and relief, kept steadily on our
course.

I afterwards learnt that my fears upon this
occasion were not unfounded. ' When General
Butler, smarting with the remembrance of my
farewell sarcasm, had beheld the letters that
Captain Cassels had taken from me, he commanded that I should be followed, and, if re-
captured, should be sent at once to Fort Warren, in Massachusetts Bay. As he issued this
order he remarked to those who surrounded
him that he would take "a leading character
in 'Beauty and the Beast.'" When the tug
returned from her fruitless chase, he was
almost beside himself with rage at being
thwarted in his revenge. This I had from
such good authority that I am confident the
General will not feel it worth his while to
contradict the statement.

At the mouth of the James River we passed
the Federal blockading fleet, and were here

boarded by a boat from the flag-ship *Minnesota*, commanded by Admiral Lee. In a few moments we had entered the James, whose waters are distinguishable from those of the Potomac by a yellow streak on the surface.

As we wended our way up the river we could see the signal-officers at the different stations busily announcing our approach, and occasionally we observed Confederate soldiers on picket duty. Every thing reminded me that I was once more drawing near to the capital of my own sunny South.

> " Amate sponde !
> Pur vi torno a riveder,
> Trema in petto e si confonde
> L'alma oppressa dal piacer."

Though exceedingly happy that I was again permitted to breathe the pure air of my native State, I did not feel completely free, for I was still under the Federal flag, and could scarcely count upon my liberty as being yet fully assured to me.

We arrived at City Point late on Friday

12

evening. This place, which could hardly be correctly dignified with the name of village, · is situate in a bend of the river. It was used as a dépôt by the Confederates, for the purpose of forwarding stores to those of their unfortunate countrymen who were prisoners in the North.

Whilst the *City of New York* was coming to an anchor, Major Mulford, his wife, Miss Goldsborough, and myself stood conversing on the hurricane-deck. Major Mulford remarked, pointing to what was apparently the Confederate flag-of-truce boat approaching, " After all, ladies, you will not have to remain on board here'to-night."

Looking in the direction indicated, we distinctly saw a steamer, which, judging from the distance between us, would in less than ten minutes be alongside. Ten minutes, however, passed in fruitless expectation; then followed twenty more of hope deferred; when Major Mulford, who began to grow very impatient, went on shore to inquire the reason of her remaining as she did—he even sent a boat to her to ascertain the reason of her detention. Major Mulford was so confident that he had seen her that the Confederate officer commanding the "Point" telegraphed the news to Richmond. Judge of our great surprise when the telegraphic reply, brought to us on board shortly afterwards, announced "that the Confederate flag-of-truce boat had left Richmond exactly at the hour we had seen her." As Richmond was more than twelve hours distant from us at the then rate of travel over that route, we could only consider that we had been deceived by a "mirage." How often must such phenomena have given rise to stories of phantom ships!

A French corvette, which had been up the river to Richmond, lay at anchor near us. This evening, in acceptance of an invitation from Major Mulford, the French captain and his lieutenant came on board to spend the evening with us; and we enjoyed their visit heartily. The next morning, when I awoke, I found that the flag-of-truce boat had arrived during the night. Captain Hatch, the Confederate exchange officer, presently came on board. We were introduced to him, and very soon afterwards were, with our luggage, safely ensconced in the snug little cabin of the ——. Here, under my own country's flag, I felt free and comparatively happy.

On our way up the river to Richmond we had to pass the obstructions situated between Chapin's and Drury's Bluffs. These places take their names from the bold appearance that the shore here presents. The obstructions designed to impede a hostile squadron became accidentally hurtful to our Confederate vessel. She ran foul of them, and it was found utterly impossible to continue the voyage.

At Drury's Bluff, therefore, we went on board a tug, in which we proceeded to Richmond. When we arrived, at eight P. M., I went immediately to the Spottswood House, and, tired and worn out with the fatigues of my journey, I retired to rest, refusing to see any one that evening.

CHAPTER XV.

Kind Reception at Richmond—I hear of my Father's Death—
Efforts of my Friends to procure my Return Home—I go
from Richmond further South—Kindness of Friends during my Illness—I am made Bearer of Dispatches—Departure from Richmond—Too late for the *Coquette*—I
take Passage in the *Greyhound.*

WHEN I came down to breakfast on the following day, my many acquaintances and friends
in the hotel were astonished to see me, for
few had expected that I should be released,
and none that I should so soon arrive at Richmond. The morning papers announced my
return in flattering terms; and, as it thus became generally known, I was at once besieged
with company, and every afternoon and evening I held a perfect drawing-room, if I may
be allowed to make use of the expression.
My reception was every thing that I could

wish; but, alas! my happiness was of short duration, and my freedom was dearly bought.

I was at a large dinner-party on a Saturday evening exactly one week after the day I had arrived. I was joyous and light-hearted, little dreaming of the blow that was to overwhelm me with sadness—little dreaming that I should be so cruelly reminded of the words of the Preacher, that "in the midst of life we are in death;" but so it was.

On Monday morning, the 14th, before I had risen, I received a little note from Captain Hatch, in which he expressed great sorrow at having to be the bearer of mournful tidings, and said that, as soon as I was dressed, he would call in person with the wife of the proprietor of the hotel. For one moment I could not imagine what he meant, but, dressing myself as speedily as I possibly could, I sent for them. They came: Captain Hatch held in his hands a newspaper. He approached me, saying,

"Miss Belle, you are aware that you left your father ill?"

In one moment I comprehended every thing, and exclaiming "My God! is he dead?" I sank fainting to the floor.

This swoon was succeeded by a severe illness; and I felt all the loneliness of my position. An exile (for the Yankees held possession of Martinsburg) and an orphan—these words described me; and, ah! how hard they seemed!

One of those strange warnings that are sometimes given to mortals, or that are, some would say, the imaginings of an excited brain shaken by sickness, ought to have prepared me for my sad bereavement.

> "Some say that gleams of a remoter world
> Visit the soul in sleep."

The night upon which my father died I had retired to rest somewhat earlier than usual. How long I slept I do not know, but I suddenly awoke, or seemed to awaken, from my sleep, although I had neither the power nor the wish to move. In the centre of the room I saw General Jackson, whose eyes rested sorrowfully upon me. Beside him stood my father, gazing at me, but saying nothing. I was dumb, or I should have spoken, for I did not feel alarmed. As I looked upon those two standing together, General Jackson turned and spoke to my father. I remember the words distinctly.

"It is time for us to go," he said; and, taking my father's hand, he led him away, adding as he did so, "Poor child!"

I afterwards learnt by a letter from my mother (the first and only communication received from her until my arrival in this country) that my beloved father, at the news of my being sent South, where I should have to battle alone with the world, had grown rapidly worse, and had expired the very next day after my arrival in Richmond. My mother and the children had been sent for, and reached my father just before he died. Although he retained his senses up to the last, he frequently spoke of me, declared that I was hovering around his couch, and would become quite restless if people in the room went to a certain spot near the bed, exclaiming that "I was being torn from him!"

Several of our senators and exchange officers, with many other influential persons, wrote to the Federal Government to try and obtain permission for me to return to my sorrowing mother. I myself wrote to the Northern President and Secretary Stanton, at the suggestion of my friends, and appealed to them as a Mason's daughter. But no, every appeal was refused.

My letters to and from my mother in Martinsburg were intercepted; and from December, the 16th, until I arrived in London, and then not until the following October, did I receive one line from her, though she had written repeatedly.

My health was very bad and my constitution greatly undermined; so in February I went from Richmond farther south, visiting Mobile, Atlanta, Augusta, and other cities, whose names have since become historical.

I cannot express one-half the gratitude that I feel to the many kind hosts whom I met in my journey through the South. During my illness in Richmond I was well cared for; and amongst the warmest of my friends must be ranked the wife of the world-renowned Captain Semmes, afterwards Admiral Semmes, of the ill-fated *Alabama*.

Mrs. Semmes treated me with as much attention as though I had been her own daughter, and invited me to visit them at their home in Mobile. I had always been termed "the child of the Confederacy," or "the child of the army;" and, no matter where I went, I was welcomed both by the gentry and the people.

In March I returned to Richmond, when, although somewhat recovered, my health still required care. I could not return home, and I felt, moreover, restless and unhappy at the death of my father. I determined, therefore, to visit Europe, so soon as I could arrange my affairs. When I made known this resolution to President Davis, he approved of the plan, considering me to need quiet and rest in some place remote from the dangers of our sorely-pressed country.

Orders were given to the Confederate Secretary of State to make me the bearer of dispatches. I commenced preparations for departure as speedily as possible.

The dispatches were ready for me on March 25th, but a brief return of illness hindered me from starting, and as these papers, being very important, could not be delayed, they were forwarded by some other hand.

At last, on March 29th, I was able to leave Richmond, having recovered sufficiently for travelling. Other dispatches were now ready, and of them I was made the bearer.

Owing to an accident on the railway, we did not arrive in Wilmington until several hours after the departure of the blockade-runner in which I was to have sailed.

This steamer would not be followed by another for at least a fortnight, because they did not run out during the brilliant nights of the full moon, lest they should fall an easy prey to Yankee blockaders. I was therefore obliged to await the arrival and departure of the next regular steamer, as, even putting aside all consideration of difficulties increased by moonlight, there was not a suitable craft in port.

One of the first vessels that arrived was the *Greyhound*, commanded by Captain Henry, formerly, it is said, an officer in the United States navy, and who had, at the commencement of the war, with many of his comrades, sent in his resignation to the United States Navy Department, and entered the Confederate service. Captain "Henry" had formerly been on "Stonewall" Jackson's staff; and, as I was acquainted with his family, I gladly accepted his kind invitation, and took passage on board the *Greyhound*, feeling doubly secure under such a skilful commander.

CHAPTER XVI.

I leave Wilmington for Europe — Running the Blockade —
— Safe Outside — *Mal de Mer* —The Federal Cruiser —
The Chase — The Yankee proves too fast — The first Shell
—The Fire grows hot — Forced to surrender — The Eng-
lish Sailor and his Flag.

On the 8th of May I bade farewell to many
friends in Wilmington, and stepped on board
the *Greyhound*. It was, as may well be imagined, an anxious moment. I knew that the venture was a desperate one; but I felt sustained
by the greatness of my cause; for I had borne
a part, however insignificant, in one of the
greatest dramas ever yet enacted upon the
stage of the world; moreover, I relied upon
my own resources, and I looked to Fortune,
who is so often the handmaid of a daring enterprise.

At the mouth of the river we dropped

anchor, and decided to wait until the already waning moon should entirely disappear.

Outside the bar, and at the distance of about six miles, lay the Federal fleet, most of them at anchor; but some of their light vessels were cruising quietly in different directions. Not one, however, showed any disposition to tempt the guns of the fort over which the Confederate flag was flying.

There were on board the *Greyhound* two passengers, or rather adventurers, besides myself—Mr. Newell and Mr. Pollard, the latter the editor of the *Richmond Examiner*. We laughed and joked, as people will laugh and joke in the face of imminent danger, and even in the jaws of death.

Gentle reader, before you accuse us of levity, or of a reckless spirit of fatalism, reflect how, in the prison of La Force, when the reign of terror was at its height, the doomed victims of the guillotine acted charades, played games of forfeits, and circulated their *bon-mots* and *jeux d'esprit* within a few hours of a violent death. Remember also that the lovely Queen of Scots and the unfortunate Anna Boleyn met their fate with a smile, and greeted the scaffold with a jest.

About ten o'clock orders were given to get under way. The next minute every light was extinguished, the anchor was weighed, steam was got up rapidly and silently, and we glided off just as " the trailing garments of the night" spread their last folds over the ocean.

The decks were piled with bales of cotton, upon which our look-out men were stationed, straining their eyes to pierce the darkness and give timely notice of the approach of an enemy.

I freely confess that our jocose temperament had now yielded to a far more serious state of feeling. No more pleasantries were exchanged, but many earnest prayers were breathed. No one thought of sleep. Few words were spoken. It was a night never to be forgotten—a night of silent, almost breathless anxiety. It seemed to us as if day would never break; but it came at last, and, to our unspeakable joy, not a sail was in sight. We were moving unmolested and alone upon a tranquil sea, and we indulged in the fond hope that we had eluded our eager foes.

Steaming on, we ran close by the wreck of the Confederate iron-clad *Raleigh*, which had so lately driven the Federal blockading squadron out to sea, but which now lay on a shoal, an utter wreck, parted amidships, destroyed, not by the Federals, but by a visitation of Providence.

At this point we three passengers began to experience those sensations which, although invariably an object of derision to persons who are exempt from them, are, for the time being, as grievous to the sufferer as any in the whole catalogue of pains and aches to which flesh is heir. Reader, may it never be your lot, as it then was mine, to find sea-sickness overcome by the stronger emotion inspired by the sight of a hostile vessel bearing rapidly down with the purpose of depriving you of your freedom.

It was just noon, when a thick haze which had lain upon the water lifted, and at that moment we heard a startled cry of "Sail ho!" from the look-out man at the mast-head. These ominous words were the signal for a general rush aft. Extra steam was got up in an incredibly short space of time, and sail was set with the view both of increasing our speed and of steadying our vessel as she dashed through the water.

Alas! it was soon evident that our exertions were useless, for every minute visibly lessened the distance between us and our pursuer; her masts rose higher and higher, her hull loomed larger and larger, and I was told plainly that, unless some unforeseen accident should favor us, such as a temporary derangement of the Federal steamer's steering apparatus, or a breaking of some important portion of her machinery, we might look to New York instead of Bermuda as our destination.

My feelings at this intelligence must be imagined: I can describe them but inadequately. "Unless," I thought, "Providence interposes directly in our behalf, we shall be overhauled and captured; and then what follows? I shall suffer a third rigorous imprisonment." Moreover, I was the bearer of dispatches from my Government to authorities in Europe; and I knew that this service, honorable and necessary as it was, the Federals regarded in the light of a heinous crime, and that, in all prob ability, I should be subjected to every kind of indignity.

The chase continued, and the cruiser still gained upon us. For minutes, which to me seemed hours, did I strain my eyes towards our pursuer and watch anxiously for the flash of the gun that would soon send a shot or shell after us, or, for all I could tell, into us. How long I remained watching I know not, but the iron messenger of death came at last. A thin, white curl of smoke rose high in the air as the enemy luffed up and presented her formidable broadside. Almost simultaneously with the hissing sound of the shell, as it buried itself in the sea within a few yards of us, came the smothered report of its explosion under water.

The enemy's shots now followed each other in rapid succession: some fell very close, while others, less skilfully aimed, were wide of the mark, and burst high in the air over our heads.

During this time bale after bale of cotton had been rolled overboard by our crew, the epitaph of each, as it disappeared beneath the waves, being, "By —— ! there's another they shall not get."

Our captain paced nervously to and fro, now watching the compass, now gazing fixedly at the approaching enemy, now shouting, "More steam! more steam! give her more steam!" At last he turned suddenly round to me, and exclaimed in passionate accents—

"Miss Belle, I declare to you that, but for your presence on board, I would burn her to the water's edge rather than those infernal scoundrels should reap the benefit of a single bale of our cargo."

To this I replied, "Captain H., act without reference to me—do what you think your duty. For my part, sir, I concur with you: burn her by all means—I am not afraid. I have made up my mind, and am indifferent to my fate, if only the Federals do not get the vessel."

To this Captain H. made no reply, but

turned abruptly away and walked aft, where his officers were standing in a group. With them he held a hurried consultation, and then, coming to where I was seated, exclaimed—

"It is too late to burn her now. The Yankee is almost on board of us. We must surrender!"

During all this time the enemy's fire never ceased. Round shot and shell were ploughing up the water about us. They flew before, behind, and above—everywhere but into us; and, although I knew that the first of those heavy missiles which should strike must be fatal to many, perhaps to all, yet so angry did I feel that I could have forfeited my own life if, by so doing, I could have balked the Federals of their prey.

At this moment we were not more than half a mile from our tormentor; for we had luffed up in the wind, and stopped our engine. Suddenly, with a deep humming sound, came a hundred-pound bolt. This shot was fired from their long gun amidships, and passed just over my head, between myself and the captain, who was standing on the bridge a little above me.

"By Jove! don't they intend to give us quarter, or show us some mercy at any rate?" cried Captain H. "I have surrendered."

And now from the Yankee came a stentorian hail: "Steamer ahoy! haul down that flag, or we will pour a broadside into you!"

Captain H. then ordered the man at the wheel to lower the colors; but he replied, with true British pluck, that "he had sailed many times under that flag, but had never yet seen it hauled down; and," added he, "I cannot do it now." We were sailing under British colors, and the man at the helm was an Englishman.

All this time repeated hails of "Haul down that flag, or we will sink you!" greeted us, until, at last, some one, I know not who, seeing how hopeless it must be to brave them longer, took it upon himself to execute Captain H.'s order, and lowered the English ensign.

CHAPTER XVII.

We are boarded by an Officer from the Yankee—The U. S.
Steamer *Connecticut*—An Officer, but no Gentleman—
Strange State of Yankee Discipline—Scenes on board of
the *Greyhound* after her Capture—"Ain't ye skeared?"—
A proud Boast.

BEFORE the acknowledgment of our surrender had been made, a keg containing some
twenty or thirty thousand dollars, equivalent
in value to about six thousand pounds sterling,
had been brought up on deck and consigned
to the deep; whilst all my dispatches and
letters of introduction, of which latter I had
many, were consumed in the furnaces very
shortly afterwards.

We were boarded by a boat's crew from
our captor, under the command of the execu
tive officer, Mr. Kempf. Mounting the side,
he walked up to Captain H. and said—

" Good day to you, Captain ; I am glad to
see you.   This is a very fine vessel, and a
valuable one.   Will you be good enough to
let me see your papers ?"

To this Captain H. replied, " Good day to
yourself, sir ; but as to my being happy to see
you, I cannot really say that I am.   I have no
papers."

The Federal lieutenant then said, " Well,
Captain, your presence is required on board
the United States steamer *Connecticut*, Captain
Almy commanding ; and, if you can prove
yourself all right, you will, no doubt, be permitted to go."

To this Captain H. made no response, but,
stepping into the cabin, donned his coat, and,
returning on deck, said, " Now, sir, I am ready ;
shall we go ?"   Without further parley the two
stepped together into the boat which was
lying alongside, and immediately pulled for
the *Connecticut*.

One Mr. Swasey was left in charge of our
luckless *Greyhound*—an officer as unfit for
authority as any who has ever trodden the

deck of a man-of-war. His subordinates were, I imagine, well acquainted with his character and abilities; at all events, they treated his orders not with respect, but ridicule.

"Now, sergeant," said he, addressing the sergeant of marines, "look out for your men, and I will look out for mine. By-the-way, though, station one man here to guard the spirit-room, and don't let any one go below; the first man I catch doing so I will blow his brains out, I will; I would not let my own father have a drink."

He might possibly have resisted the solicitations of a thirsty parent, but he proved quite unable to withstand those of the men. He had hardly finished speaking, when a seaman, whom, by his *illigant* brogue, I recognized at once for a true son of Erin, approached and addressed Mr. Swasey with all the native eloquence and pathos of his country—

"Ah, Mr. Swasey, will yees be afther lettin' me have a small bottle of whiskey to kape out the could?"

The colloquy that ensued was ludicrous in the extreme, terminating in a victory of the Irish sailor over the Federal officer. This example of successful insubordination once set, was soon followed; and in every instance Mr. Swasey yielded to the remonstrances, or rather to the mutinous appeals, of his men.

"Here," suddenly exclaimed he, catching a glimpse of myself, "sergeant of the guard! sergeant of the guard! put a man in front of this door, and give him orders to stab this woman if she dares to attempt to come out."

This order, so highly becoming an officer and a gentleman, so courteous in its language, and withal so necessary to the safety and preservation of the prize, was given in a menacing voice and in the very words I have used. I record them for the purpose of showing how admirably the Federal Government has selected its naval officers, and how punctually and gallantly they fulfilled the instructions of their superiors. *Parcere subjectis* must have been blotted out from the edition of the ancient

13

poet read in those schools which had the honor of educating them.

Mr. Swasey then came to the cabin-door and introduced himself in these brief but delicate words—" Now, ain't ye skeared ?"

My blood was roused, and I replied, " No, I am not; I was never frightened at a Yankee in my life !"

This retort of mine seemed to surprise him, as he walked away without another word. The effects of his displeasure, however, soon made themselves felt. To my ineffable disgust, the officers, and even the men, were permitted to walk at pleasure into my cabin, which I had hoped would have been respected as the sanctuary of a modest girl. In this hope, as in so many others, I calculated far too much upon the forbearance and humanity of Yankees ; and these qualities were seldom exhibited when their enemies were defenceless, and, consequently, at their mercy. .

Officers and men now proceeded to help themselves to the private wines of the captain, in spite of the protest of the sentry who had been placed in front of my door, and of whom it is but just to say that nature had qualified him to command when his superiors would have done well to obey.

While these scenes were being enacted, my maid, and a colored woman whom Captain H. was conveying to a lady in Bermuda, were subjected to the rude familiarities of the prize crew.

At this moment one of the *Connecticut's* officers, a Mr. Reveille, walked up to me and said, "Do you know that it was I who fired the shot that passed close over your head?"

"Was it?" replied I. "Should you like to know what I said of the gunner?"

"I should like to know."

"That man, whoever he may be, is an arrant coward to fire on a defenceless ship after her surrender."

To this rejoinder of mine, more sincere, perhaps, than prudent, he made no reply, but left the cabin with an embarrassed laugh.

CHAPTER XVIII.

An eventful Meeting.—A Gentleman at last.—A Wife's Apology.—Mr. Hardinge.—I am disappointed.—A pleasant
Exchange.—Farewell to Mr. Swasey.—A ludicrous Incident.—Captain Henry's best Boots.—I am discovered
through Treachery.

SCARCELY had the discomfited Yankee
betaken himself, to my intense satisfaction,
to the deck, when I noticed a young officer
who had just come over the side.

He crossed the deck by the wheel, and
approached the cabin. I saw at a glance he
was made of other stuff than his comrades who
preceded him; and I confess my attention was
riveted by the presence of a gentleman—the
first, I think my readers will allow, whom I
had met in the hour of my distress.

A woman and a wife may, perhaps, be
forgiven if, in a work which treats of more

serious adventures than those of love, she in-
dulges in a very brief reminiscence of the
impression produced upon her by her future
husband. Critics may smile; but I flatter
myself that Englishwomen, so widely and so
justly famed for conjugal devotion, will forgive
me.

His dark-brown hair hung down on his
shoulders; his eyes were large and bright.
Those who judge of beauty by regularity of
feature only, could not have pronounced him
strictly handsome. Neither Phidias nor Prax-
iteles would have chosen the subject for a
model of Grecian grace; but the fascination
of his manner was such, his every movement
was so much that of a refined gentleman, that
my "Southern proclivities," strong as they
were, yielded for a moment to the impulses of
my heart, and I said to myself, "Oh, what a
good fellow that must be!"

To my secret disappointment, he passed
by the cabin, without entering or making any
inquiries about me. I asked one of the *Connecticut's* officers, who was close to me, the

name of the new arrival in this party of pleasure. "Lieutenant Hardinge," was his reply.

Soon afterwards I heard the following conversation, which I perfectly well remember, and which I transcribe *verbatim*, between Mr. Swasey and Mr. Hardinge:—

Mr. Swasey.—" Hallo, Hardinge, any thing up? What is it?"

Mr. Hardinge.—" Yes, sir; by order of Captain Almy, I have come to relieve you of the command of this vessel. It is his order that you proceed forthwith on board the *Connecticut:* you will be pleased to hand over to me the papers you have in relation to this vessel."

Mr. Swasey.—"It is a lie! it is a lie! it ain't no such thing! I won't believe it. You have been lately juggling with the captain. Confound it! that is the way you always do!"

Mr. Hardinge.—" Mr. Swasey, I am but obeying my orders; you must not insult me. If you continue to do so, I shall report you."

Mr. Swasey cooled at once, I suppose, as I heard nothing further on his side. He promptly handed over his orders, as desired by Mr. Hardinge, jumped into the boat alongside, and I caught the last sound of his charming voice as he uttered the word of command, "Give way there!" to the boat's crew.

He returned to the *Connecticut*, and so passes out of this story. If its pages ever meet his eye, perhaps they may make him reflect that courtesy to a lady is compatible with the sternest duties of an officer, and that forbearance to the vanquished has always been the attribute of a truly brave man.

Within a few minutes of the departure of our sometime prize-master, Mr. Hardinge, now in command, issued his orders to the sergeant of marines as to how the men were to be posted; and I overheard, not without an emotion of pleasure, the sergeant telling one of our officers that, although Mr. Hardinge might be a strict disciplinarian on duty, there

was not a finer young fellow in the navy, and
that his men would follow him anywhere.

Before long, Mr. Hardinge came aft, and
bowing to me, asked permission to enter my
cabin for a moment.

"Certainly," I replied; "I know that I am
a prisoner."

"I am now in command of this vessel," said
he; "and I beg you will consider yourself a
passenger, not a prisoner."

With the commencement of Mr. Hardinge's
command—I may safely say, from the very
moment he came on board—the conduct of the
prize crew underwent a complete change; and
one of the Yankee officers remarked, in my
hearing, that, although Hardinge was young,
he knew how to command other men, and had
learned, early in life, the secret and the value of
discipline.

Half an hour, or thereabouts, elapsed, and
I was reconciling myself to my captivity, when
the return on board of Captain "Henry" was
the occasion of a ludicrous incident which
amused me more than perhaps my readers will

suppose. I despair of describing it as it appeared to me; perhaps the reaction of my own feel-
'ings (such as we experience after passing safely
through sudden and serious danger) gave it a
zest beyond its real flavor.

It was on this wise. Captain "Henry,"
coming on board, caught sight of a Federal sail-
or strutting about on the cotton-bales in a
pair of his (Captain H.'s) very best boots—
boots which the captain most particularly cherished.

"Here, you fellow, what are you doing with
my boots? Take them off at once, or I shall
report you to the officer in command for steal-
ing."

"But, sir," said the sailor, loth to part with
his contraband goods, "I bought them from a
messmate of mine, and chucked my own into
the sea."

This subterfuge, however, did not impose
upon Mr. Hardinge's sense of honor and discipline. The ancient mariner had to remove
the stolen boots, and return barefooted to his
ship.

The officers and crew of the *Greyhound*, together with my fellow-passengers, Mr. Pollard and Mr. Newell, were taken on board the *Connecticut*. The captain, steward, cook, and cabin-boy, myself and my maid, remained prisoners on board the prize.

Before we were taken—indeed, when we sailed from Wilmington—it had been agreed that "Belle Boyd" should be for the time ignored, and that "Mrs. Lewis" should take her place. It was obvious that, in the event of capture, I should run less risk, suffer fewer privations, and be exposed to less indignity, under an assumed name. Conceive, then, my surprise and indignation when I found that my secret had been revealed through the treachery of an unworthy countryman!

Captain H. told me that the *Minnie*, a blockade-runner like the *Greyhound*, which had been captured the day before by the *Connecticut*, had been the means of our own mishap. There can be no doubt that one of her officers was a traitor to the cause of his country, and had, through fear, or actuated by some other unworthy motive, sacrificed those he should have defended with his life.

It is with reluctance that I record this instance of dishonor on the part of a Southerner; but I am resolved to be an impartial historian, and although often severe to the Yankees, by dint of telling plainly their short-comings, I will not shrink from the truth when it is unfavorable to my countrymen.

CHAPTER XIX.

Bound North—We are taken in tow—Our first Evening at
Sea—We arrive at Fortress Monroe—Commodore Guerte
Gansevoorte comes on board in James River—We are
paroled by him—His Indignation against Mr. Hardinge
for flying the English Ensign—The Commodore's Conduct whilst on board—Arrival at New York—We go on
Shore—I visit Niblo's Theatre—Return aboard and departure for Boston—Love triumphant!

BOATS were continually passing to and fro
between the "Prize," as she was designated,
and the *Connecticut*, with orders and counter-
orders, until the proximity of the vessels grew
wearisome. I was relieved to hear that we
were about to start, and my pleasure did not
diminish when, at eight P. M., the command was
given to get under steam and proceed northward, keeping just astern of the *Connecticut*,
which would accompany us. Heart-sick at the

turn that the tide of fortune had taken, I retired to my couch and endeavored to sleep. But prison walls could not be banished from my imagination, and the attempt was vain.

The next morning, at daylight, I was aroused by loud hailing from the Yankee cruiser as she passed close to us, ordering that we should "heave-to" whilst she sent a boat on board. We presently learned that our destination was to be Fortress Monroe, and that we were to be towed thither behind the *Connecticut*. Hawsers were passed to us by means of boats, and, when these tow-lines had been well secured, both vessels steamed ahead.

It was the second evening after our surrender that Captain H., Mr. Hardinge, and myself, were seated together close by the wheel. The moon shone beautifully clear, lighting up every thing with a brightness truly magnificent; the ocean, just agitated by a slight breeze that swept over its surface, looked like one vast bed of sparkling diamonds, and the rippling of the little waves, as they struck the vessel's side, seemed but a soft accompaniment

to the vocal music with which Captain H. had
been regaling us.

> "Here will we sit, and let the sounds of music
> Creep in our ears; soft stillness, and the night,
> Become the touches of sweet harmony."

Presently Captain H. went forward on the
bridge and conversed with Mr. Hall, the officer
on watch.   We two were left to ourselves; and
Mr. Hardinge quoted some beautiful passages
from Byron and Shakespeare.   Then, in a decidedly Claude Melnotte style, he endeavored to
paint the "home to which, if love could but fulfil its prayers, this heart would lead thee!"
And from poetry he passed on to plead an oft-
told tale. . . . .

Situated as I was, and having known him
for so short a time, a very practical thought
flitted through my brain.   If he felt all that
he professed to feel for me, he might in future
be useful to us; so, when he asked me "to be
his wife," I told him that "his question involved serious consequences," and that "he

must not expect an answer until I should arrive at Boston."

During our voyage, Mr. Hardinge was so kind and courteous that Captain H. took a great fancy to him, and swore eternal friendship to one of whom he afterwards spoke as "the most thorough gentleman from Yankeeland that he had ever met with."

The morning which succeeded the romantic episode slightly sketched above beheld the *Connecticut* and *Greyhound* lying-to off the Capes. A fog detained us in uncertainty as to our whereabouts for some time; and, when it lifted, we steamed up Hampton Roads.

I sat on the little deck aft, watching with interest all that I saw, and listening alternately to the captain and Mr. Hardinge as they conversed on various topics. From the latter I ascertained that General Butler was in command at Fortress Monroe, and from him I could expect but little courtesy.

As we neared our anchorage, I made out distinctly the grim outline of the fortress, rising in its majesty and strength. I compared myself to the fly nearing the cunning old spider, who was eagerly watching for the moment when it should become entangled in his intricate web.

My capture had been telegraphed to those in authority. The *Connecticut* had cast off from us about half way up the river, and had gone onward to the mouth of the James, where Admiral Lee then was; but the *Greyhound*, when opposite the pier of the Baltimore steamers, came to an anchor. Mr. Hardinge went on board the flag-ship *Minnesota* to report. He was absent about two hours, and when he returned we got under way, proceeding up-stream to join the *Connecticut*. Mr. Hardinge could tell me nothing of my probable destination, and I suspected that I was to be incarcerated in Fortress Monroe—there to remain I knew not how long—perhaps forever!

After about three-quarters of an hour we again anchored, this time close by the iron-clad *Roanoke*, Commodore Guerte Gansevoorte, who was acting in the place of Admiral Lee.

The Admiral was then up the James River, ostensibly for the purpose of fighting the "rebels." But, much to the disgust of his officers and of the Federal naval department (if we may believe the journals of the day), he merely re-enacted the farce of sinking vessels and driving in spikes across the river from bank to bank, to prevent the "cowardly rebels" from doing what he dared not—giving battle.

Just after we brought up, it blew a perfect hurricane, followed by a drenching rain, which lasted for some time. Such weather was, in itself, sufficiently dreary and discouraging; nor did the sensation that we were dragging towards a lee-shore of uninviting appearance greatly comfort me. I felt, indeed, some pleasure when I thought that the Federals would, perhaps, lose their prize—a feeling which Captain H. fully shared. In this cheerful desire we were disappointed; for, as the captain afterwards remarked, "the vessel was admirably handled by Mr. Hardinge."

Amid whistling wind and pouring rain an English ensign had been flying from the stern, and the Federal flag, which had been hoisted when coming up the bay, was conspicuous at the fore. This seems to have excited the ire of the Commodore, who, when the storm had passed, boarded us, with solemn displeasure written upon his face.

I am positive that I should have had a better opinion of the man had he remained in his own vessel; for I now saw him far from sober. One of the officers remarked that "it was after four o'clock," by way of an apology to the "youngling," as he was pleased to term Mr. Hardinge.

Commodore Guerte Gansevoorte was not over-polite, and, upon reaching the deck, swore soundly and lustily, d——ing right and left, and was evidently

> " As *wild* a mannered man
> As ever scuttled ship or cut a throat."

But then, as it was a wet day, he had evidently been taking something hot within to guard him from the cold.

When the Commodore approached my cabin-door, I heard Mr. Hardinge say, " Sir, a lady is dressing there. Will you be kind enough to wait ? She is my passenger, and I am responsible for her." I had finished, however; and the colored servant, opening the door, said to Mr. Hardinge, " De lady am ready, massa." On this the Commodore remarked, " Ugh! got to that, has it ?"

His *entrée* into the cabin was truly imposing; for, stumbling over piled-up cotton, he staggered, then slipped, and made his descent and bow at the same moment. His aide, Mr. —— (executive officer, I believe) looked mortified, and seemed somewhat ashamed whilst following in the great man's rear, with less of the former's peculiar dignity.

" So," said the Commodore, " this is Miss Belle Boyd, is it ?" Just then Captain H. came in, and, turning round, he then exclaimed, " What! by ——! George, old fel——;" then, remembering his official position, stopped suddenly in the midst of the exclamation. I do not remember much of the conversation which ensued, but noticed that the executive officer was sober, and apparently disgusted with the conduct of his superior.

The Commodore at first would not be seated, but did so after a few moments' further conversation. Champagne and glasses were brought in; and he soon became exceedingly communicative, and, with an oath, swore that Captain H. should have a parole extending as far as Boston. Asking for pen, ink, and paper, which I immediately procured, he bade the executive officer write the required parole, and signed it with his own hand. Mr. Hardinge asked for the document, or, at least, a copy of the same; but he would not comply, declaring that "his orders were sufficient."

As he rose to depart, he turned to me and said, in answer to a request of mine, "You, Miss, when you arrive at New York, can go on shore, provided Mr. Hardinge accompanies you. And," he added, attempting some compliments, "I will not enforce a written parole

with you, but will take a verbal promise.
Don't be at all alarmed—you shan't go to
prison." The Commodore then left us. His
descent into the boat was executed in the
same dignified and gentlemanly manner as had
been his *entrée* into my presence; and I felt
very thankful when Mr. Hall informed me
that the great man had gone.

Half an hour may have passed, when a
boat came from the *Roanoke* to inform Mr.
Hardinge that the Commodore had ordered
that the *Greyhound* should be brought under
the lee of the iron-clad. My heart sank, for it
seemed that, after all, he had been playing
with us; still more so when, as we rounded-to
under the *Roanoke's* stern, I heard the Commodore threatening through his trumpet to blow
us out of the water. In his condition he might
have done any thing; so our anxiety may well
be imagined.

Reverting for a moment to the English
ensign before mentioned as flying aboard the
Greyhound, I may describe how the Commodore, when he saw it, shouted furiously, "Haul

down that —— rag !"   Mr. Hardinge ventured
to suggest that this was a violation of the law
regarding neutral vessels captured in time of
war.   To which the Commodore made answer
by saying, " I don't want any sea-lawyer's arguments !" and he afterwards sent a written
order to Mr. Hardinge, forbidding him to fly
the English flag.

As we lay beside the *Roanoke,* vague threats
were made, and contradictory orders given.
Now we were told to be " off at once," then
" not to think of moving at present;" until Mr.
Hardinge grew restless at such constant supervision, and, taking advantage of a command to
quit the station, steamed away, without waiting for any thing more.   Right glad were we
when the shades of night hid from our view
the monster iron-clad, and yet, thankful to
Captain Almy, of the *Connecticut,* who, *not*
being drunk, stopped us somewhat farther
down, delaying our departure for the very
sensible reason that a gale of wind was
blowing.

Early the next day a steam-tug from the

fortress went alongside of the *Connecticut*, and the officers, passengers, and men of the *Minnie* and *Greyhound* were transferred to her, with the exception of Mr. Pollard, who was sent aboard of us to proceed to Boston. When the tug steamed by, handkerchiefs and caps were waved; and I was afterwards informed that they would have cheered me had they been permitted to do so. Fresh meat, vegetables, and ice (the latter of which we esteemed a luxury, as the weather was very warm) had been procured on shore for our consumption.

At length we proceeded to sea, bound for Boston, Massachusetts, *via* New York, where it was intended that we should touch for coal. I will pass over this portion of the voyage, merely remarking that it was as pleasant as could be expected under the circumstances, and that the officers did all in their power to make things comfortable for us.

As we neared New York, thick fog completely enshrouded the coast, but our speed was not slackened. We pressed forward, often passing vessels so near as hardly to give them

breathing room. Part of one night we lay off
Barnegat; for the fog had become so thick
that the pilot did not judge it safe for us to
proceed. But when morning broke, a brisk
wind sprang up, enabling us to see the outline
of Sandy Hook. As we passed on up the
harbor the motion became less disagreeable
to me, and, a comfortable seat having been
placed on the deck-house, I enjoyed a panora-
ma of sea and shore scarce equalled in beauty
by the approach to any other city in the world.

Off Quarantine we were boarded by the
health-officer, who, after asking several questions, permitted us to go on our way; and we
came to an anchor off the Navy Yard. Mr.
Hardinge went on shore to report his arrival,
while Mr. Hall proceeded to bring the vessel
alongside the coal-hulk. When Mr. Hardinge
returned in the afternoon, the dock was filled
with gazers, who, excited by that morbid curiosity exhibited by the world in general, had come
to witness, as they supposed, my debarkation.
In this they were somewhat disappointed, for
every thing had been arranged so nicely that

not one of the many there assembled knew
when I went on shore. A Navy Yard tug
dropped alongside the *Greyhound*, and, with
the assistance of Captain H., I was soon snugly
settled in the tug's wheel-house.

Captain H. and Mr. Hardinge accompanied
me. We crossed to the New York side of the
river, and landed at the foot of Canal Street.
Procuring a carriage, we drove to a friend's
house, where I took from off my person the
money which I had concealed about me, and
the weight of which at times had almost made
me faint. This money belonged to myself and
Captain H., and was not, as Yankee papers
averred, part of the ship's money we had
thrown overboard previous to our capture.
Captain H. placed our money in the bank,
where it was safe from further molestation.

We visited Niblo's Theatre, to witness the
performance of "Bel Demonio." What a contrast did the gay, wealthy city of New York
afford at this period to my own sorrow-stricken
land! Here there was no sign of want or poverty. No woe-begone faces could I see in
14

that assemblage: all was life and animation.
Though war raged within a short distance, its
horrors had little influence on the butterflies
of the Empire City; whilst, in my own dear
native country, all was sad and heart-rending.
We were sacrificing lives upon the altar of
Liberty; while the North sacrificed hers upon
the altar of Mammon.

Next morning Mr. Hardinge called for me,
and, after having finished my shopping, we returned to the *Greyhound*, which now lay in
mid-stream. Captain H. had gone on board
before us, as also had Mr. Pollard. I forgot to
mention that this gentleman had been paroled
by Mr. Hardinge for the night.

For the rest of the time, above four hours
that we remained at New York we were besieged by visitors—old acquaintances, who
were allowed to see me. Amongst them were
several naval and military officers. About four
P. M. the pilot came on board, and, bidding
adieu to the capital of "Shoddy," away we
steamed for Boston.

The weather was lovely, the water smooth

as glass, and the sky cloudless as that of Italy.
On each side of us, along the shores of the
Sound, were beautiful residences, whose owners, as they strolled over their lawns, or sat
smoking on terrace or balcony, appeared to
think little, and care less, about the war. We
glided past many craft, which lay with white
sails that flapped against their masts. I was
melancholy; I hardly knew why. The face of
Nature wore its very sweetest smile; every
thing was propitious; yet I was not pleased,
and sought the cabin.

Mr. Hardinge, in a few moments, followed
me, and then he repeated a declaration on
which I need not expatiate, as it concerned
ourselves more than any one else. So generous
and noble was he in every thing, that I could
not but acknowledge that my heart was his.
I firmly believe that God intended us to meet
and love; and, to make the story short, I told
him that "I would be his wife." Although
our politics differed, "Women," thought I, "can
sometimes work wonders; and may not he,

who is of Northern birth, come by degrees to love, for my sake, the ill-used South?"

Then Captain "Henry" came into the cabin; and, when we told him all, he joined our hands together, saying—

"Hardinge, you are a good fellow, and I love you, boy! Miss Belle deserves a good husband; and I know no one more worthy of her than yourself. May you both be happy!"

CHAPTER XX.

Arrival in Boston—Our Plan for recapturing the *Greyhound* frustrated—Captain H——'s Escape—How it was managed—Marshal Keyes comes on Board—The Search for the Captain—A false Report of his Arrest—I communicate with him—He leaves for New York—I bid adieu to the *Greyhound*—My Quarters on Shore—I am paroled for the City—Newspaper Rumors—Mr. Hardinge proceeds to Washington in my behalf—My Mother telegraphs to the Marshal—She is not permitted to see me—Politeness of the British Consul—I write a Letter to the Secretary of the Navy—Am pronounced Insane—I am liberated—Mr. Hardinge and his Officers are placed under Arrest—Mr. Pollard is sent to Fort Warren—I leave for Canada.

WHEN we neared Boston, I saw the grim walls of Fort Warren; and a shudder passed over me as I inwardly wondered if that would be my home. All my bright dreams of "merrie England," of "bonnie Scotland," and of a tour on the Continent, were, for the time, banished. The future lowered dark and uncertain. Had

not some good spirit whispered hope, I should
scarcely have borne up against these gloomy
impressions.   But I was still "Mrs. Lewis,"
and might yet escape.

> "For, lo! the heavier Grief weighed down,
>   The higher Hope was raised."

When we were first captured, it had been
agreed that, on our voyage North, an attempt
should be made to retake the *Greyhound.*

The project, however, had been abandoned,
not from any lack of zeal, but from force of
circumstances; for Captain Almy had refused
to put on board of us our chief engineer and
first officer, whithout whom the attempt could
not possibly succeed.

Another plan, quietly prepared by us previously, and which had reference to the escape
of Captain "Henry," had better luck. Whilst
we were coming to an anchor off the Boston
Navy Yard, and Mr. Hardinge was forward,
giving orders to the men, Captain "Henry,"
Mr. Pollard, and myself were aft, seated in the
cabin.   I asked the two Yankee pilots if they

would join us and partake of a glass of wine.
To this they of course assented, and drank
freely; for doubtless such wine but seldom
passed their lips. I then nodded to Captain
"Henry," who, carelessly putting on his hat,
and taking his umbrella in his hand, walked
up on deck and went aft, where he stood for
some moments. Every thing seemed to favor
us, for Mr. Hardinge had called a harbor-boat
alongside, that he might go ashore to report
his arrival.

Before starting, Mr. Hardinge came to me
and asked "where his papers were;" when I
replied that I thought they must be "in the
lower cabin, where he had been dressing himself." He immediately went down to fetch
them; and this was the golden opportunity
for which we had waited. In less time than
it takes me to write it, Captain "Henry"
stepped into the boat, which dropped slowly
astern with the tide; and when Mr. Hardinge
reappeared, the Captain was safe on land.

The whole scene was amusing in the extreme to those who understood it, so well had

it been managed. When Mr. Hardinge found
his boat gone, he came to the conclusion that
the waterman had grown tired of waiting and
had pulled off; so, calling another, he stepped
into it and proceeded to report his prize.

In about three hours he returned, bringing
with him the United States Marshal, Keyes,
and several other gentlemen of position and influence in Boston, whom he introduced to me.

The Marshal then asked for Captain
"Henry."

"I think he is on deck," I replied.

Mr. Hardinge went to find him, leaving
the other gentlemen to converse with Mr. Pollard and myself. From me, however, they did
not learn much, for I sustained the suppositi-
tious character of "Mrs. Lewis" with becoming
gravity; and it was not until several days
after that they became quite sure that I was
none other than the celebrated "Belle Boyd."

In a few moments Marshal Keyes, followed by Mr. Hardinge, entered the cabin,
the Marshal exclaiming, "Captain 'Henry' has
escaped!"

"What!" said I; "it is impossible! only a few moments ago he was here!" and I looked very serious, though all the while I was laughing in my sleeve, saying to myself, "Again I have got the better of the Yankees!" The vessel was thoroughly searched— nay, I believe that it was fumigated, or "smoked," to get the Captain out; for Marshal Keyes was "positive" that he was on board— so he informed me on his way to the hotel.

Captain "Henry's" escape caused much sensation. Detectives, great and small, were thrown into a flutter of excitement, and the Boston police, whom Marshal Keyes affirmed to be the "best in the world," were all astir, that the fugitive might be lodged in Fort Warren. These myrmidons of Northern power were, certainly, not favored with a very accurate description of Captain "Henry." Some declared that he wore a black hat, others that he had a white covering to his head; some that his nose was aquiline, others that it was decidedly *retroussé.* Such contradictions bewildered the police, whose efforts resulted in a wild-goose chase.

Late on the evening of the escape, Marshal Keyes was jubilant over a supposed capture at Portland, Maine, whither he had tele-graphed to have any suspicious character ar-rested. The Portland captive proved to be not the gentleman of whom they were in quest, but a harmless English tourist, who was, no doubt, much aggrieved at his unlaw-ful detention.

When the Marshal informed me of the Captain's arrest at Portland, I knew that there must be some mistake, and could hardly re-strain my laughter; for all this time Captain "Henry" was lying *perdu* in Boston, under an assumed name. I was well aware of the Captain's residence, and through the medium of a friend received several communications from him. In my replies I assured him that he was already as good as free. For two days he stayed quietly at the hotel, and then I heard that he had set off for Canada, *vià* New York. Detectives had been sent all over the country to intercept him, but it was one of the best-managed escapes from the toils of the "'cute" Yankees that ever took place. Captain "Henry" actually remained for some time at one of the largest hotels in Broadway, where he saw many of his old friends, who, fortunately, did not recognize him.

Many and various were the reports of this affair that found circulation; but, singularly enough, it was the United States officers on board the *Greyhound*, and not "Mrs. Lewis," who had to bear the brunt of suspicion, though I was really the one to blame. I was delighted at being a *non-suspect*, by way of a change, and could thoroughly appreciate the chagrin of Marshal Koyes. He had prophesied that this was a case of capture with which Lord Lyons, at Washington, would not dare to interfere, as Captain "Henry"—to use the Marshal's own words—"was an officer of the Confederate navy, and therefore not an Englishman." To this view of international law I politely assented, thinking that, if Captain "Henry" could only reach a place of safety, it would matter very little how the Marshal classified him.

The *Greyhound* was hauled alongside a wharf, and an immense concourse of people assembled to witness my coming ashore; for it had been telegraphed from New York, and then again from the station in Boston Bay, that "Belle Boyd" was aboard the prize. Marshal Keyes was most courteous, and stated that he had procured a suite of rooms for me at the Tremont House, where I was to remain until my fate was definitely settled. This, he added, would be in a very few days; when he should either have the "supreme pleasure" of taking me to Canada, or the "unpleasant task" of delivering me over to the tender mercies of the commandant of Fort Warren.

The public journals were indefatigable in noticing all my movements. The Sunday-morning papers informed their readers that "Miss Belle Boyd would attend Divine service at the Old —— Church during the forenoon." The week-day news-sheets gave notice that "Miss Belle Boyd, in company with her

gallant captor, whose sympathies, no doubt,
were with the South, were seen out driving
the day before;" and, as a climax, the bulletin-
boards announced that "Belle Boyd had been
sent to the Fitchburg Jail!" Such were a
few of the many *canards* that flew abroad during my stay in the "modern Athens."

I had been there about ten days, when Mr.
Hardinge, fearing that the "Fitchburg Jail"
story might be but the shadow of a coming
event, proceeded to Washington, to procure,
if possible, my release. Having letters of introduction to many of the leading and influential men there, he induced them to use their
power in my behalf.

Although I was but thirty-six hours' rail-
way-journey from my mother, who had telegraphed to the Marshal to allow her to come
and see me, she was not permitted to do so;
and none of her letters reached me, they being
probably intercepted. But, if letters of affection were thus stopped, there were, happily,
other channels than the postal department by
which friendly comfort could arrive. Many

Boston ladies and gentlemen visited me, despite the Government spies who hovered about my quarters.

After being kept in suspense for three weeks, I forwarded, through Marshal Keyes, a letter to Gideon Welles, Secretary of the Navy at Washington, telling him that "I really was Belle Boyd, and wished to go to Canada, that I might communicate with my mother."

The Marshal received a telegram in answer, saying that "Miss Boyd and her servants should be escorted beyond the lines into Canada, and that, *if I was again caught in the United States, or by the United States authorities, I should be shot.*" This was on a Sunday evening; and the Marshal advised me to depart with all convenient speed, as I had only twenty-four hours' grace. I promised to start on Monday, at five P. M. It was impossible to go sooner, no trains running through to Montreal on Sunday.

The *Washington Republican* got possession of my letter to Gideon Welles, and published it *in extenso*, with the remark that

I was "insane," and had been, on that account, released by the Government. For this verdict of lunacy I thank them, if it contributed in any degree to mitigate my sentence. There certainly existed sufficient method in my madness to make me appreciate the advantage of having the promised shooting deferred until they caught me again; and I felt much obliged to members of Congress and others who used their influence in my behalf.

Mr. Hardinge was sent for early on Monday morning by Admiral Stringham, but he assured me that he would soon return. The day passed by, however, without any sign of him, and I began to wonder what had happened, when I received the following letter in his handwriting:—

"MY DEAR MISS BELLE,

"It is all up with me. Mr. Hall, the engineers, and myself, are prisoners, charged with complicity in the escape of Captain H——. The Admiral says that it looks bad for us; so I have adopted a very good motto, viz.: 'Face the music!' and, come what may, the officers under me shall be cleared. I have asked permission of the Admiral to come and bid you good-by. I hope that his answer will be in the affirmative."

This was written on board the receiving-ship *Ohio*. Its receipt made me feel very unhappy, for I feared that circumstantial evidence was against Mr. Hardinge, and that, ere long, he would, although perfectly innocent, share with poor Mr. Pollard a casemate in Fort Warren. But suddenly the object of my thoughts made his appearance. He informed me that the Admiral had allowed him and his officers to be paroled until sundown, and that he had availed himself of this privilege to come instantly to me.

Mr. Pollard, my fellow-passenger from Wilmington, against whom the Yankee journals were exceedingly vituperative, had on the Sunday morning been conveyed to Fort Warren, and there immured for the crime of being distasteful to those in authority. Suffice it to say of Mr. Pollard's subsequent adventures, that he was paroled to the city of Brooklyn, owing to his very bad health; since which I have not heard of him.

The time for my departure from Boston came at last. The Tremont Hotel was left,

and the railway dépôt was reached. Marshal
Keyes endeavored to make himself agreeable,
and was very busy in getting my baggage
checked and my ticket taken before the train
moved away. The Marshal, I may add, was
my courteous companion to the boundary-line
between Canada and the United States. With
a sad heart I had bidden good-by to Mr.
Hardinge, although I trusted that he would
soon rejoin me; and I enjoyed the delightful
prospect of breathing free Canadian air.

Yes, I should be free! Free from prison
bars and irksome confinement; but, alas! an
exile! Each step towards freedom carried
me farther and farther from my native land;
whilst, did I turn back, a heavy penalty awaited me. My father dead, and my dear mother
far away! Truly I was alone in the wide,
wide world! And I had left one generous
heart behind that I knew would miss me
sorely.

CHAPTER XXI.

Arrival at Montreal—Niagara—A System of Espionage still
around me — I depart for Europe—Passage across the
Atlantic—Arrival in London—I meet Mr. Hardinge once
more—Our Marriage—Comments of the Press.

UPON arriving at Montreal, I proceeded to
the "St. Lawrence Hall." Captain "Henry" and
his wife had proposed that I should join them
at Niagara; but, not having heard from them
for some time, I waited till I could ascertain
their exact whereabouts. In Montreal I met
many Southern families, refugees, and many
Confederate sympathizers. The British provinces were at this time a haven of rest for
American exiles — much as England has always been to the victims of persecution on the
European continent. I learned that my friends
at Niagara were expecting me, and accordingly

set off to join them, the Guards serenading me
just before my departure.

Niagara, with its sublime scenery, I will
not attempt to describe. We were stopping
at the Clifton House, and from my windows I
could plainly see the Yankee side of the Falls.
There, lower down, was the Suspension Bridge,
offering almost irresistible temptation to cross
from Canada to the States. We heard, on
good authority, that above a hundred thousand dollars was being expended on the reta-
king of Captain "Henry" and myself. Spies
were stationed on the bridge to watch, and, if
possible, to entrap us, should we by chance be
foolish enough to venture within their power.

About a week after our arrival at Niagara
we noticed, at the *table d'hôte*, two very fop-
pishly-dressed men, with thin, waxed musta-
ches *à la Napoléon*, and who apparently took
great seeming interest in the movements of our
entire party. We watched them closely, and
were very soon convinced beyond doubt that
they were Yankee detectives. Shortly after
this discovery, we left for Quebec. It was in

the morning, about eight o'clock, that we quitted Niagara and proceeded by rail to Toronto, where we arrived about noon. Imagine our surprise at finding the fair imitation dandies, whom we had left quietly at the "Clifton House," watching for us at the Toronto terminus! It transpired that they had seen us going, and had quietly entered another car in the same train.

The Canadian journals commented severely upon these fellows, and the system of espionage practised on us whilst we remained in the provinces.

The brace of detectives accompanied us in the steamer that left Toronto a few hours afterwards, and which plies regularly during the summer months between that place and Montreal. We noticed that they hovered round, eyeing us narrowly; and we determined to ascertain whether it was really our party that they were watching. When, therefore, we arrived at our destination, Captain "Henry" repaired to the "Donegana Hotel," whilst I went to the "St. Lawrence Hall." In a few hours I learned that one of these fellows had engaged a room at the same hotel where I was stopping; and, when Captain "Henry" called, he told me that the other detective had taken up his abode at the "Donegana"!

When we resumed our journey to Quebec, the spies still dogged us. Captain "Henry" embarked at once for Halifax. I remained some time in Quebec, previous to sailing for Europe; and when, at length, I quitted the American shores, one of the spies endeavored to secure a passage on board the same vessel! The Canadians, however, detesting this odious calling, insisted that he should be denied this opportunity.

My trip across the Atlantic was, on the whole, favored by calm weather and a smooth sea; so that I did not suffer much from my enemy, the *mal de mer*. Off the banks of Newfoundland we were, to make use of a nautical expression, "tied up" for more than a week by the fogs, amid fields and bergs of ice. The latter I had never before seen; and I gazed upon their majestic grandeur with feel-

ings of awe and amazement.   So near, at times,
did we pass them, that it is no wonder that I
felt somewhat nervous; for, had we struck, it
would have been instantaneous death to us all.
While crossing the banks we encountered a
fearful storm, and for one entire night the
steamer rolled and plunged with the force of
the waves like some living creature.

> "It was midnight on the ocean,
> And a storm was on the deep!"

But the storm in our case, though violent,
did not last long.   More moderate weather
soon came, and the passengers felt greatly relieved.

When, after entering English waters and
passing up the Channel, and my feet touched
the ground once more, I thanked God for our
safety.   I remember for a long time after, in
imagination, I could hear the whir-r-r, whir-r-r
of the screw, the creaking of blocks, the flap-
ping of sails, the hoarse, uncouth cries of the
sailors, and the clear, distinct voices of the captain and his officers.

Arrived in Liverpool, I remained there for some days at the Washington Hotel, and then proceeded to London. I soon ascertained the address of Mr. Hotze, the Confederate commercial agent, to whom I had letters of introduction from the Secretary of State. I reported to the Confederate States Commissioner that the dispatches intrusted to me at Wilmington had been destroyed when the *Greyhound* was overhauled, that they might not fall into our enemy's hands.

This report terminated Belle Boyd's connection with the Southern Government for the time being.

"So from the scene where death and anguish reign,
And vice and folly drench with blood the plain,
. . . . I turn!"

Mr. Hotze gave me a letter that had been left with him until I should reach London. Upon opening it, I found that it was from Mr. Hardinge, informing me that he had come to England, but not being able to learn my whereabouts, had proceeded to Paris, in the faint hope of finding me there. I was deeply touched at this new proof of his honest attachment, and immediately telegraphed a message to him, stating where he would find me in London. Gentle reader, you can, perhaps, imagine for yourself how joyful was our meeting, and in what manner a courtship, which had in it much of romance, was, at length, happily terminated.

Our marriage took place on August 25th, 1864, and journalists were pleased to treat the world to some portions of the romance in which we had taken part. The English press was friendly in its tone, but certain Yankee editors became marvellously indignant at the news, and even now they are subject to periodical returns of indignation.

(*Le Moniteur Universel de Paris.*)

UN MARIAGE A LONDRES.

"On écrit de Londres: Un mariage singulièrement romantique vient d'avoir lieu aujourd'hui, à onze heures, à l'église Saint-James. La fiancée était la célèbre Belle Boyd, l'héroïne de tant d'exploits aventureux pendant la guerre civile d'Amérique et surtout au moment des brillantes campagnes, du général Stonewall Jackson, dans la vallée de Shenandoah.

"Mlle. Boyd est à peine âgée de vingt ans, d'un caractère très-doux, douée de grands avantages personnels, et liée par la parenté avec quelques-unes des plus influentes familles du Sud. Il paraît que les scènes de la guerre, dont elle était témoin, depuis ces dernières années, avaient développé en elle une énergie et un courage qui se rencontrent rarement chez une femme.

"Les courses à cheval, au milieu de la nuit, à travers marais et forêts, jusque dans les lignes de l'ennemi, d'où elle rapportait aux généraux du Sud des renseignements d'une importance immense, forment le thème de nombreux récits autour des feux de bivouac dans toute l'armée confédérée.

"Elle était tombée entre les mains des fédéraux, mais un jeune officier lui donna les moyens de s'échapper et la suivit dans sa fuite. C'est lui qui, après l'avoir accompagnée en Angleterre, vient de lui donner son nom.

"Dans quelques jours, le jeune époux doit repartir pour les Etats confédérés, où il va s'enrôler comme simple soldat. Ceci a été une des conditions du mariage exigées par la fiancée, comme preuve du dévouement de son époux à une cause qu'il combattait dernièrement encore l'épée à la main.

"Le mariage a été célébré sans aucune pompe, mais ensuite un élégant déjeuner, préparé à l'hôtel de Brunswick, rue Jermyn, a réuni les jeunes mariés et tous les confédérés de marque et de distinction actuellement à Londres.

"Dans l'après-midi, les deux époux sont partis pour Liverpool, où le futur soldat du Sud va s'embarquer pour les Etats confédérés. On assure que les autorités fédérales ont mis sa tête à prix.

15

(Morning Post.)

" St. James's Church, Piccadilly, was yesterday the scene of a
romantic episode in the fratricidal war now raging on the
American continent; as, at the altar of that sacred edifice,
Miss Belle Boyd, whose name and fame are deservedly cherished in the Southern States, pledged her troth to Mr. Sam
Wylde Hardinge, formerly an officer in the Federal naval service. The marriage attracted to the church a considerable
number of English and American sympathizers in the cause of
the South, anxious to see the lady whose heroism has made
her name so famous, and to witness the result of her last captivity, the making captive of the Federal officer under whose
guard she was again being conveyed to prison. Miss Boyd, it
will be remembered, is the Virginian lady who, during the
terrible scenes enacted in the Valley of the Shenandoah, rendered such essential service to General Stonewall Jackson, by
procuring for him information of great value as regards the
position and condition of the Northern forces, and who sig-
nalized her devotion to the cause of her country by so many
other services. Capture and imprisonment did not damp her
adventurous and patriotic ardor, as she was twice immured;
once for seven months, and once for ten months. She was
again seized, and, while on board a Federal vessel, on her way
to the North, made the acquaintance of Lieutenant Hardinge,
with whom, having crossed the Atlantic, she has entered into
the bonds of matrimony. Mr. Hardinge needs no excuse for
the step he has taken in renouncing his allegiance to the Federal cause and espousing the fair 'rebel,' whom he has now
sworn to love, honor, and cherish. Though, in obedience to
the wishes of his father, he served for some time in the Federal
navy, in which service he rose to be lieutenant, his Southern

sympathies were notorious in the North, where it was well known that he had long tendered his resignation, which Mr. Secretary Welles refused to accept; and thus he was forced to continue in a service which he would gladly have renounced long since. Though more than suspected of Southern sympathies, he kept his word when he promised the executive of the Federal navy that the name he bore—a name which had descended to him from a long line of ancestors in Great Britain and America—should not be disgraced, and proved his readiness to perform his duty on many occasions.

"The bride was attended to the altar by Mrs. Edward Robinson Harvey, the bridegroom by Mr. Henry Howard Barber, and the marriage service was read by the Rev. Mr. Paull, of St. James's Chapel, in a manner which deeply impressed all present with the solemn nature of the contract entered into. Amongst the friends of the bride and bridegroom, and of the Confederate cause, who attended, were the Hon. General Williams, formerly United States Minister at Constantinople; the Hon. J. L. O'Sullivan, formerly Minister from Washington at Lisbon; Major Hughes, of the Confederate army; Captain Fearn, Confederate army; the Rev. Frederic Kill Harford (who gave the bride away); Mr. Keen Richards, of Kentucky; Mr. Henry Hotze, Mr. C. Warren Adams, Mrs. Paull, Madame Oerbelle, Mr. Reay, &c.

"At the conclusion of the ceremony, the bride and bridegroom, and their friends, proceeded to the Brunswick Hotel, Jermyn Street, where a choice and well-arranged breakfast was partaken of; and at a fitting moment, towards the conclusion, Mr. Barber, in a most eloquent speech, proposed the health of Mr. and Mrs. Hardinge, eulogizing the services the lady had performed, and prognosticating that the bridegroom would soon win fame in the service on which he is about to enter. The toast, as may be anticipated, was received with much delight, and was replied to by both bride and bridegroom, who expressed their acknowledgments to the many friends they had found in this country. The toast of 'The Queen' was afterwards given by Captain Fearn, who assured the English portion of his hearers that her Majesty was greatly revered in all parts of the Southern States of America — an assertion which was most warmly corroborated by all present, who were qualified to speak from experience. 'President Davis and General Lee,' and many other toasts, followed in due order, till the growing hours warned the bride and bridegroom that it was time to depart for Liverpool. Mr. Hardinge purposes in a few days to leave for the South, whither, in spite of the blockade, he intends to convey a goodly portion of the wedding cake, for distribution amongst his wife's friends."

The journey referred to above was taken by my husband very shortly after, for the simple purpose of communicating with my family in Virginia. Its results will be shown in the following chapters, in which he will tell his own story.

CHAPTER XXII.

Lieutenant Hardinge's Journal—Arrival at Home—A Surprise
—A silent Breakfast—Visit to Martinsburg—A pleasant
little Excitement—A Negro Welcome — "Miss Belle's
Husband "—A Portent—A Sailor's Superstition—Capture
—Poor Pat in the Toils—A high-bred General—Lieu-
tenant Adams—A Yankee Provost-Marshal—The Guard-
House — The Restaurant — A Guardsman— Ordered off
again—Arrival at Washington.

LAST November it became necessary for me
to quit the tranquil shores of England, and make,
much to my disgust, a trip across the Atlantic,
rendered doubly disagreeable to me by the
fact that I was parting for an indefinite period
from one whom I loved fondly—my wife, and
to whom I had been married but two short
months.*

---

* These papers were originally intended solely for the pe-
rusal of my wife; but, upon second thought, they have been

On the Monday afternoon after my arrival, I left Boston and proceeded to New York, where I arrived about 11 P. M., and put up at the New York Hotel. I did not sleep here, however, but went over to my mother's residence, in Brooklyn, almost immediately.

Gaining admittance to the house, and being, as you may suppose, thoroughly conversant with its internal arrangements, I mounted softly on tip-toe to my parents' room and entered. My father, aroused by the noise I made—for floors and doers will invariably creak at such times—called out as I opened the door, "Who is that?" "Martin," I replied; for I wished to surprise them as much as possible.

As soon as I had lit the gas I turned upon them and said, "Mother, how do you do?" For the moment she was struck dumb with astonishment, but the next she was in my arms, pressing me to her heart as only a mother can who loves her son devotedly.

somewhat condensed in material, and have been added to her adventures as an after-piece.

We sat for a long time, conversing upon many topics,—my wife, my future prospects, &c. About three in the morning, however, I left her and retired to my brother's room, who was at the time absent in Boston on business. I do not know why it was, but I felt like a stranger in a strange land—for my heart was with you, over the ocean, in merrie England.

All the rest of the night I sat framing a letter to you; and it was late in the morning, just as the faint glimmering streaks of dawn were flashing up from the east, and the distant hum of the city was becoming more and more audible, that I threw myself, tired, weary, and heart-sick, on the bed, and fell asleep to dream of you.

Sleep, did I say? ay, the sleep that the dog enjoys in his kennel. I think it was about nine in the morning when my mother awakened me. I sprang to my feet, and, hurriedly completing my toilet, descended, and entered the dining-room. There was very little said—a monosyllabic breakfast, one of those dismal feasts where Death seems to reign supreme.

With me it was soon over; and that same night I was *en route* for Baltimore, bound to Martinsburg, which I reached, after much delay and detention, after having enjoyed the nervous excitement of running off the track *only twice*, about 6.30 in the evening.

Here I was subjected, with the rest of the passengers, to a strict examination by the Provost-Marshal, of my passes and travelling-bag; but finally, after a quarter of an hour's delay, I was allowed to go on.

After passing several sentries and two barricades, I at length found myself at your mother's house. I did not announce my name to any one; but one of the girls rushed up to me, and, after gazing intently at me for a moment, flew out of the room.

Whilst I was revolving over in my mind this, to me, inexplicable scene, she returned, and, half laughing, half in doubt, said, "You's Miss Belle's husband, isn't you?" I of course assured her that I was. She again disappeared, but returned, accompanied by the whole sable household, who, crowding round about me, welcomed me to my home, inquiring affectionately after you, and evidently much disappointed at not finding that you were with me.

Greatly to my chagrin, your mother and sister were at Kennysville, about ten miles distant; but Mrs. G., who could not help shedding tears when she knew who I was, welcomed me as a son. All that evening we sat conversing together; and when, at last, I retired to sleep, it was in your own room; and, as I entered in at the door, I uncovered my head, and thought of you.

This was your room; here you had been held a prisoner, and had suffered the torture of an agonizing doubt as to your fate. Here lay your books just as you had left them. Writings, quotations, every thing to remind me of you, were here; and I do not know how long a time I should have stood gazing about me in silence, had it not been for my revery being disturbed by the little negro servant, who broke the silence by saying, "No one's ever sleep in dis room since Missy Bel' been gone—missus says you're de only purson as should."

So, when I retired to bed that night, and "Jim" had been dismissed from further attendance upon me, I lay for a long time thinking, looking into the fire, that glimmered and glared about the room, picturing you here, there, and everywhere about the chamber, and thinking of you sadly, far away from me in England—the exile, lonely and sad.

About midnight I fell asleep, and was only aroused from my slumbers late the next morning by Jim, who was making the fire. When I had finished dressing, I sat down near the fireplace. I hardly know what persuaded me to do so; but, if you will recollect, on the evening that we parted from one another, you placed upon my finger a small diamond-cluster ring,* telling me that there was a peculiar charm attached to it—viz., of forewarning the wearer when in danger, by dropping or being taken off. Without thinking, I did the latter.

* This ring was once the property of an African princess. —B. B. H.

Now we sailors are somewhat addicted to superstition; and I must confess that I felt nervously apprehensive about myself, which did not leave me, despite the endeavors that I made to allay my fears. I told Mrs. G—— of the circumstance when I met with her at breakfast, but she laughed at my credulity; but so firmly was I impressed with the belief, that I already began to feel that I was doomed —a marked man.

And I was. At half-past five—having previously procured a pass—I left for Baltimore; but at Monacocy station I was—judge of my surprise—arrested and kept confined all night under guard as a deserter. As a prisoner, I was of course searched; but, finding nothing upon me, the officer commanding told me that I might retire for the night.

"Where?" I asked.

"Oh! on the floor, by all means," was the response, accompanied with a horse-laugh.

The next day, at my earnest entreaty, I was sent to Point of Rocks, where I was treated more like a dog than a human being;

but, fortunately for myself, I was sent on to
Harper's Ferry, under a guard of Irish emi-
grant soldiers, who were far kinder to me than
their officers. During the journey they gave
me a long history of their wrongs, asserting
upon oath that they had been entrapped by
the oily tongue of Federal agents in Ireland,
who had given them gold and promised them
a farm, and two hundred pounds apiece more
in gold upon their arrival in the United States,
if they would only emigrate for the purpose
of tilling the land out West. Upon their
arrival in New York, however, they were
locked up as prisoners—not allowed to see
any one—and were only, after an imprisonment of over three weeks, set free, their liberty
having been purchased by their becoming
Federal soldiers.

They were also promised eight hundred
dollars bounty and three months' furlough,
which they had never to this day received,
although they had applied for it from time to
time; for no sooner had they taken the oath
of allegiance, than they were sent to the front

At the conclusion of this narration, which they swore by the "Holy Vargin" was truth and nothing more or less, one of them informed me that they had orders to shoot me if I was *impudint* to them even. "But we won't do it, me bye," they chorussed; "and, if yes says the word, we're yer min to cut over the border with yes."

This, however, was an utter impossibility, for the country was full of Yankee cavalry, looking after Mosby and his men; so I declined their proffered kindness, much to their astonishment and fright, for they begged me for the love of Heaven not to expose them. This I faithfully promised and kept; and, as I bade them good-day, just before I was conducted into the presence of General Stephenson, one of them remarked to me, *sotto voce*, "Be my sowl! young fellow, it's too bad to see yes in this condition, when ye ought to be afther mountin' into a saddle."

When ushered into General S——'s room, the General, a grizzly, gray-haired, bearded man, scanned me closely for a short time.

After enduring this as long at least as my patience could stand it, I said, "Is there any thing remarkable about me, or that you admire?"

"Yes, sir, your duplicity."

"Duplicity?" I reiterated, vaguely, seemingly unconscious of the meaning of the word.

"Yes, sir, duplicity; you are a spy, and——"

I interrupted him somewhat sharply, but recollected myself, and held my tongue.

"Where are your papers, passes, dispatches?" he asked, angrily.

"Papers I have none, except the *New York Daily News* and the *World* of yesterday. Dispatches—excuse me, did you say dispatches?"

"Yes, sir, dispatches."

"I'll save you a pun," I remarked, savagely; "I have none. As for my passes, they are there," pointing to a formidable-looking official document that had been brought on with me.

"Ugh!" was the rejoinder to this.

Lieutenant Adams just then made his appearance, and a very nice and gentlemanly fellow he was too. In striking contrast with the General, was his adjutant, the lieutenant.

"You're the husband of Miss Belle Boyd, and you ought to be hung. By-the-way, we hung one to-day; didn't we, Adjutant?"

"What are you going to do?"

"Hang you, if you can't prove your innocence—send you to Washington, perhaps. That will do, sir;" and I left the room.

In a few moments Lieutenant Adams came out, and. said, and very kindly, too, "Now, Mr. Hardinge, we'll go and get something to eat; and, if I can manage it, you shall sleep elsewhere than in a guard-house. Come into my office for a short time, until I write a letter, and then we will go."

Thanking him for his proffered hospitality, I entered the room and seated myself near the fire—for it was a rainy day, and very disagree-

able—and listened with feelings of horror and
disgust to the brutal boasts of a braggadocio
Provost-Marshal (I wish I could recollect his
name, for the sake of humanity), who boasted
of having enacted the part of Jack Ketch to
a Confederate soldier of "White's Battalion"
that very day; remarking, "By —— ! didn't
the fellow jump when the rope broke!" and
he added, "Here's a piece of the rope, young
fellow. Wouldn't you like to swing?"

"Not with you, at least, for a hangman,"
I said; and I did not attempt to suppress my
disgust from appearing.

"D—— you! I'll give you a double al-
lowance of dancing on nothing if I do!" was
the reply.

Shortly after this light and entertaining
conversation, Lieutenant A. and myself left
them; and, after a good meal and a short tour
about the town, we once more entered his
office. But this time I did not stay long; for,
although Lieutenant A. did all in his power
to keep me from the guard-house, to that delectable place I went, under the tender aus-

pices of the Provost, who endeavored to regale me with stories of men that he had "hung."

As for sleeping there, it was out of the question. A terrific fire roared and blazed up the chimney, flinging its heat into a room whose measurement might have been ten feet by twelve. In this space were packed some twenty steaming, drunken soldiers and citizens; and add to this the fact that other animals besides rats and mice were at play in the room, I think you will admit that I was at least uncomfortable.

The next morning, at a later hour, I was allowed to proceed under guard to a very seedy-looking cellar rejoicing in the name of a "Restaurant," where I succeeded in getting some stale oysters and bean coffee. Having finished this delectable breakfast, I was again reminded that I was a prisoner in the Yankees' hands by the sentinel, who carried, in addition to his gun, a watch, and who ostentatiously glanced at it, remarking, as he did so, "Time's up."

"Any news from the front?" I ventured to remark.

"No!"

"Is Mosby in the neighborhood?"

"I 'spose so."

"How often do the trains go northward in the course of a day?"

"Twice."

"Corporal," I said, "I am quite an amateur in my way. Come, you have excited my curiosity. Tell me, honestly, now, what you are; for you are the only one of the many soldiers that I have met in my intercourse with the tribe for the last three or four days who is rightly entitled to the name."

He evidently felt flattered, for it was the "Open sesame" of his tongue, and he flatly informed me that he was a deserter from the Guards, who had been stationed in Canada. "And I wish to the devil I was back out of the dirty rapscallion set that I've got into! They say birds of a feather flock together; but I'm —— if I am a bird of their stripe!"

Our conversation was brought to a close at

this period by the door of the guard-house once more being closed upon me. For want of better amusement, I stood watching the farmers or their wives from the country round, who came to procure the necessary passes to return to their homes again; and I must confess that the brutal remarks that accompanied the pass, or oftener its refusal, were enough to make the blood of any father, brother, or son, boil with indignation.

At 5 P. M., just as I was beginning to despair of ever being sent away from Harper's Ferry, a detective came to me and said, " All humbug; you're the chap, are yer? Come on!"

To this tender appeal I merely said, " I am ready; lead on."

As I passed out, he significantly pointed to a six-shooter that was buckled to his side, and remarked, " None o' yer capers."

I could not help laughing in the fellow's face; and I hardly know what would have been the *finale*, if Lieutenant Adams, who was passing in at that moment, had not said, "Treat

him like a gentleman, ——," calling him by
his name. And it is to this remark that I, no
doubt, am indebted for the little kindnesses I
received on my way to Washington.

We arrived in Washington about midnight,
and the detective, having visited the Provost's
office, I was relieved of his further attendance
upon me; and at 1 P. M. on Sunday morning I
was consigned to a horrible hole known as the
Forrest Hall, filled with every thing that was
infamous, low, and degraded.

Forrest Hall, or, as it is somewhat significantly designated by the fellows who board
here at the Government's expense, "The Last
Ditch," was without exception the most fearful
realization of a prison that it was my misfortune ever to have any thing to do with; not
that I would have you for one moment suppose that I am familiar with a convict's residence; but I have mentioned it merely from
the fact, that until I was thus thoroughly convinced to the contrary, I had always entertained the belief that, in this age of improvement and luxury, prisons had been converted

by science into luxuriously improvised hotels
—watering-places where roughs and rogues retire for a while to recruit their wasting energies.

And in this respect I have always entertained the belief that in America "they know
how to manage these things better than in
Europe, you know;" but this foretaste of St.
Giles and Billingsgate dispelled, and effectively
too, any highly-colored and very romantic ideas
that I had conceived of prison luxury; and
the rose-color tinting with which I had in
fancy painted such residences, gave way to a
most sombre picture, edged with black, that
nearly crazed me as I walked gravely back-
ward and forward, picking my way daintily
through dirty groups of sleeping men or pud-
dles of tobacco-juice with which the floor of
this place was saturated.

Situated in Georgetown, on the suburbs of
the City of Washington, Forrest Hall was,
before the commencement of this devilish struggle, used as a place of public entertainment,
where balls and suppers were held or given.
A large square-shaped room, it had nothing of

beauty to recommend it even then, much less
at the present day, when its walls are defaced
with unseemly pictures, vulgar writings, or
punctured plaster; and even in its halcyon
days it was such a room that one felt, however
warm one may have been, chilled upon entering.

Four immense windows, reaching from the
top almost to the bottom, bound with iron,
looked forth upon the street, but none of us
ever presumed to gaze from them, for orders
were given to shoot dead the audacious wretch
who should thus defy the laws. Four others
looked out upon what was known as the
"Promenade," a small enclosure where we were
allowed to walk for half an hour daily. One
feature of this "yard," as it was called, was
the hose; an instrument of torture which was
applied upon "suspects," who were supposed
to be deserters from the United States army.
Whether it was so or not, it was almost impossible to say. The manner of torturing the
unfortunate man was after the most approved
method of Yankee invention and ingenuity.

You may doubtless somewhere have read of the prisoner who was tortured by being fastened in an immovable position beneath a faucet that permitted to escape, every second, one drop of water, which fell always in one spot upon the forehead, producing a most fearful torture, resulting eventually in insanity. Well, although it was not exactly the same thing, nevertheless it approached it very nearly. For in this instance the victim was made to stand, bound securely to a post, whilst a steady stream of water, whose force was thirty pounds to an inch square, was played upon the small of the back.

It was often the case that the victim, unable to endure the torture, would, guilty or not, give in; and the consequence was, that the authorities, having witnessed the acknowledgment of his crime, would remand him in an exhausted state back to the " Hall," to be led out to execution, or conducted to the Penitentiary, where he had been sentenced for a lifetime.

Again, some, more obdurate and stubborn, would remain firm and unyielding, however fearful the torture, until fainting would ensue, or the medical attendant, who waited in person and watched closely the victim's wrist, would say, "Enough"—when he would be carried back to the room, only to be brought forth again to endure the same torture when he had sufficiently recruited his energies to be able to appear once more.

But, to revert once more to Forrest Hall. In a space little less than seventy-five feet square were crowded together over five hundred dirty, ragged, and filthy wretches, of all conditions and color, who had been immured here for many months, with the consoling remark, "Your case will be attended to." The dirt that filled the floor was something awful to reflect upon, and here they were obliged to live—here sleep. A space large enough for the promenade of the guards, who were relieved at the end of every four hours, was reserved for them; and whoever the poor wretch was that dared to invade the neutral ground—for such it was called by the residents—he was shot like a dog for his daring—

murdered, coolly and deliberately. Right over
the entrance to this room was a place called
"The Lodge." Here a corporal and three or
four sentries are placed, with the same humane
orders to execute relative to the shedding of
human blood. The place literally swarmed
with vermin, and the air is corrupt, and vile
with odors that are, at least, to be moderate,
in one's language, disgusting and nauseating
in the extreme.

It was early on a Sunday morning that I
entered this sink, after having undergone a
rigid examination of my person at the hands
of the officers who were quartered at the Hall.

This over, I was handed over to a sergeant, and conducted by him to the room that
I have endeavored to describe to you above.
It was so late, that (fortunately for me) only
some nine or ten out of the whole number that
lay huddled together on the floor were awake.
One or two stared at me for a short time, but
went on again with their play at cards.

A sentry was once more my friend in this
place. *He pitied me.* I was glad to have any

16

one's pity, even, for I felt almost like the desperate suicide at times, and the future of my life was enveloped in gloom, so dark and obscure, that it was in vain that I attempted to penetrate it.

Having passed the spot where I was standing, wrapped up in my own thoughts, he stopped suddenly and said, "You surely are not a deserter, sir?"

"You have surmised correctly," I replied.

"What are you doing here, then?" he added, with some surprise.

"That is just what I would like to know myself; and if you will inform me, I shall thank you for the information."

"An' I suppose you are one of those fellows we call political prisoners; and if you are, by Jove! there's plenty more of your same stripe that would like to have the same information you're after wanting;" and he resumed his beat.

In a short time he came to me and said, "Why don't you sleep?"

"Sleep!" I said, in astonishment.   He

grinned at the manner in which I spoke the
word *sleep*, and said—

"By ——! there'd only be a clean-picked
skeleton of you in the morning."

"Then I will try to fancy myself on the
quarter-deck for four hours;" and I commenced to promenade up and down with the
sentry, and it was not until late the next
morning that I gave up, and was forced to sit
down; but I first took my handkerchief and
brushed away the dirt on the floor as well as
I could before I did so.

As the morning wore on apace, the rascals,
who by this time were thoroughly awake,
came and stared at me, or asked me questions
of myself, business, &c. To the former I
affected a perfect indifference, but to the latter
I kept my tongue, which brought down innumerable left-handed blessings from these fellows, who saw in me, as they did not abstain
from informing their comrades, "a —— aris-
tocrat."

Taking my silence for fear, they became
bolder. One of them, a wall-eyed, villainous

scoundrel, knocked my hat off. Picking it up, I replaced it on my head, without apparently noticing the offender. Growing bolder, the cries of "Toss him! toss the swell cove! mash him! jam him!" were raised on all sides. A blanket was getting stretched for my special benefit, and I determined to act instantaneously.

Near the stove was a goodly-sized stick of wood, that was used for supporting the door when opened. I determined to get possession of it; so I walked up quietly, and, gaining possession of the instrument that was soon to decide my fate, I retreated to a corner, and waited for them.

It was not long. A party advanced, and then halted, when the wall-eyed man, who was known as "the Gouger"—a name that he had won from his prowess in tearing the eyes from out the sockets of others—came as near as was prudently safe; for I swung the stick defiantly as he advanced, and said—

"Now, young 'un, if yer don't give in, I'll

bite yer nose off! Come, now, are yer goin'
to?"

To his tender and merciful intentions as regarded my nose, I paid no attention.

"Oh, yer ain't agoin' to, then, are you!
Well, I'll have a fresh-meat breakfast, by —— !
this morning, at any rate. Come on, bullies."

I only remember one thing until the whole
affair was over; and this is the picture: the
gouger and his second advancing as I swung
my trusty weapon in a circle about me, the
pointed edge of the stick cutting into the
bridge of the "gouger's nose," and effectually
closing an eye for him, and the remaining
force of the blow being received by his second
on the temple, who fell like a lump of lead by
his leader. Then it was that I sprang forward,
slashing right and left as I went; but there
was no necessity to do murder, for they gave
way before me; and the sentry, who had been
watching the battle, received me with the
remark, as I gained his side, panting from the
exertion, "By —— ! if I hadn't have liked
you, I'd have shot you for mutiny; but you

did that well; they won't trouble you any more, I'll bet."

Nor did they. On the contrary, a "select committee," to my great surprise, waited upon me about 10 A. M., and their spokesman informed me that, by a unanimous vote, I had been chosen their president, and, if I would accept the leadership of "the Owls," it was at my command.

To their astonishment, I refused them; but, not wishing to make them my enemies, for I had no idea how long I was to remain here, I did so as politely as possible.

Fortunately for me, in the afternoon I was sent for; and, under guard, I was conveyed to the Provost-Marshal's office, in Washington City. Here I was kept for over an hour, in a place that was partitioned off for rebels, a ferocious-looking aspirant for military honors guarding me the while. Several of the clerks, who had ascertained from their superior who I was, attempted to converse with me, but in this they failed most decidedly.

Shortly after this, I was taken, under the

surveillance of Captain —— and four of his
satellites, to the Old Capitol. On my way to
that place, I was kindly permitted to partake
of some food—the first that I had eaten for
over twenty-four hours—at "Hanmack's," and
to the proprietor of that place I was indebted
for much attention.

Resuming my journey once more, after
running "a muck," so to speak, of the curious
loungers, for the churches were fast pouring
forth their inmates upon the street, and the
terrific fire of conversation from the Captain,
which was by far the worst torture I had to
endure.

On my arrival at the Old Capitol, I was
welcomed by a one-armed lieutenant, who had
"seen service," but when he did not say, and
whom I ascertained to belong to that body of
men known as the "invalid corps." I was
ordered to sit down, and, after a running fire
of questions, I was sent off to the Carroll
Prison, under the guard of two soldiers.

I was not long in reaching it, for the
political Bastile is situated not far from its

prototype, the Old Capitol. I was received by the Under-Superintendent, who, having registered my name, age, occupation, height, business, ancestry, &c., was good enough to relieve me of some money—not all, for I had been deprived of most by "the gallant knights of the greenwood," through whose merciless fingers I did not pass unscathed, and who certainly have a taking way about them. A diminutive penknife, which was also captured, although I begged to retain it as a favor, was refused, on the plea that I might injure myself.

This over, I was conducted to "Room No. 35," to keep company with a spy and a blockade-runner. On its walls, rudely executed with a piece of charred wood, I wrote our names, one day, and drew above it the English and Confederate flags, which, coming under notice of the sentinel outside, drew down upon my devoted head a whole mouthful of curses, loud and deep. Some wag, a previous inmate of this room, had written *à la* Jack Sheppard, over the door, the following very curious misnomer: "Piety Hall!"—"Piety Hall" is certainly a most deplorable spot. Four bunks, filled with bedding of a most suspicious character, occupy one-third of the space. I very foolishly slept in one of these "beds," as they are designated here, but I can assure you that I regretted it exceedingly long before morning.

It was almost an utter impossibility to tell the time correctly in this place, for the window, that opened on a passage-way without, is so completely enclosed with the cell, that has evidently been added to the building since the commencement of the war, and which is reserved exclusively for "close confinement," that it is not until a very late hour in the forenoon that daylight favors us with his presence at all. A stove in the centre of the room is used by us to cook whatever we choose to buy from the sutler, Mr. Donelly, who has had the monopoly of this prison since the beginning of the rebellion.

The morning after my arrival at the Carroll, in company with the blockade-runner, I descended into the yard, when, after refreshing myself with a hearty wash at the pump, I entered the *salle à manger* for my breakfast! I could eat nothing. The coffee is a mixture of—but I will not attempt to describe it—whilst the "hard-tack," as the old inmates call it, is the flintiest kind of flour that was ever baked and honored with the appellation of biscuit. So I walked out into the yard, and strolled listlessly about, wondering, as prisoners will, when I should be released.

About 11 A. M. I again went up to my room, and received from the sentinel a reprimand for remaining below in the yard, accompanied with the remark, that "if I didn't mind my eye, I'd have old Wood after me."

One of my room-mates said, "What was that old fool saying?"

I repeated the above remark to him, when they both laughed derisively, and said, "Don't you believe all they tell you: if you do, you will have a surfeit of gasconade, and a troublesome indigestion."

The second day after my arrival the "Colonel" entered the room and said, "Ho, ho, here we are! so you're the husband of the famous Belle Boyd, are you? Well, we haven't got her, but we've got her husband, that's next to it;" and before I had time to reply, he was out of the room; and this was the way that I first made the acquaintance of William P. Wood, the Superintendent of the Old Capitol and Carroll.

CHAPTER XXIII.

5th December.—Having procured some paper from the sutler, I wrote to Mr. Stanton,
with a simple statement of my case.

This document I forwarded to Judge Turner, who *attends* to all the cases of the prisoners held here.   That gentleman, after the ex-

piration of three days, sent for me; and having asked me, in the presence of witnesses, if I had written it, to which I answered in the affirmative, then swore me as to the truthfulness of it, and dismissed me from his awful presence, with the assurance that he would attend to it in the proper course of time.

I shall not readily forget my introduction to the inmates of Rooms 25 and 26, to which I was now transferred. I was introduced into my new quarters by Captain Mark T. "Gentlemen," he said, "allow me to introduce to this select and distinguished company, Lieutenant S. Wilde Hardinge, formerly of the United States navy, now of England, but just at present boarding with the freemen of the city at the Old Carroll Prison." (A momentary pause). "Allow me, sir—Captain McD., of Philadelphia, a counterfeiter, sir; brought here, not for an attempt to counterfeit himself, but for the crime of counterfeiting United States greenbacks, and buying Southern horses with them"—"Mr. Parker, sir" (as I was somewhat unceremoniously pushed round in front of him), "a blacksmith, not of anvils, but of the City of Brotherly Love, a forger by trade. He was brought up at the forge; and how could such an apt scholar end otherwise than in forging the United States Government?"—"Ah, H." (familiarly), "two distinguished 'colonels,' from New York, charged with ballot-box stuffing, and having the presumption to vote for McClellan; a bad case, sir, I assure you, as they [the authorities] keep putting their trial off for further evidence, which they cannot procure. However, they have an idea that they are sulky, and so they intend to keep them here. Ah, sir, this is a glorious country! nothing like it; in fact, a country whose institutions one ought to esteem, for they hang you first and try you afterwards."

Captain T. having finished his somewhat lengthy harangue, I ventured to remark, "And what, sir, may I ask, is your crime?" "Ah! mine," said he, winking complacently, "is *nothing!* but, as out of nothing came something, I presume they'll make it out of my case."

Here the introduction suddenly ceased; for,

dinner being announced, every one rushed for a seat, and devoured, somewhat ravenously, it must be confessed, every thing, except what was not eatable, upon the table; an example which I was not slow to imitate, for it had been over two weeks since I had the good fortune to get a mouthful of any thing really eatable.

December 7th.—I woke up very early this morning, and, having dressed myself, strolled about the yard below for awhile, in conversation with two or three others incarcerated here —for nothing; at least, that is the invariable answer.

By way of explanation to this, one of them said to me, "It don't do, Mr. H., to know too much in a place like this. You are a new-comer: let me advise you to ask no questions, and answer fewer. I don't mean to say there are spies here, but I wouldn't trust my own father in here;" and having finished his sentence, he left me.

I can see the ladies in the different rooms in that portion of the building devoted to them, gazing down, through their iron bars, into the yard, upon the prisoners, who are allowed to walk about here at stated intervals. I accomplished the prison feat of exchanging notes with a "close-confined" prisoner, an exploit which was executed when the Hessian sentry had his back turned upon us, and which would have been punished with bread and water in the guard-house for forty-eight hours, had it been discovered.

It is quite worthy of notice that one seems to take an indescribable pleasure in eluding the vigilance of the sentries at all times, not so much for any particular reason, but merely for the purpose of passing away the time, and proving that such a thing can be done, in spite of the "Rules and Regulations."

Captain Marsh left Room 26 to-day. He had been prisoner here for some time, but eventually was released without a trial or any satisfaction being accorded to him. His arrest was very ingeniously managed, Secretary Stanton ordering him to report for examination for colonel at Washington. Captain M. was "at

the front," *i. e.*, before Richmond, when he
received this mandate; but judge of his surprise when, upon his arrival, instead of being
promoted, he was ordered to the Carroll, and
detained there!

December 9th.—This evening, as we were
seated, conversing or playing cards, for want of
some better occupation, we were somewhat
startled by the cry of "Officer of the keys!
corporal of the guard! Post No. 7!" and almost
simultaneously with it came the report of a
musket, that sent whist-players and every one
else to their feet. Officers and men rushed to
their different stations, and the general belief,
for the moment, was that some one had been
shot in attempting to escape. Such, however,
was not the case; it proving to be only the,
accidental discharge of a fire-arm, through the
carelessness of a sentinel who had just come off
post, and was placing his piece in the rack,
when it fell, the jar causing it to go off. The
ball passed upwards through the floor, going
through a bed in 26, but fortunately without

wounding its inmate. This is not the first instance of this kind that has occurred.

Said Colonel Wood, who at that time was playing Inspector of the rooms, "That reminds me of a good story." The *good story* was as follows:—

"There was a fellow, an officer in the Confederate States Army, who received some money from a lady who was held in my residence for stubborn people. With this he bribed the sentinel who was in the yard beneath to let him attempt an escape. The sentinel agreed; but I got wind of the affair an hour before it took place; and, walking up to the sentinel, I said, 'Now, you —— ——, I've got you in my power; and, if you don't shoot that —— rebel, I'll have you hung.' So when Mr. Rebel gets out of the window, Mr. Sentinel blazes away at him, and down he drops kerflummuxed."

"What became of him?" asked one of his audience.

"Why, —— him, he died in the hospital, several days afterwards."

December 11*th.*—A captain in the Massachusetts 8th was sent into 26 to-day. He had been arrested and imprisoned in the Baltimore Jail for six weeks. In about an hour after his appearance amongst us, he was ordered out, and put into close confinement.

Captain McD., an incarcerated prisoner in 26, received the news of his sentence of court-martial through the *Star* of this evening. He was convicted of passing counterfeit money, and was sentenced to ten years' imprisonment in the Clinton Prison, New York has been cashiered the service, and disqualified from holding any office of honor, trust, and profit, under the United States Government, and to pay a fine of $5,000: this latter item, fortunately for him, is in "greenbacks."

He is a stout-built, thick-set, brawny-looking man, with black eyes and hair, and has lost a finger in the service of the Union. I watched his countenance closely as his eyes met the paragraph containing his sentence. Every one had seen it, but none cared to break the intelligence. He gave a sudden, spasmodic start, and sat for as much as ten minutes gazing at it. How he must have felt inwardly at that time, none can know but himself. It made one feel cold and nervous to see him sit there so quietly. Ten years! a lifetime for him. His hopes for the future were blighted. Farewell for him to all life's charms: he is dead henceforth and forever to the world. I would not have been in his place for thousands.

There he sat, without moving, and Room 26 was very quiet, for the occupants of it were looking at him. He evidently and suddenly became aware of this fact, and, looking up from the fatal *Star*, he said, "I'm in for it. They've done for me. Well, ten years' imprisonment! Humph!" (and he laughed), "I'm glad of that: I'll get out sooner." Then he got up and walked out of the room, and we all of us somehow felt relieved when he had gone.

December 15*th.*—Glancing up at the windows of Room 40, I saw this afternoon, whilst walking up and down the yard, a poor little child—a girl—about four years old, and standing close beside her was her mother. She clasped the iron bars of the window with childish glee, and did not seem to be aware that the cold, repelling touch of the iron that encircled her present abode was that of prison bars, that held her captive from the outer world. Her merry little laugh was truly painful to listen to.

"Aunt Lizzie" was in the sutler's at this time, so I asked her who it was.

"Who dat lady, massa? Dat's Mrs. K."

"What is her crime?" I asked.

"Oh, her husband was drafted, and she connived at his escape out ob de country, so they arrested her; an' now she's drefful feared that he'll guv hisself up in her place."

December 17th.—The ladies in Room 42 sent me a note, smuggled by ——, in which they thanked me for presents, at different times, of wine and delicacies for the table, that I had procured; for I have followed the business of blockade-runner very successfully since I have been in here; no matter if I have ill luck for an attendant outside in that dashing and very exciting business.

December 20th.—I cannot imagine why I can hear no news of you. Mr. Wood says, "You are very foolish, Mr. H., to fret: every thing is fair in love and war;" so I am forced to construe out of the latter portion of his sentence that others are employed in reading my letters. What a jolly thing military surveillance is!

December 21st.—I was introduced to the ladies in 42 to-day, and spent a very pleasant half hour in their society; and so quickly did the time slip away, that I was only reminded that the thirty minutes were gone by the officer of the keys, who, looking at his watch, said, "Time's up!" Mrs. Colonel M. spoke of you, and said "that you were undeniably the pet of the Confederacy, and would always be looked upon as its child as long as the Confederacy existed and had a name."

December 23d.—No signs of my being released yet. Mrs. Colonel M. remarked, and in the presence of Mr. Wood, to-day, "I have

material enough of Bastile life, as exemplified
in my treatment here, for a book."

"Mrs. M.," said Wood, and he laughed,
"no one will ever be able to write a truthful
account of the Capitol and Carroll Prisons. I
have a reminiscence-book, where I put every
thing that occurs of note within these walls.
If published, it would equal any of Reynolds's
novels of the Tower of London."

Then he spoke of Mrs. Horns. "I did that
girl an injustice. By ——! she was no traitor
to the South. It was I who got the papers
that condemned her friends, without her
knowledge and consent; and Mrs. G., when
she went to Richmond, ruined and completely
crushed her." Turning to Mrs. Colonel M.,
he added, "You may believe me or not, but
Mrs. G. used to write me notes, until I fairly
got sick of her, and afterwards she came out
with a vengeance against me. But, as I
rather glory in my origin, it didn't hurt
me."

December 24th.—My poor mother-in-law, in
a letter to me to-day, says: "What have I

done, a weak, defenceless woman, weighed
down with sorrow and care, that they will
not permit me to come on to Washington,
and see you?"

Had an interview with Judge Turner in
the afternoon. Judge Turner, *loquiter*, his
back to the fire, hat over his eyes (probably
from very shame), a cigar in his mouth:—

"Good-morning, Mr. H."

"Good-afternoon, sir."

"Your business, Mr. H.?"

"This, sir: can you inform me when I am
to be released?"

"Oh, one of these days."

"Are there any charges against me?"

"None, sir; that is, perhaps there may
be."

"Then why am I held prisoner here?"

"Because it pleases the Government."

"Ah! but do you call it justice?"

Judge Turner (frowning):—"Be very
careful what you say, sir. You are held here
because it pleases Mr. Stanton; besides, your
wife won't destroy any more of our army than

she has done, Mr. H., if you are held as a hostage; and Mr. Stanton has an affectionate regard for your future welfare."

What could I do? I was like the mouse, a prisoner in the cage, and at the mercy of the lion.

"I repeat my question," I said: "is it justice?"

"Justice or not," said that worthy judge, "we keep you here to make a patriot of you."

Mr. M. told me to-day two stories: one of them was of Sherman's march through Georgia. Mrs. M—— was tied to her chair and flogged, her clothes first being stripped to her waist. Leather straps were used for the purpose. A negro informed the officer that her husband had buried $20,000 in gold, and that she was aware of its hiding-place; so, finding that threats could not extort the secret, they used force.

As she stood there writhing in her agony, she appealed to the fellow, who was a "capting," for mercy; but the ruffianly scoundrel's only reply was, "D—n you ! tell us where the gold is hid, and I'll let you up." But this she could not do, and the infuriated wretches continued until she fainted, and the brutes then left her.

The other story was this, and not the less worthy of comment, as it came from the lips of a lady, both in position, as regarded her standing in society, and in wealth and accomplishments. I have no reason to urge you not to publish it to the world. Near the Rio Grande a Mrs. —— lived quietly and undisturbed, though the civil war raged about her, until a band of these "patriots for the restoration of the Union" took possession of the place for a few hours. Several of them entered her house in the night-time and ascended to her room, where she lay sick with rheumatism, and unable to move. Her servant, a young quadroon, who was waiting upon her, concealed herself in the bed; but she was dragged from her hiding-place, and these less than men, rendered furious with drink, and in the presence of the agonized and terrified lady, and in spite of her protestations and appeals for mercy, committed upon the unhappy girl the worst of outrages.

Christmas Eve.—About nine P. M. I sat down to a game of cards, and I am sorry to say that it lasted far into the morning—Sunday morning, and Christmas too; but you must excuse me, for you know that I was a prisoner. I retired to my bed about four A. M., and fell asleep almost immediately, waking up with the winter sun streaming into my face, unwell and low-spirited.

In "our room," 25, hangs, suspended from the ceiling, an evergreen wreath, with two figures pendant from it, the only thing here, in this dismal place, to recall to one's mind Christmas, save that the bells are already beginning to ring out merrily. No greetings from those you love meet your ears. Some few bid you "Merry Christmas," as you pass them by; but the look which accompanies it is low and melancholy, betokening that the one who gives the "God's greeting" says so mechanically.

Egg-nog has already commenced to flow freely in our room. Mr. Donelly's shop is much patronized this morning for whiskey and weiss-beer (the latter drink decidedly doctored, and a late importation, I should judge), eggs, and other necessaries that he doles forth, for money, to us. A glorious day, yet every one is down-hearted. I chew the bitter cud of reflection as I smoke my cigar.

Many of my fellow-prisoners have already drowned their sorrows in drink. An occasional maudlin carol comes from the barred window of some caged bird. As the day wears on apace, so does the state of intoxication increase. The sentries are maudlin, the prisoners noisy or sullen, as the liquor which they have drunk may affect them. Several are insulting. Without, drunken men and women reel through the streets. Why should I grumble, after all? There is misery and sorrow without, in this world, as well as within. I have not smiled to-day, but two or three times my eyes have been filled with tears; for I have been thinking of you, Belle, a stranger in a strange land, waiting sad and lonely for my return.

So the day creeps slowly along. The sentries are drunk, and many of the prisoners are dozing off the effects of whiskey, made up of morphine and other slow poisons.

A few moments ago one of the sentries asserted his authority with me.

Sentry (intoxicated):—"Say! where in the —— are you going to?" crossing his gun before me at the same moment.

"Are you addressing your conversation to me?" I ask.

"I don't want none of your —— palaver. Get back into that room, or I'll shoot you!"

I could stand this no longer; but I folded my arms, and, looking him straight in the eyes, I said, "I am unarmed. Shoot, if you dare; but, by Heaven! if you miss me, I shall not you."

The muzzle of his piece dropped, and, as I walk away, three cheers are given for me by the prisoners who were witnesses of the affair.

Several of the inmates of Carroll Prison

have been locked up in their rooms for being
noisy; cheering for Jeff. Davis and the Southern Confederacy, and groaning for Sherman and
Governor Brown, of Georgia.

Dinner is announced at last; goose, and
turkey, and mince-pies, for Room 26; bean-
soup and bread for the other prisoners. The
former dinner passed off in silence. Every
mouthful one takes seems like lead. Nobody
laughs or smiles: some few curse and swear.

The dinner is over. At the latter every
one scowls, grumbles, or swears, and leaves the
room—the *salle à manger* of the Carroll Prison
—chewing, by way of dessert, "hard tack."

I ask permission to see the ladies in 42.
Wood is gracious to-day, and the request is
granted, and for a few brief minutes I feel
differently. Suddenly, with a bang, the door
is flung open. In rushes Wood, utterly re-
gardless of the poor sick girl who lies writhing
with pain upon her bed—the same bed in
which you slept, in the same room; and fancy
made me always picture you as the sufferer,
as you suffered here months before—and roars

out in his loudest tones as he discourses upon
Atheism; then·off, before you are quite sure
that you have not made up your mind to
knock him down, or show him the door.

As I stood in No. 42 this afternoon, despite myself, the tears sprang to my eyes.
There, on the bed, lay poor Miss Mollie Mc-
Donough, groaning and moaning with pain,
sick and delirious; for close imprisonment had,
with its iron grasp, taken hold upon her delicate frame, and, after a brief struggle, she had
succumbed before it.

"The doctor says she must be removed,"
whispers Mrs. Colonel M. to me.

"Why, then, is it not done?" I rejoin.

"Because that renegade Virginian refuses
to let it be done."

Poor Mollie! I thought of you, Belle, as I
gazed upon her this evening, and the blood
rushed to my temples, and I clinched my
hands in silent wrath.

Mrs. Colonel M. tells me that Wood rushed
into the room this morning, and yelled out at
the top of his voice, "Hooray, Mollie! I've

got your father a prisoner." She gave one shriek, and cried out in her agony, " My God! what will become of my poor mother now ?"

Pretty scene! pretty language was that, to be used in a sick girl's room! Mrs. Colonel M., who had stood by, a silent witness of the scene, said to Mr. Wood, " For God's sake, sir, do you want to finish your work by killing her ?"

" Madam, you can't ride a high horse here." " No, sir," said Mrs. M.; " I leave that for Mr. Wood to do." Bang went the door, and he was gone, and in a few minutes he returned with Mr. McDonough.

It was at muster-roll in the evening I left for Room 25, where Colonel Wood was, swearing as usual, and holding forth upon some argument that was engrossing the attention of a crowd of tobacco-smokers lying on the beds in every conceivable position: a choice party for Sunday evening; and, in their intercourse with one another, oaths made up what their ideas lacked in the formation of their sentiments.

Finally, Wood sang a song. Give him his due: he sang it well, and with feeling. Then he left us, for which I fervently thanked Heaven. The moment that he went out, singing commenced. Every one who could not sing was compelled to make a speech, and in this manner we managed to pass the time away quickly. When it came my turn to sing, I gave them the following verses, which I had hastily written for the occasion; and, as I went on, one by one, the members who formed the company of Rooms 25 and 26 joined in the strain, until every one who could sing had done their part to swell the volume of song; and, at its conclusion, long applause greeted me from all sides. The following was the song, sung to the tune of "God Save the Queen:"—

I.

"'Land of the Pilgrims' pride,
Land where our fathers died,'
    Thy doom is read.
From every hill and glen,
In lowland, marsh, and fen,
Thy fate is written there,
    Thy glory fled.

II.

"Ambition holds her sway;
Injustice rules the day:
 Save us, O God!
Spies paid by those who reign,
Belie the freeman's fame,
And terror reigns supreme:
 Help us, good Lord!

* * * * *

IV.

"Arise, ye men who dare,
Who for your rights 'do care:'
 Uphold the laws.
Uphold them as they were,
Not as at present are:
Prove freemen as of yore—
 Uphold your cause,

V.

"What! are ye silent still!
Have ye no manly will.
 To battle them?
Yes, yes! ye will, ye come:
I hear the fife and drum!
Hark to th' increasing hum
 Of fearless men!

VI.

"Strike! for the old times gone;
Strike! for your slaughtered sons,
 And honor fled.

IN CAMP AND PRISON.

Down with the feudal horde,
Who irritate and goad,
With prison, debt, and sword,
And scoff the dead!"

You know that I do not claim to be a poet; so that should you, in glancing over these scraps, have your attention directed for a moment to their errors, forbear, if you please, from laughing at them, and recollect that they were thrown off hastily in my prison-home, and served to while away a few heavy moments on Christmas evening.

CHAPTER XXIV.

Mr. H.'s Journal continued—A Visit from my Parents—The
Order for Removal—On the March—"Do you know
Belle Boyd?"—An abrupt Introduction—Arrival in Phila-
delphia—Dismal Night-Quarters—An unpleasant Ordeal
—The Menagerie—*En route* for Wilmington—An Eight-
mile March — The Osceola — Fort Delaware — "Fresh
Fish"—"Miss Belle Boyd's Husband"—New Year's Eve
—Turned Cook—Snowballing—Sharp Practice.

On the 30th day of December, as I was
busily engaged in writing, Mr. Wilson, the
superintendent, called me down into the office
to see my father and mother, who had come
on from New York to visit me.

Previous to their coming to the Old Carroll
they had gone to Secretary Stanton to procure
the necessary pass. That gentleman expressed
himself astonished at their coming, but, after
some considerable delay, having ascertained

that the purport of their visit was purely such an one as two fond parents would be supposed to pay their son in " durance vile," gave them the necessary order, without which they could not have seen me.

Whilst we were seated together, conversing upon various topics, Mr. Wilson entered the room and said, addressing his remarks to me—

"Mr. Hardinge, you must get ready, sir."

"For what?" I said. "Is it then indeed true that I am to be sent to Fort Delaware?"

"I presume so, sir," was the reply to my inquiry.

Of course I was powerless to do aught for myself to prevent it. The scene that ensued was very affecting. My poor mother wept bitterly, and, unable to endure it unmoved any longer, I hastily quitted the room.

Whilst engaged in packing together what few articles of clothing I possessed—I do not imagine I was more than five minutes about it —I was again interrupted by Mr. Wilson with—

"Come, sir!"

"But I have not got my things together yet," I said.

"Well, if you haven't, there ain't no time to spare; so come along with you."

Seeing no possible way of obtaining a brief respite, I hastily bade adieu to those of my room-mates who were about me, and, taking my few clothes, I followed my jailer.

Down-stairs my poor mother again saw me; she was still weeping, and at times sobbed audibly. Near her, my father stood looking at me sadly.

My mother pressed forward and flung her arms round my neck, saying, as she did so, "God bless you, my son!" and then, blinded by her tears, she staggered rather than walked from the room, my father following.

I was immediately searched, then gruffly ordered to "Fall in and be d——d to you!" with the rest of the prisoners, seven in number.

The orders were then given to "Right face! Forward, march!" and away we went. In front of this modern Bastile we were again halted. Guards were then stationed on each side of us, a lieutenant marching in front with a drawn sword.

We were, upon our arrival at the depot, again halted and drawn up into line, where we remained for some time, the rain descending upon us in torrents, drenching us to the skin. We asked permission of our guards to seek shelter under a roof where they themselves were standing, but we were gruffly refused.

When the rain had ceased, we were marched into one of the railway-carriages. Lieutenant C., belonging to Major Harry Gilmore's command, sat on the same seat with me. He was, as I afterwards found, very loquacious, and, though a perfect stranger, entered into a spirited conversation, that was kept up nearly the whole way. As I have before stated, he did not, of course, know who *I* was, nor my name; and once, during a lull in our discussions, he said:—

"By-the-way, did you ever hear tell of Miss Belle Boyd?"

I smilingly assented that I had.

"Well," he said, "there isn't a Southerner who would not lay down his life for her. When I was at the battle of Winchester, I was wounded, and she came into the hospital where I was, and inquired if there were any Maryland boys there. Amongst other delicacies, she gave me some very nice peach-brandy. She and Mrs. G. were in the fort, if I err not, cheering us on when we made a charge and drove the Yankees back. When she was in Montgomery Hall, Alabama, in 1863, she attended a ball held there, and was *the* belle. She stopped a duel between two Frenchmen who were going to fight in the garden attached to the hotel. When she came back from her imprisonment she brought me a splendid uniform. You have no idea how every one loves and respects her," he added; "however, she married a Yankee, so I understand. But Miss Belle would never marry a Yankee, I am certain; I'll bet he was a rebel: indeed, I am confident of it; and——"

"And the gentleman who sits beside you is her husband," I added, interrupting him;

"and, like yourself, sir, I am a prisoner held by the Yankees.

I never in my life saw a person so thoroughly dumbfounded and confused for the moment, but finally he said—

"Well, I trust that you will pardon me for what I have said; upon my honor I did not know who you were, or I would never have done as I have."

"You have said nothing," I replied, "that a gentleman could construe into an insult; and I am happy to make the acquaintance of one who knew my wife so well." And for the rest of the way we were the best of friends.

We arrived in Philadelphia about midnight; the same systematic process of guarding us was gone through with, and as we were marched out of the carriages, sleepy passengers rubbed their eyes, and stared at the "Johnnies" as we passed by them. We were quickly moved over opposite the station. Here we were halted for a few moments, the lieutenant leaving us in charge of the sergeant whilst he went off to ascertain further infor-

mation in regard to our movements. He
returned, however, in a few moments; and,
again taking up our line of march, we filed to
the left, then to the right, in through a gate-
way, under an arch, through what had once
been a doorway, then down through a long
corridor, whose sides were filled with camp-
bedsteads, and finally a dismal slave-pen,
where there were no windows, only a narrow
grated door. This, we were informed, was to
be our quarters for the night. Our beds were
the hard boards; our covering, what we stood
in; our pillows, knapsacks or valises.

Sleep was out of the question; so, for the
consideration of ten dollars in "greenbacks"
(about two pounds sterling), I purchased,
from a calculating specimen of Yankeedom,
about *tenpence* worth of tobacco, and tried to
drown my cares and sorrows by smoking; but,
although the "smoke" vanished, my woes and
sorrows still clung to me. I felt very sore,
stiff, cross, out of temper, and indisposed every
way, which was in a measure increased the
next morning by a breakfast off tin-ware of

something. I know that I was very hungry, and ate and drank it !

Could any one be more miserable than we, under the circumstances? Soldiers, sailors, flunkeys, women, &c., came and stared at us.

"So that is him ! oh, my !" was the sentiment of a very stout, red-faced woman, staring in upon me. "Who'd a-thought it of him? What a wicked man !"

"What will they do with him?" I heard one ask of another.

"Oh, hang him," was the reply.

"Roasting's too good for him," said the other, with a laugh.

"I wonder if I can get a button or piece of his coat?" I heard some one else say.

"Ask him," said another.

This species of degrading torture I endured until noon-time, when we were ordered out, and conducted, still under guard, to the cars that we had occupied the night before on our way from Washington, now on our way to Wilmington, Delaware, where we arrived in about two hours' time.

Once more we were ordered out of the carriage. I obeyed the command with an apathetic listlessness, for I had lost all spirit, as had the rest of our party, two of whom were old gentlemen, men who already had one foot in the grave—political prisoners, like myself; men who had refused to take the oath of allegiance to the United States Government.

This time we had a journey of eight miles on foot to make. True, apparently, this was not long; but to us it was indeed so. The roads were very bad; and almost all of the way we were over our ankles in mud and slushy snow; and it was not until after three hours of this torture that we marched into Newcastle. As we passed through the principal streets, women and men rushed to the windows and doors to see us, whilst a guard of honor (?), extemporized from all the small boys and girls in the village, attended us in the front and rear, gazing at us in wonderment.

Arriving at the steamboat landing, much to our disappointment and surprise, the steamer was not to be found, and we were ordered to right about; and this time, as if to add insult to injury, we were conducted to the Newcastle jail, and confined in a convict's cell.

In this horrid place we were left to our meditations until far into the evening, when we were marched out: and this time it was with a sensation of relief that I passed on to the deck of the *Osceola*. About 8 P. M., the *Osceola* got under way and proceeded down the river, *en route* for the fortress, about twelve miles distant. Several officers stationed at that place were on board, and came aft, questioning us, scanning our attire, features, &c., and, in fact, doing every thing but poke us with sticks to make us roar.

Upon our arrival at the landing, about 10 P M., the same routine of guarding was gone through with as I have before described. At last we reached the provost-marshal's office. Here our names were registered, our age, State, when born, profession, whether citizen or soldier, &c.; and, this accomplished, it being late, we were conducted into the "Private

Barracks," and lodged in the Virginia division, in which were confined some thirteen hundred privates—a place that a gentleman-farmer in this country would not have permitted his pigs to live in, much less human beings. .

As we entered the doorway, yells and shouts from every side greeted us, of "Fresh fish! fresh fish!" Men and boys crowded around us to find out from "whence we came," "what we were held for," "who we were;" and last, but not least, "had they gone through us," in other words, and more plainly speaking, "had the sentries outside searched us."

To this last inquiry I assured my questioners that the Yankees outside had done so most effectually.

Several of them proposed "tossing us in a blanket," by way of diversion to the rest, and many were evidently in favor of it, when suddenly Sergeant B——, of the division, sprang forward, and shouted at the top of his voice—

"By Jove, boys! this gentleman is Miss

Belle Boyd's husband; you wouldn't wound her feelings by insulting him, would you?"

In an instant the shout that was raised was perfectly deafening. I was received with *empressement* by the whole body of Confederate prisoners.

In spite of this, however, I passed a miserable night, and awoke more dead than alive with the excessive cold, having no covering to shield me from the weather, the hard floor for my bed. At 9 A. M. I ate my initiatory meal at Fort Delaware, consisting of a piece of flinty bread and the smallest morsel of pork yellow with age. The latter delicacy I gave away, not having been here long enough to appreciate such dainties and eat any thing that was placed before me.

Jan. 1*st*, 1865.—I passed a dreadful New Year's Eve; cowering over the fire until far into the mid-watch, with my gloomy thoughts for sole companions—fitting company, though, for such a place as this. The floor is my bed again to-night, and I sleep as the dogs sleep— half waking, half sleeping. Once I awoke,

hearing some one engaged in prayer; deep
silence prevailed around about; and whoever
he was—the speaker, I mean—he spoke im-
pressively. Before I retired for the night I
called upon General Vance and his staff, and
passed a very pleasant evening.

Jan. 2*d.*—Some of the "boys" gave me
a blanket, and another handed me his over-
coat; so that I managed to sleep warmer than
usual. Found several friends of mine here
from Mobile, Alabama. Captain W. gave me
a very good cup of coffee for my dinner. The
days drag wearily by, God knows. Everybody treats me kindly. I have found warm
friends. Am getting accustomed to my
"feather bed of boards."

Jan. 2*d.*—Two letters. Very gloomy, and
dull, and cold. In the evening heard some very
fine singing; Captain —— sang an *aria* from
"Norma" that he rendered excellently well.

Jan. 3*d and* 4*th.*—Wrote to my friends
outside the prison to-day. Whilst engaged in
this occupation, one of General Vance's aides
brought me an invitation from the General to

dine with them.   Passed a pleasant afternoon in their society; and was introduced to Captain M., brother of General M., the distinguished Kentucky cavalry officer, and we became very warm friends afterwards.

Jan. 5th.—I attempted my first cup of tea this morning. Gods! fancy my having turned cook! My friends laughed heartily at my handiwork; *for I put the tea in the cup, then the snow upon that,* waiting for that to melt into water and boil. Meanwhile the tea suffered the natural result of such stupidity, by being burnt.

Jan. 6th.—Saw an account in the paper of my friend Mrs. Colonel —— having been sent South. Thank God, she is free!

Jan. 8th.—Received a letter from one of my friends outside to-day, smuggled in by the underground route; there is hope for me yet in Rome with Nero. Saw an account of my removal from the Carroll Prison here, headed—

"THE HUSBAND OF BELLE BOYD.—The husband of Belle Boyd, the famous Rebel Spy, took refreshments in the guard-house of the Citizens' Volunteer Hospital on Friday after-

18

noon, on his way to Fort Delaware. Dr. (?) Kenderdine was *careful to provide secure quarters for this noted individual."*

Jan. 9th and 10th. — Damp weather. Afflicted with the "blues." My feet so swollen that I cannot put my boots on.

Jan. 11th.—Whitewashed our division today. The guard kept us out in the snow that had fallen heavily. Passed the time away by snow-balling one another. One of these frozen missiles falling near a sentry, that menial deliberately fired upon us, but fortunately without doing any mischief, although the ball ploughed the snow up very near one of our party.

The places where the prisoners are held here are called "pens;" and they are correctly designated, for they are nothing more. Any one who may at any period of his life have attended a "cattle-show," can readily portray to himself the places we inhabit. These habitations, boarded and roughly put together, remind one very forcibly of old-fashioned farm-house barns, where, in the old times, your poor horse shivered the night through, standing uneasily in his stall, whilst his master slept comfortably within the chimney-corner. Officially and by courtesy they were denominated "barracks," of which there are three distinct kinds upon this island, viz., the Officers' Barracks, the Privates' Barracks, and last, but not least, the Allegiance Barracks; or, as they are commonly termed, the "Whitewashed," or "Galvanized Barracks."

In the Officers' Barracks are held some fifteen or eighteen hundred officers and political prisoners—about 150 in all of the latter.

In the Privates' Barracks, which occupy a little more space, and whose divisions are somewhat larger than those of the former, are crowded together, in their misery, some nine or ten thousand soldiers, from almost every regiment and command in the Southern Confederacy. Many of these poor fellows are but half-clad, and suffer terribly from the cold, inclement winter of the North. Many of them, by far the largest portion, are without friends in the North to whom they could apply, and are therefore indebted to the Yankees for the very little clothing that is at times given to them, but which is never given unless every vestige of the original garment has entirely disappeared, and common decency demands it. Many of them are young scions of some of the noblest and proudest families in the South; men who before this war knew naught of want and trouble; men who had from infancy been reared in the lap of luxury, and are now enduring every thing—insult, imprisonment, and starvation—willingly, and without murmuring; patriots whose names will yet live to be handed down to posterity as noblest among the noble.

And, lastly, the Galvanized Barracks. These are domiciled by Southern soldiers who have taken the oath of allegiance to the United States upon being imprisoned here. These "patriots" remain in this delectable spot for one year, and are made to work for the Government, to prove their devotion to Mr. Lincoln's Administration, by hauling wood and doing the disagreeable duties of the prison. These fellows are allowed to draw rations daily, and to live the same as the garrison in every respect as regards their food. Moreover, they are permitted to receive boxes containing clothing and luxuries which those who choose to remain constant to their principles cannot, unless they are fortunate enough to possess the influence of outside friends.

As regards their love for the "old flag," and devotion to the Union, I can hardly deem myself competent to pronounce judgment correctly. But an excellent story is told of these individuals, which is not unworthy of attention, as it may in a measure serve to show how far these *patriots* should be trusted.

General S—— and his staff once paid them a visit. Upon entering their abode the General stated to them that there was to be an exchange of prisoners, and that all those who still desired to go back to the South might do so.

"Now," he added, "all those who feel inclined to do so, step over on the left of the division."

Every one of them went over; not a man

*remaining of the many who had grown to love
the Federal Government as at present conducted.*

It is said General S—— laughed, and remarked, "Well, that will do; I only wanted
to find out whom I could trust—to ascertain
if any of you were really sincere."

These barracks or pens are divided into
divisions, each division having a stove for the
purpose of heating, in a manner, quarters that
would otherwise be untenable. They range
in length from eighty to one hundred feet, and
in breadth measure about thirty feet. They
are separated from one another by thin parti-
tions of boarding, so that really they are quite
connected, as conversations carried on in one can
be distinctly heard in the other. On each side
of these places, wide structures of wood are
built, two stories in height, which are reached
by means of wooden chats nailed to the sup-
ports. Upon these elevated platforms, each
prisoner is apportioned off so much space for
his sleeping and cooking purposes.

At night calcium lights, placed at one end

of the barracks, throw their broad glare upon
the square of something less than an acre of
mud and boards. Delectable spot in rainy
weather, with its ditches filled with muddy
yellow water! Splendid place in the summer
for disease; and many a poor fellow has
looked his last upon this earth, dying here, far
away from his home, struck down by the
small-pox or some virulent, fearful malady!

Escapes during the summer months are not
unfrequent; but in winter all such attempts
were put an end to from the inclemency of the
weather, the floating ice in the river, and the
utter impossibility of any one, however bold
and daring a swimmer he might be, living any
length of time in the water.

The regulations for the prevention of escape, &c., are rigorous enough, but they are
still more rigorously carried out.

One of the prisoners in the private barracks, rising one morning, carelessly, and without thinking of the consequences that might
ensue, threw some dirty water out of the
pigeon-hole, which answered the purpose of a

window, and served to lighten up in a manner the gloom within.

The water, splashing on the ground, attracted the attention of a sentinel who was standing guard about twenty paces distant; and, without warning, he brought his musket to a "ready," and fired hap-hazard in the direction from whence the water was thrown, hitting, not the aggressor, but an innocent youth who had just awakened, and was gazing out upon the dreary scene that presented itself before him, perfectly unconscious of his danger, or how near unto death's door he was passing.

CHAPTER XXV.

A piteous Spectacle—The Old Men's Petition—Our Guardi-
ans—Colonel W.—Mr. W.—Tom S. the Toady—How
Tom got his Situation—The Ladies' Attendants—Aunt
Lizzie—Mr. L.—The Spy discomfited—The Prison
Building—Fort Delaware—The "Galvanized Barracks"
—Galvanization and its Results—The Prison by Night—
A Reckless Sentry—Our Cuisine—Scrap Pudding—How
the Prison Officers made their Profit.

ABOUT the middle of January I saw one
of the most piteous spectacles, I think, that I
ever had the misfortune to witness. Four
men, old and decrepid, one of them tottering
on the entrance to the valley of shadows, men
whose gray beards and venerable aspects
ought to have commanded at least sympathy
from the presiding powers at Washington,
were brought in as prisoners. They were to
be held here until exchanged—men who could
18*

not possibly be of any benefit whatever to
either side, North or South.   These men were
arrested on the 3d of August last by a captain in the United States navy, who was on
shore, in command of a raiding-party, and who
brought them back prisoners on board his
vessel.   They were confined in the hold for
five months, and then transferred to the supply steamer *Massachusetts*, and sent to Philadelphia, and from thence, upon her arrival,
were forwarded to Fort Delaware.   Truly, if
this was the sole result of the brave captain's
raid, he had nothing to feel proud of.

Upon their arrival here they excited the
"commiseration" even of Adjutant Ahl, who
informed them, if they would take the oath
and draw up a petition to the Secretary of
War, that he himself would forward it for
them to the proper authorities.   Below I sub-
join the letter that they had written, by friends
who volunteered their services in the barracks,
and to which they respectively signed their
names.   One of them recounted to me his misfortunes and those of his comrades, and I con-

fess that, as I sat listening to his recital, I felt moved. "We have been treated very badly, very badly," he said, in conclusion—"confined in the hold of the vessel for most of the time; and we are all of us very old men, sir, and we never did them any harm."

"*Jan.* 16*th*, 1865.

"Capt. Geo. H. Ahl, A. A. A. Genl.

"Sir,

"In accordance with your request, we enclose you the written petition to the Secretary of War, and we solicit your kindness to have it forwarded at your earliest convenience. You have seen our condition, and can appreciate the truthfulness of our statements. If, therefore, you find it consistent with your views of duty and humanity to add thereto the recommendation of the Commanding General of this post, or such other good word in our behalf as you may deem best, you will add greatly to the obligations we are already under for your considerate attention.

"The Petitioners."

PETITION.

"*Jan.* 16*th*, 1865.

"Hon. E. M. Stanton, Secretary of War.

"Sir,

"The Petition of the undersigned humbly sheweth, that they are citizens of the State of Georgia, and residents of McIntosh County, whence we were seized and taken on the

3d of August last, by a raiding-party under the command of
Captain Colverconerris, of the United States Navy, and, after
five months of close and severe confinement on board vessel,
have been transferred to the military prison at Fort Delaware,
where we are at the present writing of this. We were, at the
time of our capture, peaceable citizens, engaged in the pursuit
of our several civil occupations, non-combatants, having never
been engaged in any military service or duty to the Confederate authorities, and are, from our advanced age and physical
disabilities, wholly incapable of such service as the field,
neither of us being less than fifty, some of us over sixty years
of age, and one of us being deprived of a leg, which was lost
by accident many years ago. Being thus incapable of con-
tributing any thing towards the continuance of this war, or
the result of this unfortunate struggle between the sections of
our once common country, and having, in the course of nature, but few remaining days to look for on this earth, we
indulge the hope, and appeal to the humanity of the enlightened Government in whose hands we are placed, that
those days shall not be shortened by the terrific rigors of an
imprisonment which cannot otherwise be endured. To this
appeal of our extreme age and helplessness, and our entirely
civil and non-combative character, we have to add that our
homes are now within your military lines as recently established by the forces under the command of Major-General
Sherman. Under this state of affairs, we humbly beg to be,
as soon as practicable, released from confinement and returned to our homes, where we engage to remain as hereto-
fore, and, as our physical condition compels, quiet and peaceable citizens. To this end we are willing and ready to sub-
scribe to the usual oath of allegiance to the United States

Government. Trusting that the petition and appeal may receive a speedy and favorable response, we shall, as in duty bound,

"Ever remain, your obedient servants,

"WM. JAMES CANNON,
"CHARLES LINGOAUT,
"WM. RILY TOWNSEND,
"WM. SOMERLIN."

Yankees generally are very susceptible to flattery, at least those in authority at Washington; and let us hope that the few masterly touches of the ingenious, if not diplomatic author, will not fail to have its desired effect upon hearts that are proverbial for their adamantine qualities. Since my sojourn here I have had ample opportunities of observing the spirit of piety and godliness amongst the Southern soldiery. A Young Men's Christian Association was organized some time ago, and prayer-meetings are held nightly in some one of the divisions, whilst prayers and readings from the Bible take place in each division every evening about half an hour before the lights are put out, either conducted by some chaplain or Confederate officer.

In their pious regard for the Sabbath day
and God's command to keep it holy, I know
of no nation which approaches nearer to the
marked devotion of the English people than
the Southerners. The Sabbath day is always
passed in a quiet and orderly manner, service
being held in different parts of the barracks.
It was my very good fortune to attend the
meeting held by the Rev. Mr. Kinsolving, in
Division 23. His service was attended by
all grades of rank, and he certainly spoke and
read with—and what is very rare with the
public speakers of the present day—much
feeling and pathos, so different from the rant
and fume of a certain sensational preacher of
the word of God that I once had the misfortune to hear in the " City of Churches."*

You will like to hear something of our
jailers. Here they are. Colonel W., our
superintendent, could be a gentleman if he
wished. With a mind cultured and at once
deep and penetrating, he appears to have bru-
talized himself by contact with those with

* Brooklyn, Long Island, State of New York.

whom he has associated. I have watched the
man closely in both phases—in one, running
about the ground like an enraged tiger, whilst
his subordinates clear to the right and left,
fearful of their tyrannical master. Finally
venting his spleen upon some unfortunate one,
he subsides into quiet, and his official dignity
now feels half ashamed of the disturbance he
has succeeded in creating about him!

I have heard him use language that modest
ears would hardly dare to listen to—not merely
commonplace oaths, but curses both loud and
deep, and horrible to hear. A fit disciple of
Tom Paine and Voltaire! for W. is an Atheist.

Atheism is his hobby. His arguments are
good in the defence of his "creed;" but, rea-
soner, and a deep one though he is, I do not
believe that he has faith in it. Conversing on
this subject one day he said, "There is my
Bible," laying his hand on a volume of Voltaire!

"And, Colonel W.," I replied, "like Voltaire, on your death-bed you will cry out in
your agony upon God to save you!"

He pondered for a moment, then said, "Well, I might. Your Bible says, that 'those who believe in Me, even in the eleventh hour, shall be saved.'"

Again, the Colonel can be as suave and polite, as affable and courteous, as any who have moved in the best society—as gentle and as tender. It is only, Madame Rumor whispers, that he is cruel when under the influence of morphia or opium. In his movements he is quick and energetic—a man of medium stature. His is a peculiar eye—keen and gray; at times cold and perfectly expressionless, at others full of shrewdness and keenness. Dressed in black coat and gray trousers and vest, his large head covered with a broad-brimmed black slouched hat, you have W. P. Wood, the Vidocq, or, better still, perhaps the Jonathan Wild of America.

Mr. Wilson, the Colonel's right-hand man, the under-superintendent, from what little I saw of him, appeared to be a gentleman, straightforward in his dealings, and a man of very few words. He dresses plainly, and wears a slouched felt hat. Every one wears felt hats now. "It is only foreigners and Southerners who carry canes and wear tall hats," said a friend of mine to me one day when in conversation with him.

Next to the Colonel, W. is the busiest man in the prison. He it is who has charge of the prisoners, and who rules supreme in the Colonel's absence. Every morning at eight o'clock he comes round and calls the muster-roll of the prisoners in their rooms, and hands them their letters, which, however, are invariably opened and read before they leave the office below.

Colonel Colby, the military commandant, who has charge of this post, I saw but little of; but we all liked him, for he was ever courteous and polite, and had always a good word for us.

Fortunately for myself, I was not under the tender guardianship of the "officers of the Keyes," so of them I can say but little, save that they attended to their business with punctilious strictness.

Another individual in this modern Bastile is a decided toady to Colonel Wood. He rejoices in the name of Tom Stackpole, and has charge of the beds and bedding, and he attempts to imitate him in his every action. In his accomplishment of swearing he is even a greater proficient than the Colonel. In his walk he outdoes him. If there is a man that he hates and fears more than all others it is certainly Colonel W——. Indeed, I think, like Jonathan Wild, the Colonel can trust his menials, because he knows a portion of their life which would not do to publish to the world.

During the late election in the United States, Tom made himself conspicuous by pulling down from the pole upon which it was hoisted the American flag, and tearing it, because it bore upon its folds the names of McClellan and Pendleton. For this hardy act he was promoted to the position that he now occupies.

The female servants of the prison, with the exception of " Aunt Lizzie," were the worst and most degraded beings I ever had the misfortune of seeing. The Five Points of New York, or the lowest dens of infamy, could not produce a worse crowd. Yet this scum were hired to wait upon the ladies who were here held—for Heaven knows what; but prisoners nevertheless.

But "Aunt Lizzie," as she was called by every one here, stood on her dignity. No one insulted her; always laughing and good-natured, Aunt Lizzie prided herself upon belonging formerly to the Snowden family. "My name, sah, am Aunt Lizzie Snowden, sah, and I'm berry proud of it, sah." Straightforward and ever scrupulous, in her Colonel W—— had one faithful attendant. She was not to be bribed nor cajoled. None could see her smiling face and feel gloomy : a good word she had for everybody. She it was who mended our linen and washed our clothes. Aunt Lizzie was certainly a good feature in this prison, and many besides myself will, I am sure, remember her with feelings of gratitude.

Mr. L—— is another gentleman who rejoices in belonging to the corps that is commanded by Colonel W——. He is the "Jerry Sneak" of this institution. His nose is everywhere, and his eyes are upon every thing. If a visitor comes to see a friend confined here, Mr. L—— stands near at hand, noting down in his memory the conversation, whilst apparently engaged in trimming his nails, or fixing his eyes on dreamland, as he notes down their words. If in the court when the prisoners are walking about, he is always looking on and smiling, or has some soft word of " endearment " to say to new-comers, to bring against them when their time comes. I was particularly the object of his hatred, and our hate was mutual.

I grievously offended him. One day a gentleman called to see me. Our interview was interesting—one purely upon personal matters. Upon entering, I seated myself close to the gentleman. Mr. L—— took a chair, and, placing his legs between us, stretched himself complacently at full length, and prepared, as was his custom, to listen.

Of course, our hope of a conversation was, to all appearances, at an end. For some moments I stood it calmly, but at last I could stand it no longer. "There are," I said, very quietly, "in this prison spies; bearers of stories, ever ready for any thing mean and contemptible, but the meanest and most contemptible of them all is— I beg your pardon, sir," turning suddenly to him, "is yourself, Mr. L——."

"I can't help it," said that individual, looking piteously at me. But the shot had taken effect: Mr. L—— removed his chair to the fire, and our conversation was uninterrupted.

Of the *cuisine* of Fort Delaware there is not much to be said in praise. Two meals are served out to us daily, consisting of one piece of peculiarly constructed bread, and one ditto of indescribable salt, yellowish-colored pork, or meat that has had its nutriment entirely boiled out of it in the making of soup for the garrison, previous to its being apportioned out to the prisoners.

Occasionally a mixture, designated by our persecutors as soup, and containing an ample sufficiency of maggots, is doled out to us in tin pots. It is an indescribable *olla prodrida* of soups of every kind, and in its appearance reminds one irresistibly of the sty and the trough. Coffee and tea are luxuries never seen in the shed where we receive our rations. Only those who are fortunate enough to have money are ever enabled to procure these articles from the sutler; who, although selling a very good kind, does not forget to charge a very exorbitant price for his considerate (!) kindness.

These meals thus served out to us are called, respectively, breakfast and dinner—misnomers for such luxuries in the outside world, however poor they may be. What would our English friends, who are, I believe, by no means averse to good cheer, think, if they could try it for afew weeks, of "the nutritious food, the unparalleled good treatment of the prisoners held here, of which the Federals. boast so loudly?"

These pleasant meals are served to **us** at nine in the morning and three in the afternoon. The cook-house, as it is named, from **whence**

this food is served out to us by its grinning
demons, is a large room, in length about one
hundred feet, by sixty in width, filled partially
with long and very narrow tables, constructed
of pine boards. Upon two generally, though
sometimes there were more, are placed at regular intervals our pieces of bread (by courtesy)
and our ditto of meat. About half-past eight
some subordinate of the cook-house shouts out
the command to "fall in, 28!" or "31!" and
whichever portion of the officers' barracks may
be first mentioned, the inmates immediately
respond by coming forth from their separate
divisions, and falling in, by trios or threes,
march up to the entrance of the cook-house.

Here we are generally kept waiting for
several minutes until the door is thrown open,
when we enter and file in single column down
the table, taking our allotted rations as we
pass on, until the end of the table is reached,
when on again, face to the right about! re-
tracing our steps out of the room, when we
are once more fain to return to our dens, or eat
in the open air. The latter alternative, how-

ever, is not very often chosen, as it is winter, and we are but scantily clothed.

Each division, during the cold weather, is provided with a stove for the purpose of heating, in a measure, places that would have otherwise been untenantable. Over this some one or more of us are generally pretty much occupied in cooking nondescript dishes, some plate composed of odds and ends, and which I find from experience are not altogether unsavory after once conquering the repugnance felt upon being brought into contact with such very unaccustomed food. Coffee-pots, tea-pots, and oftentimes mugs and dippers, are piled upon every conceivable spot or space large enough to admit of such packing; and in cold weather to approach anywhere near the stove is a thing utterly impossible, owing to the numbers surrounding it.

Political prisoners have the privilege of procuring their meals from the kitchen, provided they can make some arrangement with the heads of that department, and have the money necessary to back them in such ar-

rangements. After I had been imprisoned for
two weeks, I managed to have " an interview "
with the presiding dignitary of this steaming
sanctum, which resulted favorably ; and henceforth, instead of living, as I had for the past
fourteen days, upon bread and water (for I
never ate the pork), I dined regularly upon
meat, potatoes, and coffee for breakfast, dinner,
and supper, having for my comrade and messmate Major R——, quartermaster on General
Ramseur's staff.

Several messes of this description were
thus formed, many of them having from six to
eight members. By feeing the " cook-master,"
we managed to get several extras occasionally,
so that, altogether, we contrived to get along
better than we should had we been without money or without friends.

For a consideration, some one of the lower
class of men confined here enacts the duties of
cook, and sets and clears off the dishes (tin-
ware) from the table (in our case a cheese-box
on legs), and announces the meals when ready
for us. We might have fared better, but

Rumor whispers that the sutler and presiding officials at the fort are leagued together, and that the order prohibiting luxuries being forwarded here by friends was made as much for the benefit of themselves as for the irritation that it occasioned us, as it is utterly impossible to procure any thing unless through the shark of a sutler, who charges exorbitantly for his politeness.

CHAPTER XXVI.

Miss McDonough—A brutal Outrage—Treatment of Mr. W. R. Coyner—The "Court-Martial"—Sentence—"Tossing in a Blanket"—The Torture by Fire—Fort Delaware—A Box of Clothing—A Man of Consequence—Adjutant and General—The Blankets at last—The "Softest Plank."

I HAVE already spoken of poor Miss Mc-Donough. She was taken prisoner last summer, upon the charge of having murdered a Federal officer. At the time of this alleged murder, Miss McDonough was nowhere in the vicinity, and it was only in hopes that her brother would be advised of her arrest, and surrender himself in her stead, that this shameful seizure was made.

James McDonough was a Lieutenant in Mosby's command, somewhere in the Valley of the Shenandoah, and Captain B. was shot by him (not murdered) when, during a skirmish, he refused to surrender himself prisoner. It was for this justifiable act of war she was made to suffer. Miss McDonough was compelled to remain in a room* perfectly stifling with noisome smells. Add to this the fact, that she was continually fretting for fear that her brother would deliver himself up for her. Can it then be wondered at that she should have died there, far away from her friends and those she loved?

During my sojourn in the Carroll Prison, I one evening called upon Mrs. ——, a lady prisoner from Galveston, Texas, who tended Miss McDonough with motherly care during her illness. Poor Mollie was then in a state of semi-insensibility, and was barely conscious of what was going on about her, when W—— the superintendent of the prison, burst into the room, shouting out at the top of his voice "Hooray! Jem McDonough's caught, and will swing, by ——! before the week is out."

Miss McDonough slowly raised herself in the bed until nearly upright, stared wildly

---

* The same in which Belle Boyd was held so long.

about her for an instant, and, uttering a pier-
cing shriek, fell insensible upon the floor.

I sprang forward, but Mrs. —— was beside her before me; and I, turning full upon
the author of this outrage, remarked excitedly,
"By ——! Colonel W——, if I ever catch you
in Virginia when I get a command, you shall
swing for this, sir!"

Another instance of Yankee brutality and
vindictiveness was related to me by the young
gentleman himself, Mr. R. Coyner, a private in
the old 7th Virginia regiment of cavalry. At
the time of his capture he was on furlough at
Moorfields, Virginia. On the 12th of October,
1863, he was taken prisoner by a force of Federal infantry, under Captain Jarbon, and conveyed to Petersburg, Western Virginia, when
he was handed over to Colonel Mulligan, who
not only paroled him, but treated him with
kindness and attention. Here he remained
until the 24th of October, when he was sent,
under a strong guard, to New Creek Station, on
the Baltimore and Ohio Railroad, where he
arrived late at night on the 25th. Here his

sufferings began. He was thrown into a large, damp cellar, where were huddled together about seventy Yankee deserters, murderers, and bounty-jumpers, where he was kept until the 26th, subsisting upon hard biscuits and cold water, which were served to them twice during the day. On the 26th he was taken from thence and carried to Baltimore. Upon his arrival he was placed in Campbell's slave-pen, then under the charge of the infamous Colonel Fish, who was afterwards sentenced to the Albany Penitentiary for various crimes. Early on the morning of the 27th, Mr. Coyner was again ordered out of his place of confine-ment, and conducted, still under guard, to Fort McHenry, which he reached about eleven A. M., of the same day, and was immediately placed in what is known as the "Solitary Cell."

Here the company was as select as that at New Creek Station, comprising as it did mur-derers and thieves, and other wretches of the deepest dye. In this solitary cell, where he was doomed to pass a weary interval of time, no windows admitted the light of day, no lamp was permitted at night. The apartment, or rather den, was cold and noisome; its walls thick with mildew, the floor covered with filth of every kind, and literally swarming with insects; none of the prisoners held here being ever allowed to leave the place for any purpose whatever.

Here young Coyner, upon entering, found two other Confederate soldiers with ball and chain attached to their legs; the cause assigned for this treatment by the Yankee authorities being simply that they were *Confederates*. Young Coyner himself had not remained here more than an hour when the sergeant entered, and with the assistance of his men placed a 42-pound ball and chain upon his left ankle, adding that if he attempted to take it off, he would shoot him. He remained here, and in this condition, for three months and a half, and his sufferings, as he related them to me, were certainly horrible in the extreme.

The first night that he passed in this "hell upon earth," as he termed it, could never be

obliterated from his memory. A mock court-
martial was held, before which he was arraigned upon the charge of being a rebel and
guerrilla; the remainder of those in the den
looking on, laughing spectators of the scene.
Of course, the result of this court-martial may
be inferred: he was found guilty, and the
court pronounced the following sentence upon
him, viz., "To be tossed in a blanket *until
lifeless.*" This was immediately carried into
effect, the Federal guards looking on, amused
spectators of the scene, taking no heed of his
piteous appeals to them for mercy or protection, but on the contrary inciting his persecutors by words and gestures to carry the sentence into effect.

Handed over to them, he was tossed
thirteen times, each time falling heavily upon
his head or sides; when, finally, more dead
than alive, he was permitted to crawl off
amidst the jeers and laughter of his tormentors, who were highly elated at the manner
in which they had eventually succeeded in
eliciting groans from their unfortunate martyr.

Thoroughly sick, and feeling like one more dead than alive, poor Coyner, bruised and sore, endeavored to court sleep, and to thus, in a measure, drive off the fearful thoughts that were at times nearly driving him mad. He eventually fell into an uneasy slumber, and may have slept for an hour, when he was awakened by fire being applied to his feet by the "judge advocate" of this mock court, who gloried in the name of Kelly, and who exultantly boasted of having murdered his captain for greenbacks.

This fresh torture of young Coyner was considered the very acme of pleasure and amusement by his tormentors, some of whom held him, whilst others applied the burning paper to his feet, the fire being supplied to them for this purpose by the sentries. He showed me the scars caused by the severe burns that he had received—scars that he will take with him to the grave.

It was in vain that he appealed for mercy At last, wearied out, they permitted him to go free for the time being. "By these miserable

19*

brutes," said young Coyner, "I was not permitted to speak in defence of my country, nor yet assert my rights: If I remonstrated with them, I was knocked down and kicked by my brutal persecutors, oftener beaten.

"This kind of treatment I endured for a period of three months and a half, when I was ordered out of this horrible place by the Provost-Marshal, whom I found to be kind and compassionate, and who in my case was but obeying his superiors. He placed me in a very nice and comfortable room which the Confederate officers held, and removed from my ankle the ball and chain that had so long been my companions in my misery.

"Here I remained until the 12th of May, when I was removed to Fort Delaware to serve out a sentence of court-martial, viz., 'Hard labor for the war'—that had been passed upon me by my tyrannical captors."

It is worthy of remark that, out of those nine officers who composed one of the most atrocious military commissions that was ever assembled, and before whom he was arraigned, all, with the exception of one of its members, have already met a violent death. Eight were killed before the 20th of June by Southern bullets, and the remaining one lies already at the point of death, struck down by consumption's fatal shaft, which is slowly but surely working out his fate.

"Here I am for the present," he said, in concluding his narrative; "how long I am to remain I know not; but I am willing to suffer any and every thing for my country and her cause."

Previous to my incarceration in Fort Delaware, and whilst I was yet a prisoner in the Carroll, I received a letter from my mother, in which she mentioned that she was about to forward to me a trunk filled with winter clothing and some few little articles necessary for my comfort, but before it came I was sent to the fort. Here the *régime* was much stricter, and prohibited the prisoners from receiving any thing whatsoever in the shape of food, and it was only by special permit that even clothing was allowed to be sent here, the different expresses refusing to accept parcels unless they had pasted upon the outside the passport of the fort. Desirous of keeping myself warm at least, I wrote to the Assistant Adjutant-General of the post, George W. Ahl, the following letter :—

Jan. 4th, 1865.

"Officers' Barracks,

"Fort Delaware.

"Capt. Geo. W. Ahl,

"Sir :— Will you permit the undersigned to receive two blankets, and a box that has already been forwarded to him from his mother's residence, Brooklyn, Long Island ?

"And I am, Sir,

"Respectfully,

"S. Wilde Hardinge."

This I forwarded to him by mail, although my friends scouted the idea of my ever receiving an answer to it; and their conjectures were correct, for Captain Ahl did not deign to notice it. Whether it was owing to the weight of his official duties, or to his supreme contempt for rebels, I was never able to ascertain.

Finally, however, one day, as I sat thinking

upon my dreary imprisonment, of you my
wife, and home associations, affected decidedly
with the "blues," Mr. J., whose misfortune it
was to have been a Democrat and the editor of
a Baltimore journal, said, "Well Mr. H., have
you received a reply to the letter you wrote
the other day?"

"No, sir," I responded, gloomily.

"Well, try the General: he ranks several
grades above an adjutant, and is, therefore, not
so important as the lesser bird."

"By Jove!" I replied, "the idea is a good
one;" and forthwith I wrote.

Certes, the General was far more polite to
his prisoners than his adjutant; for the next
day I received by mail the following order:—

——, Paste on the outside of the Box.

—Any thing not mentioned in this Permit will be Confiscated.

Head-quarters,
Fort Delaware,
Jan. 10th, 1865.

Mr. ——,
Supt. Old Carroll Prison,
Has permission to send :

(1) One box, now in his possession, provided it contains
clothing,
To Sam W. Hardinge,
Political Prisoner,
A Prisoner of War at this Fort.
By command of
Brig.-General A. Schoepf,
G. W. Ahl,
Capt. & A. A. A. Genl.,
P. S. Hemings.

Of course, this was all that was desired;
and in a few days I had the extreme pleasure
of overhauling the contents of this much-
coveted box. And, oh! you of the outside
world, who have never in winter slept without
blankets, nor indulged in that very dubious

luxury, " the softest plank," for a bed in some
modern Bastile—you, I say, can never conceive
the joy that I felt swelling up within me as
" I laid me down to sleep" that night, wrapping myself up in this warm embrace. You,
doubtless, would not envy me the luxury;
and yet there were plenty of poor fellows here,
without money and without friends, sleeping
calmly and peacefully around me, as I have
slept, without blankets to cover them, only
their martial cloaks—and they are very ragged
—for a covering.

CHAPTER XXVII.

Wanted at the Fort—The Order for Release—Farewells—
Free at last—A cool Reception—An undignified Costume
—No Conveyance—The Walk to Wilmington—Home
once more—Conclusion of Mr. Hardinge's Journal.

On the 3d of February, whilst seated with
Major R. and Adjutant C——, talking of our
anticipated exchange, the sergeant of the barracks came into the division and inquired for
me. I immediately descended from my perch,
and presented myself before him, inquiring as
I did so the purport of his visit.

"You're wanted at the Fort—General
P—— wants you. Follow me," was the
reply.

Half wondering what it was, and drawing
closer about me my apology for a blanket, for
it was a very cold afternoon, I followed my

conductor until I reached the fort, when I was immediately ushered into the august presence of the commandant, who stared hard at me, without, however, saying any thing. One of his aides, evidently a secretary, handed me, after a few moments had elapsed, the following document, which was to be my safe-conduct by sea and land:—

"Special Orders
    "No. 62.   "Head-quarters,
                             "Fort Delaware, Del.,
                                  Feb. 3d, 1865.
    " S. Wilde Hardinge (Political Prisoner) is hereby released from confinement at this Post, in compliance with the following telegram from the War Department, dated Feb. 3d, 1865:—
    "'Brig.-Genl. A. Schoepf,
        "'Fort Delaware,
    "'The Secretary of War directs the release of S. Wilde Hardinge, a Prisoner at Fort Delaware. Acknowledge receipt, and inform me when Mr. Hardinge leaves the island.
                    (Sgd.)   "'JAMES A. HARDEE,
                                "'Col. and Insp.-Genl.'
                    (Seal)   "A. SCHOEPF,
                                "Brig,-Genl. Comg."

The General then remarked, "Mr. H——,

you have now our permission to leave the island. Will you go to-night or to-morrow morning? Do you go to Baltimore or New York City? I presume you will leave for Europe by the *first steamer?*"

To this I made answer, saying, "I will go now. My destination is New York; and I thank God I am free! Rest assured that I shall not trouble the Government by remaining longer than I can help. Good-afternoon, sir;" and, turning, I left the room and walked rapidly back, still accompanied by the sergeant, to the barracks, that soldier remarking, " By ——! you're an awfully lucky chap."

I was not long, I can assure you, in packing up what few things I had; and then came the final adieux and partings. I confess that I felt badly as I took Major R—— by the hand, and bade him good-by; for he had ever been a good friend and counsellor of mine. I am not ashamed to confess that my eyes were filled with tears, as one after another of my friends gathered around, shaking hands with me, wishing me a " God speed you, Hardinge!" "God bless you, my boy!" "Hope to meet you in Dixie soon," "Write to me," etc.—words that I shall never forget, for they came from the lips of some of the bravest spirits in the Southern Confederacy. It was very fortunate that I had taken the precaution to hide these notes carefully about my person; for, upon re-entering the guard-room previous to leaving the island, my bundle was first thoroughly inspected, then my pockets, the lining of my felt hat, and my boots. But here the soldier employed for that purpose luckily stopped. I was then permitted to step on board of a small steam-tug which lay at the wharf. This in a few moments cast off from her moorings, and we slowly glided away from the Château d'If of America, daintily picking our way through the miniature bergs that impeded our progress to the mainland, which, although only about seven miles distant, we were nearly two hours in reaching.

It was with feelings of unmistakable pleasure that I felt my feet pressing once more *terra firma*, and experienced the gratifying

sensation awakening itself within me that I
was once more my own master. So, drawing
my tattered blanket about me, I stepped into
the hotel that stood near the landing, and inquired the distance to Wilmington.

The proprietor of this country place eyed
me suspiciously; the dog who had been bask-
ing at the fire rose and growled at me; and
the frequenters of the place, who were seated
round the stove smoking or drinking, by their
looks inferred as plainly as tongue could
speak, "He is an escaped prisoner." And no
wonder, when I describe to you my presentation dress upon the occasion.

A felt hat, remarkable only for its being
crownless, adorned my head; a ragged blanket
sufficed—only in a measure, however—to keep
the cold from my coatless body; a pair of
"inexpressibles," horribly dilapidated, encased
my lower extremities; a boot on one foot, and
the other wrapped up in old rags. Is it a
wonder, then, that I was an object of doubtful
character?

Seating myself near the fire, I called for a

glass of wine, which was handed to me by the bar-tender, who muttered something about a desire that he had of seeing "the color of my money."

To this I replied by drawing out my pocket-book, and offering him a fifty-dollar greenback, desiring him to give me small moneys for it. In an instant the conduct of those present underwent a complete change; the bar-tender was all smirks and bows, and, with an urbanity that was all the more strikingly apparent from his former behavior, desired to know if I wished to have an apartment.

"No, I wish to go to Wilmington. How far is it from here?"

"Sixteen miles," was the reply.

"Is there any conveyance that will take me there to-night?"

There was none.

"Hem! not if I will pay you well for it?"

"I wouldn't let a dog of mine go out this night," was the answer.

"Then I will walk," I said.

"Walk!" was chorussed simultaneously, with astonishment depicted on their countenances.

"Yes, walk!" I reiterated, desperately.

"Well, if you get to Wilmington safely, you will do more than I expect you will, in that garb especially;" and the speaker looked at my costume with a sneer.

"Nevertheless, I am going," I said; and, suiting the action to the word, I rose, and, attended to the door of the hotel by the group of astonished villagers, I commenced the journey.

It had been snowing and raining alternately throughout the day, and the roads in this part of the country, never at any time when I saw them remarkable for their goodness, were ankle-deep with mud. I shall never have the recollection of that night obliterated from my memory. Several times I was on the point of lying down on the roadside; but the love of life and the thought that—God willing—I should soon be at home, were strong within me, and I staggered on through the freezing rain and slushy snow.

Twice on the way I inquired at the door of some farm-houses the direction that I was to take, and once the "gude wife" of the quiet homestead where I gained admittance prepared for me with her own white hands a cup of coffee, and pressed me to stay all night at her hospitable place—an invitation in which she was seconded by the rest of her family. Herself and husband were both English, and I shall not forget their kindness to me; and when I at last rose to depart, the husband, wife, and children bade me a kind adieu, the husband accompanying me down the road some distance.

At last, just as the clock was striking ten, I staggered into the dépôt at Wilmington, just in time to catch the train for New York. I had accomplished the distance in four hours, but it was fully a week before I was able to walk or sit even with any degree of comfort.

Early in the morning I arrived in New York, and drove immediately to my brother's place of business. He was perfectly amazed at seeing me, and laughed immoderately at the deplorable figure I cut.

Eventually, having procured a suit of clothes, and enjoyed the luxury of a bath and the inexpressible feeling of delight that one has in finding his body once more in contact with clean linen, I bade adieu to the United States, and started directly for the shores of hospitable and peaceful England.

CHAPTER XXVIII.

Conclusion of Mrs. Hardin e's Narrative.

My memoirs were written, and a portion of them already in the hands of the publishers, when the startling news came which has thrilled all Europe and filled her inhabitants with horror—the assassination of Abraham Lincoln, President of the United States.

It was always the boast of Americans, were they Northern or Southern in their sentiments, that theirs was the only history that could show to the world a clear, untarnished record of successful Republican rule.   But their annals can be no longer so regarded; for, in the sudden demise of Mr. Lincoln by the bullet of an insensate fanatic, that peculiar institution of Europe, the school of the assassin, has transferred itself to the shores of

20

America; and that country can no longer uphold her former boast, that crime such as this had never been perpetrated under the Government commenced by George Washington.

Personally I had no animosity against the honorable gentleman who has wielded the sceptre of Northern power for four long years. His has been a trying position. No man probably in the pages of History took his seat under more inauspicious circumstances. The Press of the world warred furious warfare upon him. He was jeered and scoffed at; he was pronounced uncouth, vulgar, low, servile, and abject; disappointed politicians and opposition cliques vied with each other in calling him upon every occasion the "rail-splitter;" and wiseacres of soothsaying proclivities speedily predicted that, with such a man as Abraham Lincoln at the head of the Government, the Union would most assuredly be split, with as much precision and as quickly as Mr. Lincoln had been known to split rails when a backwoodsman in the Western wilds.

Although a member of Congress previous to his elevation to the presidential chair of all the United States not in rebellion, and having for his political opponent in his presidential campaign that great statesman, the late Mr. Douglas, Mr. Lincoln was not a forensic success.

His speeches and arguments, teeming with wit and dry humor, were better calculated to attract the backwoodsman, by whom he was looked upon as a leading man, than the more mature and riper intellects with which he was in after-days brought into contact. I can appreciate and admire fully the character of such men who exemplify the sentence, "out of nothing came something." As such I looked upon Lincoln, when, month after month, and then year after year, of his presidential term rolled by, and I saw how well he governed the Northern Republic, and how firmly he held the reins of the Federal cause, which from time to time toppled upon the verge of a yawning chasm.

Now all is changed. Can any one believe

that Mr. Johnson is the man who is to restore
the Republic to what it was, save the nation
from bankruptcy, and bring peace and good-
will to America? It might not have been
impossible with Mr. Lincoln; for that gentleman held out the olive-branch, concealing no
deadly weapon beneath it, to General Lee and
his little band of heroes. With Mr. Johnson
at the head of the Government of the North,
who can foresee any thing save anarchy and
dissolution? He will fiddle whilst Rome is
burning.

Politically I did not like Mr. Lincoln, for
in him I saw the destroyer. As long as it
served his purpose, Mr. Lincoln boldly advo-
cated the right of *Secession*. I trust that the
accusation will not startle my readers; but
such was the case; and I will cite one instance
—when, as a representative, he openly avowed
" that any nation or people, in any portion of
the world, had a right to rise up and rebel
against the mother government if they wanted
to."

When the North, in 1860–61, declared that

she would usurp all rights, and have, whether
or no the South wished it, and in direct violation of the Constitution, a strictly Northern
President, Abraham Lincoln, still true to his
former assertion of the right of Secession,
accepted the nomination of the Chicago platform, and by this act inserted the wedge in
that log called the *Union*. The log was
ultimately split, through force of circumstances.

There are those who maintain that in this
world women have no right to interfere in the
affairs of state, in politics, in plots, and coun-
ter-plots. Others there are who, more chivalrous, are willing to admit that women have as
much right to act, think, and speak, as men.
I do not set myself up as an advocate of the
woman's-rights doctrine, but would rather
appear in the character of a quiet lady
expressing her sentiments, not so much to the
public as to her immediate friends. There
fore, I trust that the former class of gentlemen
will here forgive what to them may appear
presumption; especially as, in the preceding

chapters of my book, I have endeavored to avoid politics as much as possible.

But to return to my subject. The North boldly declared that she did not care much if the South did secede; and the South, never doubting the intentions of the North, took her at her word — seceded; and the consequence has been a civil war, whose magnitude has never been surpassed, and whose slain can be counted, not by tens, but by hundreds of thousands. Mr. Lincoln, as the representative of his nation, took the oath of office to uphold the Union "as it was." Then, after a while, "as it was" became "as it is."

"The Constitution as it is," said the notorious "Senator Jim Lane," of Kansas, "is played out; and I am ready to see any man shot down who favors the Union as it was talked of by Mr. Lincoln." And on the evening of the very next day after Mr. Lincoln had favored a conciliatory treatment towards the South, he was shot down!

Englishmen! I appeal to your impartial judgment. I look to you for the discounte-

nancing of the foul charge which Mr. Stanton
has thrown upon the shoulders of the Southern
leaders, that he might thereby induce the
European powers to withdraw their recognition of Southern belligerency. It is not the
chivalrous sons of the South who have done
this deed. The papers, indeed, make the assassin use the words, "*Sic semper tyrannis!*"
But if this be true, then, as a Virginian woman, I say, never was the State motto of
Virginia more unworthily abused.

And, in truth, our people have even more
to regret in the death of President Lincoln
than have the people of the North. When
our noble old chieftain, General Lee, heard of
the assassination, he covered his face, and
refused to listen to the details of the murder;
whilst, in the Libby Prison, where were confined a large number of Southern soldiers, the
inmates on one of the floors held a meeting,
and denounced the murder, passing resolutions
that they were soldiers, and could not therefore applaud assassins.

Yet Mr. Secretary Stanton, with a hatred

and malignity that is unsurpassed, charges the commission of this deed upon the South. There are those in the Northern States who will yet move heaven and earth to prove that it was the South; and to prove it, money will be spent, bribes given, and, where money and bribes fail, threats will be used. But I appeal to Europe to judge discriminately between North and South. Do not pronounce too hastily your judgment, nor cast upon a brave and chivalrous people the stigma of assassination

Many have advised me to suppress this volume, urging that its publication will probably cause my life-long banishment. But I cannot—I will not recede. I firmly believe that in this fiery ordeal, in this suffering, misery, and woe, the South is but undergoing a purification by fire and steel that will, in good time, and by His decree, work out its own aim.

THE END.

Lightning Source UK Ltd.
Milton Keynes UK
UKHW022052160223
417160UK00003B/379